Advance Praise for *Welfare for the Rich*

"Conyers and Harvey describe—in infuriating detail—all the ways that the wealthy and the well-connected use the power of the state to divert your money into their pockets. **This robust defense of free markets is both timely and terrifying.**"

—Katherine Mangu-Ward,
Editor in Chief, *Reason*

"The political left has long demanded government intervention to reduce economic inequality. Increasingly, the political right is joining in this call. Yet as Harvey and Conyers make crystal clear, government itself is a major contributor to inequality and more government programs will only make things worse. **Far better would be to heed Harvey's and Conyers's humane proposition for *less* government by simply eliminating the government's costly 'help-the-rich' programs.**"

—Donald J. Boudreaux, Professor of
Economics, George Mason University

"As governor of New Mexico, I became all too familiar with government programs and policies that favored the wealthy and well-connected at taxpayer expense. **Today, citizens of all political persuasions can surely agree that taxpayer money should not be channeled to those who need it least.** Thanks to Phil Harvey and Lisa Conyers for demonstrating the scope of this waste."

—Gary Johnson, Presidential Candidate 2016,
Former Governor of New Mexico

"Harvey and Conyers offer concrete, feasible, fair solutions to end the thousands of government programs that are taking from the poor to give to the rich. *Welfare for the Rich* **is based on thorough research that will make any normal person's blood boil,** as one ripoff after another is brought to light. Get angry. And then get real. Kudos to Harvey and Conyers for offering a realistic path to an equitable and just society."

—Dr. Tom G. Palmer, George M. Yeager
Chair for Advancing Liberty, Atlas Network,
Senior Fellow, Cato Institute

"*Welfare for the Rich* masterfully documents how governments violate free market principles by passing laws that bestow special favors, subsidies, and power to the wealthy. Readers will share the righteous indignation of authors Phil Harvey and Lisa Conyers when they discover how their **tax dollars are being wasted on pet projects and programs for the rich.**"

—Scott G. Bullock, President and
General Counsel, Institute for Justice

Phil Harvey   Lisa Conyers

WELFARE FOR THE RICH

How Your Tax Dollars End Up in Millionaires' Pockets —And What You Can do About It

Post Hill
PRESS

A POST HILL PRESS BOOK
ISBN: 978-1-64293-414-4
ISBN (eBook): 978-1-64293-415-1

Post Hill Press
New York • Nashville
posthillpress.com

Published in the United States of America

For Judith Appelbaum (1939-2018),
who made us better writers

Contents

Figures

Acknowledgments

We are grateful to Karl Weber for his masterful editing of this book and for the guidance he has provided us throughout the process. Thanks to Chris Edwards and others at the Cato Institute, who provided valuable analytical and content advice. We thank Christina Ballas, who grappled patiently with the labyrinthine requirements of the Chicago Manual of Style in executing footnotes and figures. Thanks also to Heather Hunt for creating a striking cover for our book, and to Kathy Bell for typing from Phil's cacophonous handwriting.

Foreword
David Boaz, Cato Institute

merican political debates over the past generation or two have often revolved around the size and scope of the welfare state. We debate whether the United States has the least generous social safety net among the major industrialized countries, or on the other hand, whether our growing entitlement programs are going to bankrupt us. Arguments are particularly fierce over the portion of the welfare state actually directed at the poor—the programs we know as welfare, Medicaid, food stamps, subsidized housing, and more.

We focus much less on what Phil Harvey and Lisa Conyers call welfare for the rich—taxpayer subsidies and benefits that go to millionaires and billionaires, owners of farms, and businesses. It's about time we did look at those programs, and this book is a good opportunity to start that debate.

Economists call such programs "upward redistribution of wealth." When we hear the word *redistribution*, we usually think of Robin-Hood-like programs that take money from the rich to give it to the poor. Those "downward redistribution" programs have always been controversial.

Upward redistribution—taking from the poor or the middle class to benefit more affluent people—should be less controversial. Who would favor that? And yet, as this book demonstrates, there are many such programs. Why do they persist? The ostensible reasons are different from the fundamental ones. Take farm subsidies: farm owners support the subsidies because they get money. But they use arguments that appeal to the public interest: they say the programs are intended to guard against volatile food prices, to ensure that Americans will have food in time of war, to preserve rural America, or indeed to ensure that we don't starve to death. As the slogan goes, "no farms, no food." There's a similar purportedly public-interest defense of every subsidy, tariff, regulation, mandate, and license. In the end, though, the programs persist because the rich and powerful interest groups that benefit are able to persuade politicians to renew them.

One problem with upward redistribution is its fundamental unfairness. Most people don't mind paying modest taxes to help people in need. But they would be most unhappy if they knew how much of their tax money goes to people better off than themselves.

Samuel Brittan of the *Financial Times* has written that "reassignment," an economic policy that changes individuals' ranking in the hierarchy of incomes, is far more offensive than a policy of redistribution, which, in his idealized vision, would merely raise the incomes of the poorest members of society to some reasonable minimum. Reassignment, the use of government to make privileged people better off than others who served customers better, can create justified resentment of those who benefit.

There's a long history of government-created privileges for businesses and the wealthy, even in generally free enterprise America. In his 1977 book *The Governmental Habit*, Jonathan R. T. Hughes described subsidies, price regulations, and monopoly franchises going all the way back to colonial and early federal days. And one of the most stirring attacks on government for the privileged was delivered in 1832 by President Andrew Jackson as he vetoed the renewal of the Second Bank of the United States:

> It is to be regretted that the rich and powerful too often bend the acts of government to their selfish purposes. Distinctions in society will always exist under every just government. Equality of talents, of education, or of wealth cannot be produced by human institutions. In the full enjoyment of the gifts of Heaven and the fruits of superior industry, economy, and virtue, every man is equally entitled to protection by law; but when the laws undertake to add to these natural and just advantages

artificial distinctions, to grant titles, gratuities, and exclusive privileges, to make the rich richer and the potent more powerful, the humble members of society—the farmers, mechanics, and laborers—who have neither the time nor the means of securing like favors to themselves, have a right to complain of the injustice of their Government.

Old Hickory would endorse this book.

Economists study such ideas that underlie upward redistribution, such as protectionism, the "too big to fail" rule, and "concentrated benefits and dispersed costs." Harvey and Conyers give us chapter and verse on how those phenomena influence us. They present story after story of subsidies going to billion-dollar companies or billionaire owners. In the energy chapter, they dig up a report from an obscure blog about an energy lobbyist's frank presentation of the return on investment (ROI) his company got from New York Governor Andrew Cuomo's nuclear power bailout after the company's "lobbying and public relations campaign."

They write, "Governments at the federal, state and local levels provide favors to wealthy businesses and individuals through outright subsidies, regulations that favor the well-connected over the little guy, targeted tax holidays, taxpayer guaranteed loans, and zoning laws that have created wealthy enclaves that working men and women can't afford."

It would take more than one book to cover all the examples. My Cato Institute colleague Chris Edwards finds more than two thousand federal programs offering "subsidies to individuals, businesses, nonprofit groups, and state and local governments...subsidies for farmers, retirees, school lunches, rural utilities, the energy industry, rental housing, public broadcasting, job training, foreign aid, urban transit, and much more." These subsidies don't all go to the rich, but it helps to be well-connected. And of course, there are many more subsidy programs at the state and local level: for stadiums, film production, big businesses like Amazon and Foxconn, small businesses, "redevelopment," and so on.

What are the costs of all these programs that redistribute wealth and income upward? There's the unfairness, of course, of taxing people to subsidize those richer than themselves. And the direct financial costs in taxes and added borrowing. There's the inequality that is often *caused or worsened* by government itself. And then there's the inefficiency that regulations and subsidies create. The value of a market economy is that it directs resources to their most valued uses. Subsidies and regulations by definition override the decisions made by consumers in the competitive marketplace and redirect resources to politically favored recipients. If subsidized companies were economically viable—that is, if they were serving consumers better than alternatives—then they would make a profit. They wouldn't need subsidies.

Billionaire investor Warren Buffett, who knows how to make a profit, explained why his companies are in the wind energy business: "We get a tax credit if we build a lot of wind farms. That's the only reason to build them. They don't make sense without the tax credit." So that tax credit is channeling resources away from efficient uses and toward companies that, at least in some cases, are run by billionaires.

In a paper for the Cato Institute, Brink Lindsey wrote about another aspect of upward redistribution: policies that he called "regressive regulation"—"regulatory barriers to entry and competition that work to redistribute income and wealth up the socioeconomic scale." He asked why such policies, generally criticized by libertarian, conservative, and progressive policy experts, persisted. And he concluded that it was because they are "guarded by 'dragons'—the powerful interest groups that benefit from the status quo, all of which can be counted upon to defend their privileges tenaciously."

And that's why Harvey and Conyers conclude, "at the end of the day, the only way to reduce the intensity of the lobbying enterprise is to reduce the amount of government spending." Books like this can infuriate and inspire Americans to demand change.

Introduction

This book is designed to inform Americans—especially taxpayers who are footing most of the bill—about the massive movement of money from millions of middle- and lower-income Americans to much wealthier people and corporations that do not need and should not be entitled to these favors.

Most Americans recognize the importance of a safety net for America's poorest. Welfare programs for those in serious need, though often flawed, are means tested and generally reach deserving parties.

However, there is simply no justification for providing cash benefits and subsidies to America's rich. Yet for many decades, too many of our government's policies have taken wealth from taxpayers of modest means and provided a big chunk of it to the rich. The same perverse policies are in place today, and there is every reason to believe that they'll remain in place for the foreseeable future—unless we act as citizens to demand change.

What's most remarkable about these policies is their variety and ubiquity. Governments at the federal, state, and local levels provide favors to wealthy businesses and individuals through outright subsidies, regulations that favor the well-connected over the powerless, targeted tax loopholes, taxpayer-guaranteed loans, zoning laws that create wealthy enclaves that working men and women can't afford, and many other mechanisms. While today's politicians—especially those vying for the presidential contest in 2020—are proposing ways that the government should act to reduce income and wealth inequality, we ask, at the least, that *the government stop making inequality worse*. Ironically, this is one area of economic policy that the vast majority of Americans of all political persuasions are likely to agree upon. Liberal or conservative, socialist-leaning or libertarian, Republican, Democratic, or independent—practically everyone will acknowledge the absurdity of having government take from the poor and the middle class to give to the rich. Yet that's exactly what happens, every day, in many ways, large and small.

The ways by which government policies transfer taxpayer funds to the wealthy break down into four basic categories.

1. *Cash and in-kind payments directly to wealthy individuals and companies.* The U.S. farm program is the most egregious example of this. Originally designed during the New Deal to assure adequate food supplies to the poor and to help struggling farmers, the farm program hasn't truly served those purposes for decades. The U.S. today is a major food exporter, and farmers as a group are no longer needy. Indeed, according to the Environmental Working Group, which tracks farm subsidies and crop insurance payments, fifty billionaire members of the Forbes 400 got over $6.3 million in farm subsidies between 1995 and 2014. [1] A report issued by Oklahoma Senator Tom Coburn in 2011 reveals that 1,617 millionaires received $16.9 million in farm payments in 2006 alone, an average of more than $10,000 each going to individuals whose incomes exceeded $2.5 million that year. [2] This is a shocking abuse of funds that are paid by millions of middle-class citizens who make only a fraction of that amount.

2. *Regulations that favor large companies and investors over smaller, less wealthy ones.* An example: Mattel, a toy maker with revenue of $1.79 billion in 2016, lobbied in support of a 2008 federal regulation that imposed strict compliance standards on materials and processes used to make children's furniture and toys. This regulation, the Consumer Product Safety Improvement Act, was justified on the basis of product safety, but the act went well beyond that standard, requiring complex and costly tests and inspections that only big companies like Mattel could afford. It ended up destroying the livelihoods of thousands of at-home small furniture crafts persons and toy makers whose toys and

chairs were perfectly safe.[3] Similarly, the Dodd-Frank Bill of 2010, designed to make banks more resilient in financial crises, now favors large banks over small ones, and many small banks have gone out of business as a result.

3. *Tax laws and targeted subsidies that favor the rich.* Our tax code is riddled with loopholes only the rich can slip through. "Carried interest," for example, is a special tax privilege that allows hedge fund managers and private equity executives to classify the income they receive on investment gains as low-tax capital gains. Oil and gas companies, whose earnings in 2018 topped $181 billion dollars, also get special tax breaks and lots of subsidies.[4] Exxon Mobil's 2011 upgrades to its Baton Rouge refinery in Louisiana, for example, are still generating benefits from a $119 million state subsidy, according to an investigative report in *The Guardian*.[5]

4. *Government policies that provide favors to the rich for which American consumers must pay.* The sugar program is the biggest offender in this category. A combination of tariffs, guarantees, and import quotas force the cost of sugar in the United States up to nearly double the world price. As a result, everyone who buys sugar-containing products, from ketchup to candy to bread, pays more, benefiting wealthy sugar growers. This program is particularly egregious because even those too poor to pay income taxes must buy food, and they, especially, should not be forced to subsidize wealthy sugar barons.

How do these public payoffs to the wealthiest people and companies happen? It's no secret. Special interests line up at the trough in Washington, where the big guys have loud voices. The major players include many of our biggest corporations, trade associations, and unions, and many other interest groups, from the American Association of Retired Persons to Lockheed Martin. Together, organizations like these paid a total of $3.45 billion to registered lobbyists in 2018.[6] In a recent study, the Sunlight Foundation, a nonprofit that promotes government accountability, found that "between 2007 and 2012, 200 of America's most politically active corporations spent a combined $5.8

billion on federal lobbying and campaign contributions. Those same corporations got $4.4 *trillion* in federal business and support" during those five years, including subsidies, tax breaks and favored government contracts. [7] "After examining 14 million records," Sunlight concluded, "we found that, on average, for every dollar spent on influencing politics, the nation's most politically active corporations received $760 from the government." That's a rate of return that almost compels companies and other interest groups to get into the game.

The amount of talent and energy that goes into these efforts is staggering. There are twenty registered lobbyists for each of the 535 members of Congress, and they work hard. They labor to preserve government favors—from farm payments to tax loopholes to export subsidies—lest any group lose the privileges they already have. And they also work to create new favors every time Congress passes a budget, creates a new agency, or debates changes to regulations.

The stated rationales for these political maneuvers range from protecting vulnerable family farms to promoting useful industries to enhancing public safety. But although the programs involved do little to promote these goals, the programs live on. Government largesse to the rich is so well-entrenched and so well-guarded by the efforts of lobbyists that few objections to it are ever raised. So rich farmers get more money, wealthy individuals enjoy more arcane tax breaks, and big companies get even bigger subsidies. Meanwhile, middle- and low-income taxpayers get pinched, including entrepreneurs and small businesses that are being stymied by regulations and tax levies that don't affect the big boys. The process exacerbates income inequality in America, which is both unnecessary and wrong. Why should the government systematically make the rich richer at the expense of everyone else?

When we first dug into this material, our reactions were deeply personal. Lisa was furious. "I pay taxes," she said. "I pay a lot of taxes! And making ends meet can be a challenge. Why should these millionaires be getting my money?"

Phil pays income taxes in six figures and was equally appalled at the basic unfairness—the downright immorality—of present laws and policies. His reaction: "The payments to wealthy corporations and individuals, out of taxpayers' pockets, are enormous, growing, and utterly inexcusable."

In the months that we've been researching the details, we've heard the same sorts of reactions from almost everyone with whom we share our findings.

In the chapters that follow, we'll draw on extensive research to reveal the increasing size and scope of the problem of welfare for the rich. We'll provide insights from interviews conducted around the country with subsidy recipients, lobbyists, and investors who support these policy anomalies, and with citizens, activists, and community leaders who are working to change them. And we'll offer advice and a host of ideas concerning what you can do to support the movement to reform our government's laws, regulations, and policies so that welfare for the rich can finally begin to shrink.

1   Robert Coleman, "The Rich Get Richer: 50 Billionaires Got Federal Farm Subsidies," Environmental Working Group AgMag, April 18, 2016, https://www.ewg.org/agmag/2016/04/rich-get-richer-50-billionaires-got-federal-farm-subsidies

2   Tom A. Colburn, M.D., "Subsidies of the Rich and Famous," November 2011, http://big.assets.huffingtonpost.com/SubsidiesoftheRichandFamous.pdf

3   Yvonne Zipp, "A New Law Hurts Small Toy Stores and Toymakers," *The Christian Science Monitor*, January 9, 2009, https://www.csmonitor.com/The-Culture/The-Home-Forum/2009/0109/p25s23-hfgn.html

4   M. Garside, "U.S. Gas and Oil Industry Annual Revenue 2010-2017," Statista, September 26, 2019, https://www.statista.com/statistics/294614/revenue-of-the-gas-and-oil-industry-in-the-us/

5   Damian Carrington and Harry Davies, "US Taxpayers Subsidising World's Biggest Fossil Fuel Companies," *The Guardian*, May 12, 2015, https://www.theguardian.com/environment/2015/may/12/us-taxpayers-subsidising-worlds-biggest-fossil-fuel-companies

6   Erin Duffin, "Total Lobbying Spending in the U.S. 1998-2018," Statista, April 29, 2019, https://www.statista.com/statistics/257337/total-lobbying-spending-in-the-us/

7   Bill Allison and Sarah Harkins, "Fixed Fortunes: Biggest Corporate Political Interests Spend Billions, Get Trillions," Sunlight Foundation, November 17, 2014, https://sunlightfoundation.com/2014/11/17/fixed-fortunes-biggest-corporate-political-interests-spend-billions-get-trillions/

Unhealthy Harvest: Millionaire Farmers and the Hand That Feeds Them

The more alfalfa he did not grow, the more money
the government gave him, and he spent every penny
he didn't earn on new land to increase the amount of
alfalfa he did not produce…[he] sprang out of bed at
the crack of noon…just to make certain that the chores
would not be done.

—Joseph Heller, *Catch-22*

The story of farm subsidies and supports begins in the depths of the
Great Depression, when they were introduced to help farmers cope
with precipitous drops in crop prices, to secure the nation's bread-
basket in times of war, and to help rural farmers get their crops to the
growing cities where hungry people needed food.

Congress passed the first Agricultural Act in 1933, and that act—
commonly referred to simply as the Farm Bill—has been renewed every

five years ever since then. Its seventeenth iteration, passed in 2014, allocated $489 billion for the period from then through 2018.[1]

Much of that money covers the cost of nutrition programs for the poor, which were added to the Farm Bill in the 1970s in order to make it more palatable to Congressional liberals.[2] Farmers themselves understand the politics of the Farm Bill. John Komoyen, an Indiana farmer who raises subsidized crops on his 750-acre farm, told us "There's a reason the food stamp program is always going to be in the Farm Bill, because that way legislators can argue that they can't possibly reduce farm subsidies because then the poor will go hungry. If you separated the two, the problems with farm subsidies would be a lot clearer, but this way the flaws with the subsidy system are hidden from the taxpayer."[3]

The subsidy part of the latest Farm Bill—$98 billion—is provided through several different programs. We'll discuss these programs and how they work below. The various kinds of spending mandated by the bill are illustrated in Figure 1-1.

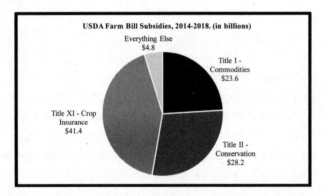

Figure 1-1: USDA Farm Bill subsidies, 2014-2018. (in billions)
Source: Congressional Budget Office, Cost Estimates for Agricultural Act of 2014, January 2014[4]

The natural assumption is that the subsidies provided in the Farm Bill are needed to keep small farmers in business. But a look at the list of subsidy recipients paints a different picture. Here are a few examples.

Philip Anshutz, CEO of AEG Entertainment and founder of Major League Soccer, got $606,514 in farm subsidies between 1995 and 2014.[5] His net worth is $9 billion.

Penny Pritzker, also a billionaire and an heiress to the Chicago Mill & Lumber Company, was Secretary of Commerce under President Obama. She got $1,604,288 in subsidies for her farm properties between 1996 and 2006.[6]

Topping that figure, partners in the Racota Family Ranch—including Kristi Noem, a Republican member of Congress from South Dakota— got $3,058,152 in farm subsidies between 1995 and 2008, with Noem herself getting an estimated $503,751.[7] In 2017, Noem announced her candidacy for governor, and opposition to cuts in the farm subsidy program became part of her successful campaign.

Also in South Dakota, Doug Sombke got $1,335,523 in subsidies between 1995 and 2019 while Sombke Farms was averaging earnings of over $500,000 a year.[8] Subsidy payments also went to his son's pheasant farm, a private venue for pheasant hunters who pay to hunt there. In a 2017 newspaper article, Sombke, an investor in those pheasant farms, complained about possible cuts in the next Farm Bill, noting that "past cuts to the Conservation Reserve Program eventually led to less interest from pheasant hunters" in his area.[9]

At the same time that the government was subsidizing those pheasant farms in South Dakota, it was paying out $35.4 billion to Texas farmers (years 1995-2017).[10] The top recipient, Alamo Freight Lines, Inc., got over $5.6 million in 2014 alone, qualifying for those subsidies because of farmland it leases in West Texas, even though its primary business doesn't involve farming or farm property.

These are just a few examples of the many wealthy people and businesses that benefit from federal farm subsidies. In 2011, more than ten thousand individual farming operations reaped federal subsidies worth between $100,000 and $1 million apiece, with twenty-six getting subsidies of $1 million or more to supplement their substantial farm earnings.[11]

The sheer number of recipients is staggering. Ninety percent of farmland in America is covered under a farm program subsidy, and most of the money goes to big farming operations. As Vincent Smith, an economist at Montana State University, noted in a 2015 *Wall Street Journal* article, the farmers who receive the bulk of all subsidies are worth somewhere between $6 million and $10 million on average.[12] A report from the Heritage Foundation notes that 69 percent of farm households rank in the top half of all U.S. households in terms of income. The median net worth of farm households ($801,980) is ten times that of total U.S. households ($81,200). And only 2 percent of farm households are in the bottom half of all households in terms of both income and wealth.[13]

No other demographic in America receives this kind of income support. No one else can earn hundreds of thousands, or even millions of dollars per year, then turn to the taxpayers and ask for more. Yet that is exactly what keeps happening with farm subsidies. The Environmental Working Group, which has been tracking federal farm subsidies for many years, provides a map on its site (ewg.org) that allows viewers to click on farms throughout the country and find out the name of each farm and the amount of subsidies each received through 2017.[14] In the past, the database included farmer's names and affiliations, and as a result farmers found themselves subject to pressure (and public disdain). Lobbying ensued, and the resulting changes in the 2014 Farm Bill have made it much more difficult to identify individual farmers who receive subsidies.[15]

Subsidies have become a major part of our nation's agricultural economy. According to estimates by the U.S. Department of Agriculture, close to $12 billion of 2017 net farm income came from federal payments, almost 14 percent of U.S. farmers' total profits that year.[16]

The Congressional Budget Office's long-term forecast model predicts a drop in the cost of these programs between 2018 and 2024, but the agency provides no justification for that estimate. Given the upward trend in costs virtually since the farm program began, getting these costs down seems unrealistic. Meanwhile, the costs overrun are paid for by borrowing. As the farmers get richer, America's debt inexorably increases.

While the Wealthy Benefit, Others Struggle

Why should America's wealthy farmers receive government handouts?

Manuel Cunha, president of the Nisei Farmers League, which supports the interests of farmers in the San Juaquin Valley of central

California, has an answer. "Farmers need the support. Look, we are growing the food that feeds the country. We are national security, and we employ so many people. We have so many risks to contend with; weather, floods, fires, pests…it's a hard, hard job."[17]

Cunha's arguments are not without merit. But under the current system, small farmers in America don't have the same opportunities as rich ones. Despite the Department of Agriculture's insistence that it is expanding its services to small farms and younger farmers, 79 percent of all farm subsidies are paid to the largest 10 percent of farm operations, and "farmers in the top 1 percent in terms of income, average $1.5 million in annual farm subsidy welfare checks," according to Professor Vincent Smith. [18]

And what about the farmers who are excluded from the subsidy program? We sought out some of them to learn their stories.

One example is Cheri Lynne. Nestled in the rolling hills outside of Raleigh-Durham, Lynne's modest-sized Mountainview Farm includes a robust chicken population, a large greenhouse to start seeds in the spring, and a permaculture design including small ponds and water catchments. She has plans for on-site grey water processing, which will reduce the demand for fresh water and increase her farm's sustainability. Asked whether she participates in any USDA programs, she shakes her head. "No. Farmers like us can't get any help." [19] She is probably better off without government aid, as some of the examples that follow will illustrate.

Lynne is not the only small farmer who is ineligible for government help. As explained by the organization Physicians for Responsible Medicine:

> The USDA refers to fresh fruits and vegetables as "specialty crops." Specialty crops do not receive subsidies. In fact, farmers who participate in commodity subsidy programs are generally prohibited from growing fruits and vegetables on the so-called "base acres" of land for which they receive subsidies. This provision, enacted in 1996, restricts the ability of both small and large commodity farmers from diversifying their crops and including fruits and vegetables as part of their production.[20]

Other farmers opt out of the system voluntarily. Greg Gunthorpe, who farms 270 acres in North Central Indiana, has chosen to take no subsidies. With twenty full-time and ten part-time employees, he produces a million pounds of meat and poultry a year on his farm, including 120,000 chickens, 12,000 ducks, 10,000 turkeys, and 2,500 pigs.

Gunthorpe leases some of his land from a local landowner who also rents to his neighbors, and many of them do receive subsidies. As we drove the road between his farm and theirs, Gunthorpe observed wryly, "Who wouldn't want a guaranteed rent floor, except an idiot like me? Because of those subsidies, all my neighbors can afford to pay higher rents, and the landowner knows it, so my rents keep going up as those farmers rake in more money. I've only ever gotten hassles from the government, never any help. The government has no idea how to support sustainable niche agricultural enterprises like ours. They only support big commercial farms." [21]

The Sour Side of Sugar

Then there are the billionaire Fanjul brothers, Alfy and Pepe, dubbed "the first family of corporate welfare" by *Time* magazine. They raise sugarcane on 200,000 acres in the Florida Everglades and on another 200,000 acres abroad. Along with a few close relatives, the brothers own the Fanjul Corporation, whose brands include Domino, Florida Crystals, Redpath, Tate & Lyle, and C&H.

The Fanjuls are among the biggest beneficiaries of federal government price supports for sugar. The sugar program got its start in 1789, when the government passed its first sugar tariff to generate federal revenue. Between 1789 and 1930, Congress passed thirty pieces of legislation that, in combination, transformed sugar policy from a revenue source to a protectionist program. In the 1930s, price supports and import quotas for sugar were solidified, and the extreme protectionist measures have been in place ever since.

Today, the Farm Bill's sugar program heavily regulates the sugar industry, giving cane and beet growers subsidized loans, imposing import tariffs on sugar from abroad, setting quotas that affect how much sugar can be imported and how much can be sold, and fixing market prices. It is widely recognized as the least free market portion of the Farm Bill; no other crop is managed as heavily. A 2011 *Vanity Fair* investigation found that the Fanjuls were receiving about $65 million in price supports annually. Although the price of sugar on the world market was ten cents per pound at the time, the government paid American sugar growers, including the Fanjuls, twenty-one cents per pound (see Figure 1-2). And if sugar growers overproduced so that the price of their crop fell, the government bought the surplus. All told, growers got about $560 million in price supports that year, which meant that consumers had to pay $1.4 billion more for products containing sugar at the supermarket.[22]

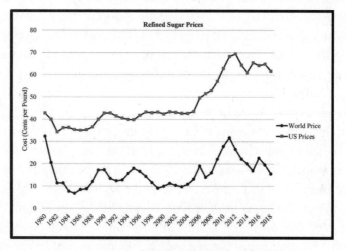

Figure 1-2: US and world refined sugar prices, 1980-2018.
Source: Bureau of Labor Statistics, 2019

The sweet deal enjoyed by sugar growers is no accident. A 2015 exposé by Amy Bracken in *Al Jazeera America* noted that the sugar industry "gave more than $5 million to members of Congress in the last election cycle…What the industry gets in return…are domestic controls and import tariffs that keep prices up and profits high for U.S. sugar producers, perpetuating a controversial system."[23]

David Guest, an attorney with Earthjustice who has fought the powerful sugar industry for over twenty years, with a special focus on Florida, noted in a 2011 interview that Big Sugar trades cash in the form of campaign donations for political favors in the form of subsidies. "They aren't in the agricultural business, they are in the corporate welfare business."[24]

Senator Mark Kirk (R-IL) has fought the sugar program for years. Along with senators Jeanne Shaheen (D-NH) and Pat Toomey (R-PA), he introduced the Sugar Reform Act in 2013, which would have brought an end to the worst parts of the sugar program.

Under heavy lobbying from the sugar industry, the bill failed.

We have often wondered how the relative handful of senators and Congressional Representatives who have constituents in the sugar business manage to convince their fellow lawmakers—a great many of whom represent non-farm city folks—to vote in support of the obviously unfair, biased, and dysfunctional sugar program. The answers are complex and include vote trades ("you back my priority project, and I'll back sugar"), but campaign contributions are an important part of it.

The Fanjul brothers, for example, have used their political clout to survive a heavy onslaught of media criticism and exposure. In addition to the articles we've already mentioned, popular author Carl Hiaasen parodied the family in his book *Strip Tease*. In 2006, Jodie Foster and Robert De Niro teamed up to make a movie, *Sugar Land*, that they hoped would tell the story of a class action suit brought against the Fanjul brothers by the migrant workers in their Florida cane fields. The Fanjuls got the case thrown out on a technicality, and the movie was never produced. However, a documentary, *Sugar Daddies*, tells the story of the slavery-like conditions on the two hundred thousand acres of Dominican sugar cane fields owned by the Fanjuls.

None of this bad publicity has moved Congress to scale back the sugar program. Perhaps not surprisingly, the Fanjul brothers donate equally to Republican and Democratic candidates. In the 2016 election cycle, they hosted major fundraising events for both Donald Trump and Hillary Clinton. Thus, no matter who is in office, the Fanjuls and other sugar growers win.[25]

Other businesses, however, are big losers. Candy makers and other companies that use sugar have moved out of the United States to avoid these costs, taking American jobs with them. Consider Judson-Atkinson, a San Antonio-based candy company. Because of the sugar program's subsidies, quotas, and tariffs, the company's owner, Amy Atkinson Voltz, was forced to pay more than twice the international price for sugar, which added $2 million to her annual costs. "It's totally unfair competition," she said. Largely as a result of these inflated sugar prices, Judson-Atkinson went out of business in 2011 after making candy for over a hundred years. "It's been really hard," Voltz says. "We had to bring in employees who had worked here 20-plus years and tell them that we were not going to produce candy."[26]

A Close Look at Crop Insurance

Another problematic portion of the Farm Bill is the Crop Insurance program, which began in 1938, in response to the Great Depression and the Dust Bowl, which had devastated American farmers. The program was small and experimental, and only covered a few crops. Over the years, the program has grown dramatically, and now most farmers participate.

Ralph Pistoresi, a California rancher, explains why he believes that he and other farmers need the insurance support:

> You know what farming is? Farming is nothing but risk, risk, risk. You buy the land, you've got a mortgage to pay, you're taking a risk on that land panning out. You go and buy seed, more risk, you've just spent money and gambled on those seeds growing. You till the land and plant those seeds, and then you tend them all season. Anything can happen, and I've had it all happen to me—rain, hail, drought, pests, labor problems. Risk, risk, risk. And then you harvest the crop, and then the buyers come and tell you what they'll pay, and you've got to take what they offer because you've gone all in— *all in*—and you need the money for the next year. There is no other job like it."[27]

Pistoresi's lament rings true. Sometimes, however, the crop insurance—like so much else in the realm of government subsidies—doesn't work as intended. Pistoresi shared his favorite crop insurance story while visiting with us in his broker's office in Fresno. "I had a freak hailstorm hit my plum trees when the plums were less than a quarter-inch around. As they grew, the skins of the plums developed scabs where they were damaged. The scabs looked just like this." He reached down and touched his worn tan leather cowboy boot. "There were these scabs on all my plums. When they grew to full size, we picked a sample for the buyer, and they said they wouldn't take them because consumers wouldn't buy the prunes if they had these scabs on them."

In an effort to recoup his losses, Pistoresi filed a claim with the insurance company. "They wouldn't accept the claim, saying they were applying a 'fingernail test.' They said that if an adjuster's fingernail could pierce the skin of the fruit at the damaged location, then the scab wasn't considered unacceptable, and thus the fruit was considered acceptable for sale."

He rolled his eyes, remembering the conversation with the bureaucrat on the other end of the line. "The fingernail test." He sighed. "So I had a crop I couldn't sell, and I couldn't recoup the loss because the insurance company said I could sell them. I tried selling them to a grape juice concentrate company while they still had juice in them, but by the time they got back to me, they had atrophied on the vine. That was a claim I never got payment for, and a whole field of plums lost."

Mostly though, the crop insurance system works, Pistoresi says. When it does, it can play a helpful role in mitigating the significant risks inherent in the business of farming.

Unfortunately, there are other, less savory, reasons for the popularity of the farm insurance program among wealthy farmers and their supporters on Capitol Hill. "Congress channels the largest portion of farm subsidies through its insurance programs in order to obscure the identities of wealthy recipients," Chris Edwards of the Cato Institute observes. An expert on farm policy, he notes that news stories often identified the millionaires receiving farm subsidies, which was embarrassing to Congress. Insurance subsidies are less transparent.[28]

At a cost of $41 billion for 2014–2018, the Farm Bill's crop insurance program lets farmers purchase crop insurance, with the federal government paying part of the costs.[29] And then, if a farmer puts in a claim for a loss, the government covers the deductible.

These handouts are available to farmers through a program called Multiple Peril Crop Insurance (MPCI), which must be purchased before the growing season. As the name implies, MPCI covers losses from several perils—drought, moisture, freeze, and diseases—and it includes price-loss provisions that mitigate losses in revenue because of low yields or falling prices.

Thanks to the price-loss provisions, farmers can supply predictions of what their revenue will be at the end of a season, using an established national price per crop, and then make claims against their policies if actual revenue falls short of predicted revenue once the season is over, whereupon their government-paid insurance issues payment to make up for the shortfall. In 2018, 1.1 million crop insurance policies worth $106 billion in liability protection, covered almost 90 percent of all farmland in America—311 million acres.[30]

Attempts to rein in Farm Bill largesse have included setting income limits for farmers who qualify for certain benefits. The income limit specified in the current Farm Bill stands at $900,000 a year, which is more than ten times what the average American makes annually.[31] However, this income limit does not apply to the crop insurance program, which probably explains why it's the fastest growing and most expensive portion of the Farm Bill.

The commodities program is another kind of farm insurance program that was started following the Great Depression in the 1930s. Unlike crop insurance, which insures against physical crop damage and losses, the commodities portion of the Farm Bill helps farmers cope with market fluctuations in prices once certain crops are ready to harvest, especially corn, wheat, soybeans, cotton, rice, peanuts, and dairy products. Its Price Loss Coverage (PLC) and Agricultural Risk Coverage (ARC) programs were predicted to cost $24 billion from 2014 through 2018.[32]

Using the PLC and ARC programs, farmers can either provide figures for the worth of their crops when they plant them, and insure them at that value (the Harvest Price Exclusion Option), or they can predict the amount that the crops will sell for at market time and insure them at that value (the Harvest Price Option). Either way, if a farmer gets less than the insured price, the government makes up the difference. On the other hand, a farmer whose crops sell for more than the insured price gets to pocket the difference.

As a result, farmers using this kind of insurance usually run no financial risks on any crops covered by the program. If a farmer predicts earnings of $100,000 in a given growing season, acquires insurance to cover that yield, and then doesn't earn the predicted amount, the farmer will still get the full $100,000 through the taxpayer-funded insurance.

Noting that 83 percent of farmers choose the Harvest Price Option, scholars at the American Enterprise Institute call it the "Cadillac Option." They estimated that it would cost taxpayers $2 billion more than other forms of subsidized insurance over the life of the 2014 Farm Bill.

"The problem with subsidized crop insurance," as Professor Smith has noted, "is that it allows farmers to operate in ways that increase the risk of crop and other forms of financial loss." Knowing "that any losses they incur will be covered by taxpayers, farmers have responded rationally by, for example, planting crops on poor-quality land, cutting back on things like pesticides and fertilizer that reduce the risk of crop losses, and reducing the extent to which they diversify their enterprises."[33]

These subsidies "encourage the worst kinds of farming," says Blaine Hitzfield, a farmer in Northwest Indiana who dropped out of the crop insurance program. "The insurance does nothing to encourage stewardship of the land. Instead, it encourages farmers to grow the worst crops and to abuse the land to get high yields."[34]

Gay Brown, a North Dakota farmer who doesn't participate in either the commodities program or the crop insurance program, has a story to tell about the results of incentives to mismanage crops. While his hayfield was standing tall in the autumn sunshine, ready for harvest, several of his neighbors had filed loss claims stemming from their poor crop management. The neighbors called to ask him to cut down his hay so the insurance company wouldn't see that the damage to their crops wasn't due to weather. "Hell, no," Brown said, and left his hay in the field.

Paying Farmers Not to Farm

The Conservation Reserve Program was enacted in the 1950s, originally as a "soil bank" program designed to protect soils at risk from erosion by taking them out of production and planting them with stabilizing native cover crops.

The conservation program is predominantly used to pay farmers to grow their crops on fewer acres, although it also provides incentives to minimize ecologically harmful practices by using methods such as drip irrigation that protect against soil erosion.[35] Compensation comes through the program's Land Rental provisions which pay "rent" to farmers for acres they leave fallow.

Of America's 360 million acres of farmland, as many as twenty-five million are now eligible for the Land Rental Program, down from thirty-six million acres a couple of years ago. This number varies depending on how many farmers choose to participate in any given year. The program paid farmers more than $1.7 billion in 2016, an average of $72.61 per acre taken out of production.[36] Typically, farmers commit to taking specified numbers of acres out of production for ten to fifteen years, but they can change the amount at any point depending on crop price fluctuations. In years when crop prices are high, more farmers are likely to use acreage for growing crops. Conversely, when crop prices are low, more farmers choose to compensate for the loss of crop income by converting land to land rental property in exchange for money from the government.

Leaving land temporarily fallow does have some benefits, but novelist Joseph Heller had it basically right in the passage from his satirical novel *Catch-22* quoted at the start of this chapter: American taxpayers are paying farmers not to grow food.

Overseas Aid as Handout to the Wealthy

Farm program money also goes to the Foreign Market Development Program (FMDP) and the Market Access Program (MAP), two federal programs that are supposed to promote U.S. crops abroad. The FMDP doles out $27 million a year to groups such as the Mohair Council and the National Sunflower Association, which generally chip in 70 percent of the cost of programs for promoting their products overseas. And as John Sandbakken, President of the National Sunflower Association, notes, "American embassies even provide market intelligence to us, doing the research to discover where our products will have the best chance of success, and what the market is like in the host country. It's great. If we had to pay for that research, it would cost us a lot of money."[37]

As for the Market Access Program, it pays $174 million a year for activities that promote commodities and branded products in foreign markets, focusing heavily on promotion, usually via advertising.[38] Recipients include a producer of chili-pepper-infused honey, the Wine Institute, the Popcorn Board, the Pet Food Institute, and the Distilled Spirits Council.

The Ethanol Boondoggle

In addition to all of the above, the Farm Bill offers funding for some technical assistance to farmers in developing countries, and for biofuels, biochemicals, and bioplastics industries, including substantial amounts for the ethanol program.

U.S. ethanol derives from corn, the largest crop in America, with about 97 million acres grown annually. Corn is also our most heavily subsidized crop, with subsidy payments to corn growers totaling close to $90 billion between 1995 and 2010. Yet the corn industry long ago stopped being about feeding people.[39] The 2007 Independence and Security Act mandated use of 36 billion gallons of biofuels by 2022 in the United States, giving a huge boost to the ethanol industry—paid for by the taxpayers. Today, more than 40 percent of the corn grown in the United States is converted to ethanol; another 40 percent is used for animal feed, and close to 15 percent is exported.[40] The remaining 5 percent is mostly used to make high fructose corn syrup.

The ethanol boondoggle has hurt Americans in a variety of ways. Because of corn's use for ethanol, there's less corn for food and feed, and that drives up food prices. As Jillian Kay Melchior noted in *National*

Review, the Congressional Budget Office estimated that American consumers would spend $3.5 billion more on groceries in 2016 because of the ethanol mandate.[41] What's more, the ethanol mandate "has triggered an environmental disaster," says William F. Shughart II, a senior fellow at the Independent Institute. Because ethanol demands huge amounts of corn, diverse prairie lands are being plowed under, "destroying the prairie ecosystem…that previously served as habitat for more than eight hundred species of birds and monarch butterflies and honey bees."[42]

It's not surprising to learn that some of the nation's most powerful political influence brokers benefit from the ethanol mandate. The Koch brothers have firmly denied supporting the mandate. "Koch Industries opposes all forms of corporate welfare—even those that benefit us," Charles Koch declared in a 2016 letter to the *Washington Post*, adding that the "government's ethanol mandate is a good example.[43] We oppose that mandate, even though we are the fifth-largest ethanol producer in the United States."

Charles Koch and his brother David Koch (who died in August 2019) spent a fair portion of their combined net worth of $100 billion quietly buying up ethanol processing plants. "The company philosophy is against all subsidies," said Jeremy Bezdek, vice president of a Koch Industries subsidiary. "But ethanol is a moneymaker."[44]

Still More Subsidies

Rich cattle and dairy ranchers and rich peanut growers are among the other groups that benefit from government subsidies. Cattle ranchers save money by feeding their cattle with subsidized fodder. Dairy farmers benefit from the Margin Protection Program in the 2014 Farm Bill, which protects milk prices in much the same way that other crops are protected from price declines. And peanut farmers got bonuses in the 2014 Farm Bill, which not only expanded their dedicated subsidy program, but also made them exempt from all limits on the amount of money they can make while remaining eligible for subsidies.[45] Peanut subsidies will total nearly a billion dollars over the life of the current Farm Bill.[46] Some of that money will go to businesses such as Carter

Farms, the famous peanut farm of President Jimmy Carter, whose net worth reaches into the millions.[47]

The fact that the target price the government set for peanuts in 2014 was much higher than any price paid to peanut farmers in any recent year became an incentive for farmers to switch from other crops to peanut farming—and many of them did. The result was a glut of overpriced peanuts. In a truly bizarre move, the USDA then decided to ship most of those excess peanuts to Haiti as food aid. As the *Washington Post* reported, that aid represented "subsidized foreign competition for Haiti's peanut growers, who are struggling to supply the local market, with support from—you guessed it—the U.S. Agency for International Development."[48]

In short, the government subsidized our peanut farmers to grow more peanuts than they could sell. Then the government bought the excess peanuts. Then they shipped those peanuts to a country where 500,000 Haitians were involved in peanut production, undermining local efforts to earn a living.[49]

Poultry farmers have gotten in on the act as well. In 2013, the National Chicken Council, a trade industry group that represents the chicken industry, approached the Department of Agriculture with a dilemma: Their members had raised too much chicken—fifty million pounds' worth. They convinced the USDA to buy it and give it away in the food assistance program. The USDA paid four producers a total of $50 million for the fifty million pounds of excess chicken.[50] "Members of the National Chicken Council are most appreciative of USDA's timely action," the organization declared.[51] American taxpayers were not consulted.

One of the most appalling uses of taxpayer dollars was the slaughter of half a million dairy cows under a "herd retirement program" between 2004 and 2008. The goal was to drive up the cost of dairy products. According to the *Washington Post*, "From 2004 to 2008, milk producers' prices rose 66 cents per hundredweight of milk. By the end of the program in 2010, it was responsible for a cumulative increase in milk price revenue of $9.55 billion."[52]

This is one of the relatively rare cases in which egregious corporate welfare was exposed, and in some measure, reversed. An anti-trust lawsuit was brought against the dairy farmers. Steve Berman, speaking for one of the law firms that brought the suit, said, "The biggest dairy producers in the country, responsible for almost 70 percent of the nation's milk, conspired together in a classic price-fixing scheme, forcing higher prices for a basic food item onto honest consumers and families."[53] In 2017, the suit was settled for $52 million. The Cooperatives Working Together group, a conglomerate of dairy suppliers, admitted no wrongdoing but agreed to refund purchases of dairy products sold during this time.

The scheme would have never seen the light of day had not the dairy farmers been receiving milk subsidies in the first place. A free market would have encouraged only the production of as much product as the market could bear, and a half-million cows would have been spared "early retirement."

Are Farm Subsidies Necessary?

Farm subsidies certainly have their defenders. One is Tony Mellenthin, president of the Wisconsin Soybean Association. Sitting in the office on his seven thousand-acre farm, planted half in soybeans and half in corn, Mellenthin shared his opinion of the Farm Bill. "I think the current crop insurance subsidies are a good thing," he told us. "They create stability for farmers, removing some of the uncertainty that comes with farming. Having the price guarantees means we can invest in seed, fertilizer, and equipment with some peace of mind."[54]

As for conservation, he sees putting land into a conservation status as a "CD for farmers":

> "We put land into the conservation easement for ten years and get the annual payment from the government from doing so, and then at the end we have land that has increased in value and we've earned some 'interest' on it. People outside of the system don't understand how important these subsidies are to the whole economy of the Midwest. If this economic support were to go away, there would be a trickle-down effect that would impact

whole towns—tractor companies, farm feed operations, car dealerships, retail…that money gets spread around way beyond just the farm that gets it, and really helps the whole state economy. It would be a disaster if those funds were cut off."

Another farmer we spoke to went further: "Don't knock the Farm Bill—it is our bread and butter. We farmers are the foundation of this country, and the country has a responsibility to support us. Heck, where would we be as a country if America stopped supporting the very farms that feed us? I think you're crazy if you think that would work out. It's the way the whole system works."

One farmer who refused an interview expressed his anger at the bad press that agricultural subsidies have inspired. "I'm not going to speak with you, and you're not going to find any farmers that will. We've all been vilified and misrepresented in the press too many times. People don't understand us and what we do."[55]

Darin Von Ruden, President of the Wisconsin Farmers Union, disagrees. A third-generation dairy farmer, Darin has never carried crop insurance on his 230-acre dairy farm. Asked about the income limits on farmers who qualify for subsidies, he noted that the Farmers Union is actively researching the issue and plans to make a recommendation to Congress that the income limit be dropped from $900,000 to $75,000. "Most farmers I know, including myself, want to be paid by the consumer, not the government. We want to participate in a free and open market. Period. It is the big corporate farms who get the bulk of these subsidies, and they do so by pretending that each of the family farms they've swallowed up is still an independent entity so that the farmers qualify for the benefits."[56]

Asked why the Food Stamp Program falls under the Farm Bill, he smiles. "There's no way the Farm Bill would pass without the Food Stamps being a part of it. Everyone knows that. The Food Stamps are the way to get the urban support from Congress for the rest of the Farm Bill."

Helping to meet the nutritional needs of the poor was indeed one of the original purposes of the original Depression Era Farm Bill. Beyond the Food Stamp Program, however, the current U.S. Farm Bill does little to make low-cost food available to the poor, or to improve American diets. According to an American Enterprise Institute report called *Poverty, Hunger and Agricultural Policy*, farm programs do not affect food prices in a direction that protects the poor, and the people whose incomes are most improved by farm policies are not the same people who are at risk of poverty and hunger. "In short," the report declares, "the time is long past—many decades past—for thinking of US farm policies as a good way of helping the poor."[57]

In addition, farm subsidies tend to encourage a heavy diet of processed foods, producing a nutritional landscape overloaded with cereal grains. Kathryn Doyle, writing for Reuters, noted that "Current federal agricultural subsidies help finance the production of corn, soybeans, wheat, rice, sorghum, dairy, and livestock, which are often converted into refined grains, high-fat and high-sodium processed foods, and high-calorie juices and soft drinks (sweetened with high-fructose corn syrup)."[58] According to a report in the American Medical Association's journal *Internal Medicine*, "The more people eat of foods made with the Farm Bill's subsidized commodities, the more likely they are to be obese, have abnormal cholesterol and high blood sugar."[59]

Farm subsidies have also been blamed for distorting the best farming practices, focusing farmers' attention on how to play the program for maximum dollars rather than working on the long-term productivity of their land. The New Zealand experience graphically illustrates how improved agricultural productivity can follow the phasing out of government involvement.

Until the early 1980s, New Zealand farmers were generously subsidized. "It got to the point that a third or more of our income was being supplied from the central government," says Bill Cashmore, a New Zealand farmer whose family owns a five thousand-acre farm.[60] Part of the subsidy was tied to the number of sheep being raised, irrespective of their weight or condition. Cashmore called this "the skinny sheep policy," as the weight of farmers' ewes went down. Combined with stifling restrictions on imports of farm equipment and on other parts of the economy as well, the New Zealand economy was in serious trouble in the early 1980s. In response, the government passed radical reforms, virtually eliminating agricultural subsidies and also lifting many of the most onerous import restrictions.

Without the subsidies, many farmers had to struggle, but, a few years later, New Zealand was on the way to becoming one of the most efficient agricultural producers in the world. "Same number of ewes. Same number of cows," Cashmore reported. "But they're providing thirty to fifty percent more [return]." Overall, New Zealand farm productivity gains went from one percent per year to nearly six percent. "I'd never go back," Cashmore says. And most New Zealand farmers agree.

Many American farmers have come to believe that our own subsidy program is equally destructive of good farming practices. Blaine Hitzfield, one of seven brothers farming the Seven Sons Farm in North Central Indiana, provides an example. Lulled by the guarantees of the Farm Bill programs, Blaine and his family got careless, slipped into monoculture farming that depleted the soil, and began overusing fertilizers and other chemicals that ultimately contributed to Blaine's mother's deteriorating health. Realizing the need for radical change, the Hitzfields sold two-thirds of their original fifteen hundred acres, foreswore all government subsidies, and started farming sustainably on the remaining five hundred acres. The farm is now thriving without government support, selling directly to consumers who sign up for monthly deliveries of fresh produce. When asked whether he and his family are ever wistful for the days of the subsidy program, Hitzfield shakes his head. "We would never participate in that system again."[61]

The sectors of American farming that operate largely free of subsidies further illustrate that agriculture need not be dependent on government largesse. American vegetable farmers grew 3.7 million tons of lettuce in 2015, plus more than a million tons of carrots, onions, and watermelons. Most of those results were achieved without government assistance, although even here a few subsidies have crept in. A number of fruit and nut growers have access to subsidized water for irrigation, especially in the West, and subsidy payments for crop insurance premiums are common for the major vegetable growers.[62]

However, these subsidies are relatively trivial compared to the funds doled out to the major food grain growers. And mostly without federal help, vegetable farmers have managed to earn close to $20 billion through the produce they grow each year. The outlook for vegetable farmers remains rosy, as noted in a 2017 report by IBISWorld, a financial services research firm:

> A push toward healthy eating has increased the market for higher-margin fresh vegetables…Despite slight cost increases, industry operators have managed their supply contracts well, shielding and even increasing their profit margins. Drastic changes are not expected within the industry over the next five years. Vegetable consumption will remain near current levels, as industry associations promote healthy eating through marketing campaigns that tout the benefits of eating vegetables.[63]

D'Arrigo Brothers Farms, famous for their Andy Boy brand, is a case in point. They farm 37,000 acres of fennel, broccoli, cauliflower, and lettuce in California, earning revenues of $239 million a year in the process. They are sufficiently confident of their profitability to provide roughly a million dollars a year to philanthropic causes.[64]

Despite the many problems with farm subsidies, and the strong arguments against them, once such programs become entrenched, they are difficult to dislodge. In fact, it's all too easy to find reasons to launch new handouts.

In 2018, and again in 2019, President Donald Trump authorized farm "relief" payments of $12 billion and $16 billion to selected American farmers.[65] These payouts were intended to compensate farmers for their losses suffered as a result of Trump's new tariffs on Chinese goods, in response to which the Chinese, expectedly, slapped tariffs on U.S. farm products.

For many farmers, Trump's contributions represented one subsidy too many. "We want to make a living in the market, not from handouts," was a frequent response. Jennifer Poindexter-Runge, a South Dakota veterinarian interviewed by *The Washington Post* about these latest farm bailouts, scoffed at their potential effects: "The [farm] bailout package is like putting a Band-Aid on a bleeding artery. It's not going to save anybody."[66]

These comments capture a final, potent argument against farm subsidies—namely, the psychology of it all. For many thoughtful farmers, the payments and subsidies feel like welfare. "They don't want to admit it, [but] they're ashamed," said a farmer we encountered in a feed store in Indiana. "American farmers have this aura, this history, of being rugged individualists, braving nature's worst to raise crops for their fellow citizens. And reality now is so far from that. When you come right down to it, farmers today are just high-end welfare cheats feeding at the public trough, and I can tell you this much—their granddaddies are rolling over in their graves."

1 "Budget Issues That Shaped the 2014 Farm Bill," *Every CRS Report*, April 10, 2014, https://www.everycrsreport.com/reports/R42484.html.

2 "Projected Spending Under the 2014 Farm Bill," United States Department of Agriculture Economic Research Service, https://www.ers.usda.gov/topics/farm-economy/farm-commodity-policy/projected-spending-under-the-2014-farm-bill/.

3 John Komoyen (Indiana Farmer), interview by Lisa Conyers July 2017.

4 "Projected Spending Under the 2014 Farm Bill," United State Department of Agriculture Economic Research Service, August 20, 2019, https://www.ers.usda.gov/topics/farm-economy/farm-commodity-policy/projected-spending-under-the-2014-farm-bill/.

5 "Microsoft Word - Billionaire Chart BW_RC," 1, https://cdn.ewg.org/sites/default/files/blog/Billionaire_Chart_BW_RC.pdf?_ga=2.83119636.360598995.1497477451-842112084.1489101636.

6 "Microsoft Word - Billionaire Chart BW_RC," 9.

7 Andrew Breiner and Alan Pyke, "How Republicans Who Took Millions in Farm Subsidies Justify Cutting Food Stamps," *ThinkProgress*, June 18, 2013, Climate Progress, https://thinkprogress.org/how-republicans-who-took-millions-in-farm-subsidies-justify-cutting-food-stamps-6dc850ed748a/.

8 "USDA Subsidy Information for Doug Dallas Sombke," Environmental Working Group, https://farm.ewg.org/persondetail.php?custnumber=A07736446.

9 Patrick Anderson, "What Trump's Budget Would Mean For South Dakota," *Argus Leader*, May 23, 2017, updated May 24, 2017, https://www.argusleader.com/story/news/2017/05/23/what-trumps-budget-would-mean-south-dakota/339573001/.

10 "Texas Farm Subsidy Information," EWG's Farm Subsidy Database, https://farm.ewg.org/region.php?fips=48000&progcode=total.

11 "Crop Insurance in the United States," EWG's Farm Subsidy Database, https://farm.ewg.org/cropinsurance.php?fips=00000&regionname=theUnitedStates&_ga=2.130354696.682960410.1505326591-842112084.1489101636.

12 Vincent H. Smith, "Should Washington End Agriculture Subsidies?" *Wall Street Journal*, July 12, 2015, Business Leadership, https://www.wsj.com/articles/should-washington-end-agriculture-subsidies-1436757020.

13 Daren Baskt, ed., *Farms and Free Enterprise: A Blueprint for Agricultural Policy* (Washington, D.C.: The Heritage Foundation, 2016), 13, http://thf-reports.s3.amazonaws.com/2016/Farms_and_Free_Enterprise.pdf.

14 "The Database Tracks $368 Billion in Farm Subsidies from Commodity, Crop Insurance, Disaster Programs and Conservation Payments Paid Between 1995 and 2017," *EWG's Farm Subsidy Database*, https://farm.ewg.org/?_ga=1.147549623.1607116893.1473806254.

15 "EWG's Farm Subsidy Database," Environmental Working Group, https://farm.ewg.org/search.php.

16 "Data Files: U.S. and State-Level Farm Income and Wealth Statistics," United States Department of Agriculture Economic Research Service, https://www.ers.usda.gov/data-products/farm-income-and-wealth-statistics/data-files-us-and-state-level-farm-income-and-wealth-statistics/.

17 Manuel Cunha (Nisei Farmers League President, San Joaquin Valley, California), interview by Lisa Conyers, July 2018.

18 Vincent H. Smith (Professor of Economics, Montana State University), interview by Lisa Conyers, July 2017.

19 Cheri Lynne (Farm Owner, North Carolina), interview by Lisa Conyers, August 2017.

20 "Dietary Studies," *JAMA Internal Medicine* (commentary), July 5, 2016, https://media.jamanetwork.com/news-item/dietary-studies-commentary-in-jama-internal-medicine/.

21 Greg Gunthrope (Indiana Farmer), interview by Lisa Conyers, August 2017.

22 Marie Brenner, "In the Kingdom of Big Sugar," *Vanity Fair*, January 5, 2011, Business, https://www.vanityfair.com/news/2001/02/floridas-fanjuls-200102.

23 Amy Bracken, "A Sweet Deal: The Royal Family of Cane Benefits from Political Giving," *Aljazeera America*, July 23, 2015, http://america.aljazeera.com/multimedia/2015/7/fanjul-family-benefits-political-donations.html.

24 Virginia Chamlee, "How Big Sugar Get What It Wants from Congress," *The Colorado Independent*, September 20, 2011, https://www.coloradoindependent.com/2011/09/20/how-big-sugar-gets-what-it-wants-from-congress/.

25 Guy Rolnik, "Meet the Sugar Barons Who Used Both Sides of American Politics to Get Billions in Subsidies," ProMarket (blog), September 19, 2016, https://promarket.org/sugar-industry-buys-academia-politicians/.

26 Daniel Rivera, "U.S. Sugar Program Hurts Businesses and Kills Jobs," Competitive Enterprise Institute (blog), November 10, 2011, https://cei.org/blog/us-sugar-program-hurts-businesses-and-kills-jobs.

27 Ralph Pistoresi (California Rancher), interview by Lisa Conyers, August 2018.

28 Chris Edwards, "Agricultural Subsidies," Cato Institute, April 16, 2018, https://www.downsizinggovernment.org/agriculture/subsidies.

29 Anne Weir Schechinger and Craig Cox, "Double Dipping: How Taxpayers Subsidize Farmers Twice for Crop Losses," Environmental Working Group, November 14, 2017, https://www.ewg.org/research/subsidy-layer-cake.

30 "Crop Insurance Acreage Sets New Mark in 2017," National Crop Insurance Services, February 6, 2018, https://cropinsuranceinamerica.org/crop-insurance-acreage-sets-new-mark-2017/; "Facts & Figures," Crop Insurance, https://cropinsuranceinamerica.org/about-crop-insurance/facts-figures/.

31 Ron Durst and Robert Williams, "Farm Bill Income Cap for Program Payment Eligibility Affects Few Farms," United States Department of Agricultural Economic Research Service, August 01, 2016, Farm Economy, https://www.ers.usda.gov/amber-waves/2016/august/farm-bill-income-cap-for-program-payment-eligibility-affects-few-farms/.

32 Schechinger, "Double Dipping: How Taxpayers Subsidize Farmers Twice for Crop Losses."

33 Smith, "Should Washington End Agriculture Subsidies?"

34 Blaine Hitzfield (Northwest Indiana Farmer) interview by Lisa Conyers, July 2017.

35 Daniel M. Hellerstein, "The US Conservation Reserve Program: The Evolution of an Enrollment Mechanism," *Land Use Policy*, no. 63 (April 2017): 601-610, https://doi.org/10.1016/j.landusepol.2015.07.017.

36 John Newton, Ph.D., "Change on the Horizon for the Conservation Reserve Program?" American Farm Bureau Federation, May 15, 2017, https://www.fb.org/market-intel/change-on-the-horizon-for-the-conservation-reserve-program.

37 John Sandbakken (National Sunflower Association President), interview with Lisa Conyers, June 14, 2017.

38 "MAP Funding Allocations—FY2019," United States Department of Agriculture: Foreign Agricultural Service, https://www.fas.usda.gov/programs/market-access-program-map/map-funding-allocations-fy-2019.

[39] Jonathan Foley, "It's Time to Rethink America's Corn System," *Scientific American*, March 5, 2013, https://www.scientificamerican.com/article/time-to-rethink-corn/.

[40] "Production and Exports," U.S. Grains Council, 2019, Corn, https://grains.org/buying-selling/corn/.

[41] Jillian Kay Melchior, "Trump's Support for Ethanol Is Bad for Taxpayers and Their Cars," *National Review*, January 21, 2016, https://www.nationalreview.com/2016/01/donald-trump-ethanol-subsidy-support-bad-taxpayers/.

[42] William F. Shugart II, "How the Ethanol Mandate Is Killing the American Prairie," *Investor's Business Daily*, April 13, 2017, Commentary, https://www.investors.com/politics/commentary/how-the-ethanol-mandate-is-killing-the-american-prairie/.

[43] Charles G. Koch, "Charles Koch: This is the One Issue Where Bernie Sanders is Right," *The Washington Post*, February 18, 2016, Opinion, https://www.washingtonpost.com/opinions/charles-koch-this-is-the-one-issue-where-bernie-sanders-is-right/2016/02/18/cdd2c228-d5c1-11e5-be55-2cc3c1e4b76b_story.html.

[44] Mario Parker, "Koch Brothers Build Biofuel Giant Aided by Mandates They Abhor," *Bloomberg*, November 2, 2016, https://www.bloomberg.com/news/articles/2016-11-02/koch-brothers-build-biofuel-giant-aided-by-mandates-they-abhor.

[45] Dennis A. Shields, "U.S. Peanut Program and Issues," Congressional Research Service (report), August 19, 2015, https://www.fb.org/files/2018FarmBill/CRS_Report_on_Peanuts.pdf.

[46] Editorial Board, "America's Nutty Farm Subsidies Cause Damage at Home and Abroad," *The Washington Post*, April 26, 2016, https://www.washingtonpost.com/opinions/americas-nutty-farm-subsidies-cause-damage-at-home-and-abroad/2016/04/26/22f51fa6-07fb-11e6-bdcb-0133da18418d_story.html?utm_term=.46697ddb0f26.

[47] "List of Presidents of the United States by Net Worth," Wikipedia, https://en.wikipedia.org/wiki/List_of_Presidents_of_the_United_States_by_net_worth.

[48] Editorial Board, "America's Nutty Farm Subsidies Cause Damage at Home."

[49] Clare Leschin-Hoar, "U.S. to Ship Peanuts to Feed Haitian Kids; Aid Groups Say 'This Is Wrong'," *NPR*, May 5, 2016, Food For Thought, https://www.npr.org/sections/thesalt/2016/05/05/476876371/u-s-to-ship-peanuts-to-feed-haitian-kids-aid-groups-say-this-is-wrong.

[50] Staff, "USDA Awards Contracts for Chicken Purchase Program," Sosland Publishing Company, September 27, 2013, Meat+Poultry, https://www.meatpoultry.com/articles/8806-usda-awards-contracts-for-chicken-purchase-program.

[51] "National Chicken Council Thanks USDA for Special Purchase of Chicken," National Chicken Council, August 16, 2011, https://www.nationalchickencouncil.org/national-chicken-council-thanks-usda-for-special-purchase-of-chicken/.

[52] Samantha Schmidt, "'Herd Retirement': A Nice Dairy Industry Term for Slaughtering 500,000 Productive Cows," *The Washington Post*, January 19, 2017, Morning Mix, https://www.washingtonpost.com/news/morning-mix/wp/2017/01/19/herd-retirement-a-nice-dairy-industry-term-for-slaughtering-500000-productive-cows/?utm_term=.87b8c23b3cb9.

[53] Schmidt, "'Herd Retirement': A Nice Dairy Industry Term for Slaughtering."

[54] Tony Mellenthin (Wisconsin Soybean Association President), interview by Lisa Conyers, November 2018.

[55] Farmer, interview with Lisa Conyers, July 18, 2018.

[56] Darin Von Ruden (Wisconsin Farmers Union President) interview by Lisa Conyers, November 2018.

[57] Daniel A. Sumner, Joseph W. Glauber, and Parke E. Wilde, "Poverty, Hunger, and US Agricultural Policy: Do Farm Programs Affect the Nutrition of Poor Americans?", *American Enterprise Institute*, January 9, 2017, http://www.aei.org/publication/poverty-hunger-and-us-agricultural-policy-do-farm-programs-affect-the-nutrition-of-poor-americans/.

[58] Kathryn Doyle, "Foods from Subsidized Commodities Tied to Obesity," *Reuters*, July 5, 2016, Health News, https://www.reuters.com/article/us-health-diet-farm-subsidies/foods-from-subsidized-commodities-tied-to-obesity-idUSKCN0ZL2ER.

[59] Dong D. Wang, MD, MSc, et al., "Association of Specific Dietary Fats with Total and Cause-Specific Mortality," *JAMA Internal Medicine* (August 2016), doi:10.1001/jamainternmed.2016.2417; Karen R. Siegel, PhD, et al., "Association of Higher Consumption of Foods Derived from Subsidized Commodities with Adverse Cardiometabolic Risk Among US Adults," *JAMA Internal Medicine* (August 2016), doi:10.1001/jamainternmed.2016.2410.

[60] "Trailblazers: The New Zealand Story," Free to Choose Network, directed by James Trusty and Maureen Castle Trusty, 2016, https://www.freetochoosenetwork.org/programs/new_zealand/credits.php.

[61] Blaine Hitzfield (Seven Sons Farming, Indiana), interview by Lisa Conyers, July 2017.

[62] Isabel Rosa and Renée Johnson, "Federal Crop Insurance: Specialty Crops," Congressional Research Service, January 14, 2019, https://fas.org/sgp/crs/misc/R45459.pdf.

[63] "Vegetable Farming Industry in the US - Market Research Report," *IBIS World*, May 2019, https://www.ibisworld.com/industry-trends/market-research-reports/agriculture-forestry-fishing-hunting/crop-production/vegetable-farming.html.

[64] Kim Hughes, "94-Year-Old Family Produce Biz Andy Boy Gives Millions to Charity," *SamaritanMag*, May 28, 2014, https://www.samaritanmag.com/features/94-year-old-family-produce-biz-andy-boy-gives-millions-charity.

[65] Alan Rappeport, "A $12 Billion Program to Help Farmers Stung by Trump's Trade War Has Aided Few," *The New York Times*, November 19, 2018, https://www.nytimes.com/2018/11/19/us/politics/farming-trump-trade-war.html; Katie Mettler, "Extreme Weather Is Pummeling the Midwest, and Farmers Are in Deep Trouble," *MSN*, May 30, 2019, Money, https://www.msn.com/en-us/money/markets/extreme-weather-is-pummeling-the-midwest-and-farmers-are-in-deep-trouble/ar-AAC9bTJ#page=2.

[66] Annie Gowen, "'I Don't Know How We're Going to Survive This.' Some Once-Loyal Farmers Begin to Doubt Trump." *The Washington Post*, June 21, 2019, National, https://www.washingtonpost.com/national/i-dont-know-how-were-going-to-survive-this-once-loyal-farmers-begin-to-doubt-trump/2019/06/21/04a32c65-c385-4052-8cd7-5cb4ef2119cc_story.html?utm_term=.5d6455d9939a.

2.

The Tariff Trap: Taxing Millions to Enrich a Few

Blockading squadrons are a means whereby nations seek to prevent their enemies from trading; protective tariffs are a means whereby nations attempt to prevent their own people from trading. What protectionism teaches us, is to do to ourselves in time of peace what enemies seek to do to us in time of war.

—Henry George

I'm a tariff guy.

—President Donald J. Trump

Tariffs are usually thought of as an arcane element of economic policy. But today, tariffs are making headlines and attracting a national debate. It started when President Trump declared himself "a tariff guy" and began using tariffs as a tool of economic and foreign policy—first against American allies, like Canada, then against rivals like China. The president's self-proclaimed trade war against China has leaned heavily on the use of tariffs—to the detriment of American citizens, since the tariff fees paid by companies are almost always passed through to consumers in the form of higher prices.

In the year 2000, tariffs levied on imports into the United States cost each American between $269 and $660 a year, depending on income.[1] In 2018, the National Bureau of Economic Research did an in-depth study of the effects of President Trump's trade war, and concluded that "Over the course of 2018, the U.S. experienced...complete passthrough of the tariffs into domestic prices of imported goods...[W]e find that the full incidence of the tariff falls on domestic consumers, with a reduction in U.S. real income of $1.4 billion per month by the end of 2018."[2]

By 2019, with the imposition of more and more tariffs, Nien Su, a former chief economic adviser to the House Foreign Affairs Committee, projected yearly costs of between $800 and $1,000 per consumer due to President Trump's ongoing trade war, but this number was likely understated; according to a 2019 Trade Partnership Worldwide analysis, the trade war with China alone will cost American families about $2,300 a year.[3] The New York Federal Reserve Bank estimated that, to mid-2019, the Trump administration's tariff policy had cost median earners $831 per year each.[4]

Trump's trade war has sparked a national debate.

But the perverse harm done by tariffs is nothing new. The U.S. has always had a long list of tariffs that tend to discriminate particularly against people of low to modest income. Tariffs raise prices and consumers pay more.[5] These costs fall heaviest on the poor.[6] Many of the products that have traditionally carried the highest tariffs are basic necessities like inexpensive shoes (duties on shoes range from 6 percent to 48 percent) and basic food items that low-income citizens depend on.

Dan Ikenson, Director of Trade Policy Studies at the Cato Institute, noted in 2016 that "The United States has relatively low tariffs on average—less than 2 percent. But tariffs on clothing (18 percent), footwear (14 percent), and food products (10 percent) are especially high... Imports of life's basic necessities—food, clothing, and shelter—are subject to some of the highest taxes."[7]

A 2017 study on the impact of tariffs gives this example of the hurdles for low- and middle-income Americans: "[F]or a family doing their back-to-school shopping, backpacks of man-made fibers carry tariffs of 17.6%; non-mechanical pencils and crayons about 4.3%; markers 4%; mechanical pencils 6.6%...Meanwhile, there are no tariffs applied on imports of cross-country snow skis, sailboards, or archery equipment."[8]

In 2018, Tyler Moran, an economist at the Peterson Institute for International Economics, analyzed the impact of tariffs on Americans by household income (Figure 2-1). He found that the less money a family earned, the higher the percentage that goes towards paying the cost of tariffs on the goods they purchase. Thus, those earning less than $10,000 pay the highest percentage of their income as a result of tariffs (12–14 percent), while those earning over $150,000 pay the least (5.25 percent).[9]

Annual Household Income (pretax;in dollars)	Tariff Impact (percent)
Less than 5,000	12.1
5,000 to 9,999	13.95
10,000 to 14,999	11.5
15,000 to 19,999	11.16
20,000 to 29,999	9.85
30,000 to 39,999	10.39
40,000 to 49,999	9.14
50,000 to 69,999	8.14
70,000 to 79,999	8.29
80,000 to 99,999	7.93
100,000 to 119,999	6.52
120,000 to 149,999	6.11
150,000 and more	5.25

Figure 2-1: The impact of tariffs on households at various levels of pretax income.
Source: Bureau of Labor Statistics, Consumer Expenditure Survey; United Nations Conference on Trade and Development, TRAINS

It's hard to imagine that any rational legislator would deliberately propose such a scheme.

The Tariff System—Mind-Numbingly Complex

The U.S. International Trade Commission maintains a list called the Harmonized Tariff Schedule, which in its ninety-nine chapters and twenty-two sections lists over seventeen thousand items that are subject to a tariff. These do not include the additional tariffs imposed by President Trump. U.S. Customs and Border Protection is the agency responsible

Basic Name	Tariff Code	US Tariff Rates (general)
Tobacco	2401.10.65	350%
Peanuts	1202.41.80	163.80%
Canvas Shoes	6404.11.59	48%
Glassware	7013.99.40	38%
Waterproof Footwear	6401.10.00	37.50%
Tuna	1604.14.10	35%
Men's Shirts	6105.20.20	32%
Women's Shirts	6106.20.20	32%
T-Shirts	6109.90.10	32%
Sweaters	6110.30.30	32%
Baby Shirts	6111.30.20	32%
Brooms, Brushes	9603.10.60	32%
Baby Sweaters	6111.30.40	30%
Cantaloupes	0807.19.20	29.80%
Apricots	2008.50.40	29.80%
Women's Suits	6204.63.11	28.60%
Baby Pants	6111.30.10	28.20%
Men's Coats	6101.30.20	28.20%
Women's Coats	6102.30.20	28.20%
Ceramic Tableware	69.12.00.20	28%
Meat	0201.10.50	26.40%
Bras	6212.30.00	23.50%
Gloves	6216.00.38	23.50%
Glassware	7013.42.20	22.50%
Dates	2008.99.25	22.40%
Corn	0709.99.45	21.30%
Linen	6302.21.50	20.90%
Suitcases	4202.12.21	20%
Orange Juice	2008.30.35	11.20%

Figure 2-2: US tariff rates.

Source: U.S. International Trade Commission Harmonized Tax Schedule, 2019

for interpreting the traditional tariffs and advising businesses trading in potentially dutiable goods. Available online, the schedule is mind-numbingly complex—an example of what happens when government policies are set in response to political pressure and lobbying efforts by an array of competing interest groups, each seeking to bend the system in their favor. Figure 2-2 is a table showing some of the highest and most disruptive tariffs prior to President Trump's trade war, culled from the three thousand-page schedule.

Some tariffs decrease by formula as the value of the item being imported increases, which means that the cheaper version is automatically slapped with a higher tariff rate than the more expensive one. Glassware is one example (Figure 2-3):

7013	Glassware of a kind used for table, kitchen, toilet, office, indoor decoration or similar purposes (other than that of heading 7010 or 7018):	
7013.42.20	Valued not over $3 each	22.50%
7013.42.30	Valued over $3 but not over $5 each	11.30%
7013.42.40	Valued over $5 each	7.20%

Figure 2-3: US tariff rates on glassware.
Source: U.S. International Trade Commission Harmonized Tax Schedule, 2019

There are many examples of the startling advantages enjoyed by many makers of upscale products. For instance, the Apple Watch, costing $399, is completely exempt from tariffs, as is perfume. Cars are taxed a reasonable 2.5 percent.

Interpreting the Harmonized Tariff Schedule is the job of employees of the International Trade Commission. The following sample correspondence provides a hint of the complexity and effort involved in maintaining these well-entrenched tariffs. The author, Gwenn Kirschner, a tariff expert whose job is to impose tariffs on imported goods, received a request to classify one men's knit jacket from China. The minutiae of detail included in her reply gives us a small sense of the impact of the harmonized tariff schedule. Every variation requires a classification and a tariff determination. And of course, all such work is done by federal government employees on the taxpayer's payroll.

Ms. Elizabeth Orzol
Diesel USA, Inc.

RE: The tariff classification of a men's knit jacket from China.

Dear Ms. Orzol:

In your letter dated February 4, 2014, you requested a tariff classification ruling...

Style "05D308–FABERDEEN" is a men's jacket constructed from 51% cotton, 49% polyester, finely knit, French terry fabric. The garment has a lined self-fabric hood with a drawstring; a full front opening with a zipper closure; long raglan sleeves with rib knit cuffs; front pockets below the waist; and a close fitting rib knit bottom.

The applicable subheading for Style "05D308–FABERDEEN" will be 6101.20.0010, Harmonized Tariff Schedule of the United States (HTSUS), which provides for: Men's or boys' overcoats, carcoats, capes, cloaks, anoraks (including ski-jackets), windbreakers, and similar articles, knitted or crocheted: other than those of heading 6103: of cotton: men's. The rate of duty will be 15.9% ad valorem.

This ruling is being issued under the provisions of Part 177 of the Customs Regulations (19 C.F.R. 177).

Sincerely,
Gwenn Klein Kirschner
Acting Director
National Commodity Specialist Division[10]

Bear in mind, however, that practically all imported products were in danger of getting hit with tariffs in late 2019. As we'll explain later, the uncertainty of how tariff rules may change in the future adds to the dysfunctional nature of the tariff system, making life more complicated for business managers, and creating an extra drag on the national economy.

The Arbitrary Impact of Tariffs on Specific Products

One reason welfare for the rich is such a persistent problem in a free, democratic society like the United States is a phenomenon that economists and political scientists refer to as "concentrated benefits and dispersed costs." When a law enriches a relative handful of people or companies at the expense of other Americans, the small group of beneficiaries has a powerful incentive to do everything possible to defend that law. Meanwhile, the costs are spread out among millions of their fellow citizens, each of them losing just a few dollars a year in the process—often without even realizing it. As a result, those millions see little reason to rise up in arms against the law, which makes reform extraordinarily hard.

There's no better example of this problem than import duties or tariffs on items used by millions of Americans every day, especially food. While the special interests that benefit from such tariffs—sugar growers and orange juice distributors for example—lobby extensively to maintain these taxes, millions of Americans pay a little more at the supermarket every week, unaware of the reason for higher prices. Vincent Smith, senior fellow at the American Enterprise Institute and a professor at the Montana State University, has studied tariff issues, with a focus on the American food supply. In a 2017 article, Smith noted:

> In particular, tariffs and quotas on imports and marketing orders designed to restrict market supplies—especially for sugar, dairy products, orange juice and tomatoes—increase food prices paid by all consumers. Compared to wealthier households, low-income households spend substantially higher percentages of their incomes on food. As a result, increases in food prices, resulting from trade barriers and other supply-control policies, impose greater burdens on those low-income households.[11]

When tariffs are levied on foods, consumers pay more and manufacturers benefit. Orange juice, for example, carries a tariff of $.18 per liter. This extra eighteen-cent tax on imported orange juice means that the Florida Orange Juice Company can continue to sell its juice for $4.12 per liter (2018). [12] Without the tariffs, orange juice from Mexico and the Dominican Republic would reach the U.S. at lower prices—creating a bigger competitive challenge for U.S. companies, but benefiting consumers.

Here are a couple of other examples of the seemingly arbitrary tariffs applied to various kinds of goods.

Tariffs on shoes. Sorting out the different duties on footwear alone employs hundreds of federal employees. The Harmonized Tariff Schedule has a particular fondness for footwear. It includes 127 entries such as this one:

> ...shoes of which over 90 percent of the external surface area (including any accessories or reinforcements such as those mentioned in note 4(a) to this chapter) is rubber or plastics and not suitable to be finished into footwear (1) having foxing or a foxing-like band applied or molded at the sole and overlapping the upper, or (2) designed to be worn over, or in lieu of, other footwear as a protection against water, oil, grease or chemicals or cold or inclement weather...[13]

Generally speaking, cheaper shoes bear the brunt of higher tariffs, while expensive shoes get a pass. Is this a deliberate Congressional effort to make life worse for poor people? Almost certainly not. These tariff anomalies, like so much of federal legislation and rulemaking, are the result of focused lobbying efforts over many years, log-rolling (i.e. the trading of favors among legislators), and even the side effects of other legislation.

In the 1930s, when the original shoe tariffs were instituted, there were many American manufacturers of canvas and rubber shoes, but virtually no U.S. makers of fancy leather shoes—hence, no one demanding tariffs on expensive foreign footwear. Sneaker makers, on the other hand, made their voices heard and got a substantial 48 percent tariff on those shoes during the Great Depression.[14] Today, tariffs for such shoes have been reduced to the 20 percent range—but most makers of expensive shoes still pay no more than 8.5 percent.

These anomalies are driven by lobbying efforts that continue to this day. New Balance, one of the few remaining running shoe manufacturers that make their shoes in the U.S., lobbied hard against the Trans-Pacific Partnership (TPP), the Obama Era trade deal that was later scrapped by President Trump. New Balance was worried that if the tariffs levied against imported athletic shoes were dropped, its American-made running shoes would no longer be price competitive.[15] Now that TPP has been jettisoned, New Balance will continue to enjoy tariff protection, probably indefinitely.

Furthering the theme of hitting the working class hardest, work boots draw higher tariffs than almost any other kind of footwear. According to the Harmonized Tariff Schedule, work boots "incorporating a protective metal toe-cap" can carry a 7 percent tariff. Industrial work boots—that is, footwear designed to be worn over, or in lieu of, other footwear as a protection against water, oil, grease, or chemicals, or in cold or inclement weather—have tariffs that run up to 66 percent. But ski boots and fancy leather women's clogs and shoes made of pigskin have no tariff duties at all.

This undisciplined potpourri of tariff rates has no coherent rationale. Indeed, the Harmonized Tariff Schedule is nonsensical. But like everything else in Washington, once these rules are established, they are very hard to change.

Even many in the shoe industry agree it is time for footwear tariffs to be examined. According to a 2017 statement from the Footwear Distributors and Retailers of America:

> With 99% of all footwear [including running shoes] sold in the U.S. imported, footwear tariffs…no longer protect American jobs…Rather than pay $3 billion in footwear duties in 2018, companies could have used those funds to innovate and hire new workers in the fields of design [and] marketing and [provided] blue collar jobs at ports, warehouses, and in trucking. [This] would have saved American consumers $7 billion in

2018 on their shoes at retail...Footwear tariffs are also some of the highest on any consumer good, averaging 11%, but reaching upwards of 48% and 67.5% on certain footwear types. Meanwhile, items like iPhones have no duty rate. Tariffs directly increase the cost of footwear at retail, hitting hard working families the hardest, as lower cost basic shoes face significantly higher tariffs than men's leather dress shoes.[16]

Tariffs on tires. Chinese tires have historically been the focus of substantial tariffs. In 2009, ostensibly at the urging of American union workers in the tire industry (many of whom had lost their jobs during the recession), the Obama administration imposed a 35 percent tariff on imported Chinese tires. This tariff was also touted—bizarrely—as a way to rein in tire prices, but it had little effect on these, as Figure 2-4 shows. There was a brief dip in the price of American-made tires immediately after the tariff was imposed, but then prices continued to rise at only a slightly slower pace than before the imposition of the tariffs (13 percent vs. 13.8 percent over three years).[17]

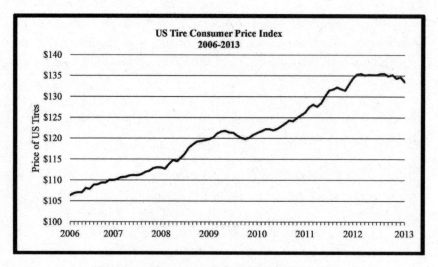

Figure 2-4: U.S. tire consumer price index from 2006 to 2013.
Source: United States Department of Labor; September 2019

The tariffs on Chinese tires, rather than benefitting American job seekers and consumers, mostly benefitted workers in other countries in Asia, including Thailand, South Korea, and Indonesia. Tire manufacturers in those countries began building tire plants of their own and shipping those tires to the U.S.—sometimes with direct investment from the Chinese.[18] And although union employment in the tire industry rose briefly during the tariff period, overall employment in the tire industry fell, with the industry losing twenty-five hundred retail jobs between 2009 and 2012.[19]

The tariff expired in mid-2012. Today, over 60 percent of new tires sold in the U.S. are imported.

Tariff Engineers and the High Cost of Tariff Dodges

In addition to the detrimental impact on free trade and the higher cost of taxed products, the price of tariffs includes the time and effort companies spend on compliance, and when possible, on avoidance. Today, many industries employ "tariff engineers," whose job it is to find creative ways around tariff restrictions. As Bryan Riley, an economist at the Heritage Foundation, explains, "Companies will employ tariff engineers to make sure products come in at a lower tariff rate, and you can't tell me there is not a better use for their talent. It would be a lot easier if companies could just focus on producing what American consumers want, instead of trying to design products to get around the most harmful aspects of U.S. trade barriers."[20]

However, under the existing complicated tariff regime, many companies feel they have no choice but to employ tariff engineers. Here are a few examples of their work.

Snuggies are "blankets with sleeves." Made in China, they sold in huge numbers in the U.S. after their introduction in 2008. Some years later, they became involved in a protracted tariff dispute. At issue was whether the Snuggie is a blanket or a form of "pullover apparel." The difference is not just semantic: imported blankets face a tariff of 8.5 percent, while items of pullover apparel face one of 14.9 percent. In 2017, the Court of International Trade ruled that the Snuggie is in fact a blanket, not a pullover—a nice victory for the Snuggies folks.[21] Of course, a good deal of time, effort, and money would be saved if the tariffs on both blankets and pullover apparel were simply eliminated.

How about feathers and feather dusters? In 1991, a feather importer was found guilty of "artifice" for arranging offshore manufacturing of feather dusters that the company had no intention of selling as such. The reason? Feather dusters carry a much lower tariff (20 percent) compared to the tariff rate for feathers (up to 80 percent). Once in the United States, the feather dusters were disassembled, and the feathers were sold to crafters for use in hats, boas, and fishing lures.[22] Creative? Yes. But wasteful, and frankly idiotic.

An even more wasteful tariff dodge was described by the *Washington Post* in 2018: "Brand-new Ford Transit Connect vans, made in Spain, are dropped off at U.S. ports several times a month. First, they pass through customs—and then workers hired by the automaker start to rip the vehicles apart. The rear seats are plucked out. The seat belts in back go, too. Sometimes, the rear side windows are covered with painted plates. Any holes left in the floor are patched over."[23]

Why? According to David Boaz at the Cato Institute, "Because there's a 25 percent tariff on imported pickup trucks and work vans, but only a 2.5 percent tariff on passenger vans. So even with all the extra effort of building a passenger-quality van and then dismantling it, it's still cheaper to do that than to pay a substantial tax on the import."[24]

Sometimes, when lobbyists try to manipulate tariffs to benefit them, their efforts backfire. That appeared to be the case with Boeing's 2017 demand for a prohibitive import tariff of nearly 300 percent on Bombardier's C-Series aircraft built in the U.K. and assembled in Canada.

Boeing claimed that Bombardier was receiving government subsidies and selling their aircraft too cheaply in the U.S. They demanded that the U.S. impose tariffs as a way of combating this unfair support from the public sector. However, Boeing's demand was widely recognized as hypocritical, since Boeing itself is near the top of the list of companies that seek and get government subsidies. Noted *The Economist*:

> Aviation executives think that Boeing is attempting to
> destroy the competition with trade cases against both

Bombardier and Airbus. But worst of all, in the process of pursuing these, the American firm is hurting its own shareholders and employees by alienating its international customers. Boeing predicts that around 80% of orders for civil jetliners over the next twenty years will be from outside America. But they won't stick around to buy from Boeing if it continues to follow a nationalist agenda. As Adam Pilarski, the former chief economist of McDonnell-Douglas (now part of Boeing), astutely notes, if the global plane-making giant wants to "act like a little whiny American company," it will lose out as a result.[25]

Boeing brought an international trade suit against Bombardier, claiming its tactics were illegal and should justify the imposition of harsh tariffs. But in early 2018, the United States Court of International Trade ruled Boeing was not being harmed by Bombardier and threw out the case.[26]

Tariffs in Trump's America

In spite of overwhelming support among economists for removing and reducing tariffs, President Trump's original trade plan, announced in March 2017, included large increases in tariffs. Two intended beneficiaries were announced in January 2018: Whirlpool, the manufacturer of washing machines, and Suniva Inc. and SolarWorld Americas, two manufacturers of solar panels.

Whirlpool argued that they were facing unfair competition from the South Korean washing machine manufacturers Samsung and LG, who were importing cheaper washing machines into the U.S., and so, cutting into Whirlpool's profits.[27] In response, the Trump administration announced that starting in 2018, the first 1.2 million imported washing machines would be faced with a tariff of 20 percent, while further imports would face a tariff of 50 percent. This tax was supposed to phase out after three years, assuming it had been successful in forcing South Korean washing machine companies to raise their prices.

Of course, these higher prices hurt American consumers. Noted columnist George Will, "The government is poised to punish many Americans, in the name of protecting a few of them, because in the government's opinion, too many of them are choosing to buy foreign-made washing machines for no better reason than that the buyers think they are better."[28] And of course, cheaper.

Meanwhile, it's worth noting that, in 2018, Whirlpool controlled more market share than Samsung and LG combined. The CEO of Whirlpool, Mark Bitzer, earned over $11.7 million in 2018.[29]

The argument for tariffs on imported solar panels is even more dubious. The panel manufacturers were protected with a 30 percent tariff aimed at fending off competition from Chinese producers. Yet most of the U.S. solar industry opposed the tariff, recognizing that the loss of access to inexpensive Chinese solar panels would dramatically reduce the demand for solar energy conversions. Upon hearing the announcement, the Solar Energy Industries Association Board of Directors issued a sharp rebuke:

> The decision effectively will cause the loss of roughly twenty-three thousand American jobs this year, including many in manufacturing, and it will result in the delay or cancellation of billions of dollars in solar investments.
>
> While tariffs in this case will not create adequate cell or module manufacturing to meet U.S. demand, or keep foreign-owned Suniva and SolarWorld afloat, they will create a crisis in a part of our economy that has been thriving, which will ultimately cost tens of thousands of hard-working, blue-collar Americans their jobs...
>
> It boggles my mind that this president—any president, really—would voluntarily choose to damage one of the fastest-growing segments of our economy.[30]

But Trump was just getting warmed up. In February 2018, he dismayed many members of his own party and nearly all economists when he announced 25 percent tariffs on imported steel and a 10 percent levy on imported aluminum, including imports from Canada, Mexico, and the European Union, though some exceptions for individual companies were proposed. The announcement came on the heels of a report from the Commerce Department claiming that an American decline in steel and aluminum production could pose a national security threat, and the administration used this report to justify invoking a little-used trade law that allows for tariffs to protect national security. But few experts agreed with the report.[31] And Republican Senator Pat Roberts, who chairs the Senate's agriculture committee, noted, "Every time you do this, you get a retaliation. Agriculture [will be] the number one [retaliatory] target. I think this is terribly counterproductive for the agriculture economy."[32]

Job losses due to the tariffs soon materialized. In a scathing opinion piece, the editorial board of the *Wall Street Journal* described how the American Keg company, a Kentucky-based manufacturer of steel kegs, had responded to the threat of price increases for steel by laying off a third of their workers in 2018. Meanwhile, a tsunami of exemption requests was flooding into the Department of Commerce from companies seeking relief from the tariffs.

In July 2018, Trump's trade war escalated. Twenty-five percent tariffs were imposed on $34 billion worth of goods from China, including thousands of machinery items, pumps, lathes, drills, hay-balers, and other farm equipment. A second round of tariffs imposed in August 2018, included a 25 percent tariff on $16 billion worth of goods, including lubricants, plastics, vinyls, polymers, and chemicals; iron, steel, and aluminum; and machines and equipment, such as railroad cars and motorcycles. A third round of tariffs imposed in September 2018, began at 10 percent and was raised to 25 percent, affecting another $200 billion in goods from China, including hundreds of food items from meat to seafood to shellfish, as well as vegetables and fruits, nuts, oils, alcohol, and tobacco, plus chemicals, construction materials, leathers, handbags, furniture, and more. In September 2019, yet another round of tariffs was slated, covering $300 billion in imports.[33]

There is no way to predict how long these tariffs will remain in place, but there is no question that they severely harmed the U.S. economy in 2018 and 2019.

Trump's Trade War and Agriculture

Darin Von Ruden is President of the Wisconsin Farmers Union, a member-driven organization committed to enhancing the quality of life for family farmers. We spoke with him over coffee one rainy morning in a breakfast deli in Eau Claire, Wisconsin, at a time when the agricultural tariffs imposed by China in response to Trump's levies on Chinese goods had already hit Von Ruden's community.

"There will be a lot of food wasted and lost," Von Ruden said. "I have a couple of members who have decided they are selling out to big corporate farms. At the end of the day, all these tariffs do is accelerate the consolidation of farms into large corporate farms. The little guy can't compete in this environment."[34]

We asked Von Ruden about the compensation payments the administration had arranged to soften the blow to farm incomes. The payments to farmers had been paid out in two tranches: one in 2018 for $12 billion, a second in 2019 for $16 billion.[35] Von Ruden was unimpressed. After the current year, he figured, there would be no more payments, so nothing really had changed. What's more, as is usual with handouts to farmers, the biggest farm interests, plus at least a thousand city residents, got most of the money.

However, many of those who opposed the compensation payments took them. Greg Gunthorpe, the Indiana pig farmer we interviewed about the Farm Bill, was asked about those payments while speaking at an Indiana Farm Bureau event in late 2018. "Well, yeah, we went ahead and took them," he said, grinning a bit sheepishly. "The rule was supposed to be that you had to be adversely impacted in order to get them, so we filled out the paperwork and said we were adversely affected. It didn't amount to much—about four dollars a hog, I think—but we took it."[36]

Gunthorpe is not the only one who benefitted from the pork subsidies. In a truly baffling development, Smithfield Foods, a Virginia company owned by a Chinese conglomerate and the largest pork producer in the United States, also qualified for the subsidy payments. The Chinese owners of Smithfield were, we assume, happy to get the money, courtesy of U.S. taxpayers. JBS, a Brazilian company, was another foreign-owned beneficiary of the tariff compensation payments. [37]

At least two U.S. senators who had lobbied for the tariff relief were also taking payments: Charles E. Grassley (R-Iowa) and Jon Tester (D-Mont.).[38] Senator Grassley, a farmer and longtime supporter of the Farm Bill, is worth $3.5 million, while Senator Tester has a net worth of $1.3 million.[39] These are not the kind of "family farmers" that, in theory, were supposed to benefit from Trump's trade war and its compensation subsidies.

Another group of Americans often supposed to benefit from tariffs are members of labor unions. In fact, unions frequently lobby in defense of tariffs, seeing the protection they represent as a way to preserve jobs. But such protectionism often backfires. As economist Milton Friedman has pointed out, the benefits of a tariff are visible. Union workers can see they are "protected." The harm which a tariff does is invisible. It's spread widely. There are people that don't have jobs because of tariffs, but they don't know it.[40]

Tariffs hurt. Free trade, anchored since 1995 by the World Trade Organization—which was created with major assistance from the U.S.—has generated enormous wealth around the globe. The open trade that comes with globalization has benefitted Americans and the people of all countries everywhere. Re-imposing trade barriers and creating new ones, as President Trump has done, is a terrible mistake.

A final devastating impact of the current trade war—yet one that's little understood—is the economic effect of uncertainty. Paul Krugman, the *New York Times* columnist and a Nobel Prize winner in economics, discussed the problem in a 2019 column. "[W]hy do Trump's tariff tantrums seem to be having a pronounced negative effect on near-term economic prospects?" Krugman asked. "The answer, I'd submit, is that he isn't just raising tariffs, he's doing so in an unpredictable fashion..." Krugman concluded, with some dismay, "...it's hard to see what can reduce this uncertainty. U.S. trade law gives the president huge discretionary authority to impose tariffs."[41]

Uncertainty makes it difficult for business leaders to make decisions about future investment. Rather than spend money to hire employees, launch new products, or build new plants that may end up being rendered less valuable by new tariffs and further trade reductions, managers are more likely to hold back, thereby retarding economic growth. Many observers believe this is already happening. In July 2019, the *Wall Street Journal* declared, "Business investment has been cool since last year's third quarter when the President revved up his trade brawl with China. Executives have reported delaying investment decisions since they don't know the impact of his multifront trade war on cross-border supply chains." *The Journal* went on to observe, "Foreign investment in the U.S. has been declining, with capital flows from China falling 87.9% between 2016 and 2018...The U.S. economy needs more domestic investment, which requires more business confidence and an end to Mr. Trump's trade folly."[42]

We couldn't agree more. Not only do we hope that President Trump's trade war will be short-lived, but we'd like to see the entire complicated, costly structure of tariffs eliminated once and for all. Americans would be better off without these nonsensical taxes.

1 Jason Furman, Katheryn Russ, and Jay Shambaugh, "US Tariffs Are an Arbitrary and Regressive Tax," *Vox*, January 12, 2017, https://voxeu.org/article/us-tariffs-are-arbitrary-and-regressive-tax.

2 Mary Amiti, Stephen J. Redding, and David Weinstein, "The Impact of the 2018 Trade War on U.S. Prices and Welfare," NBER Working Paper no. 25672, Cambridge, National Bureau of Economic Research, Massachusetts, March 2019, https://www.nber.org/papers/w25672.

3 Mercy A. Kuo, "Upping the Ante in the US-China Trade War: Insights from Nien Su," *The Diplomat*, May 21, 2019, https://thediplomat.com/2019/05/upping-the-ante-in-the-us-china-trade-war/; Mahita Gajanan, "Trump's Trade War with China Could Cost the Average Family Up to $2,300 a Year, Report Estimates," *Time*, May 14, 2019, https://time.com/5587197/trump-china-trade-war-cost-families/.

4 Frederick W. Smith, William Brock, and Charlene Barshefsky, "We Need to Get Back to a Pro-Trade Consensus. But It'll Take a Fight." *The Washington Post*, August 18, 2019, Opinions, https://www.washingtonpost.com/opinions/we-need-to-get-back-to-a-pro-trade-consensus-but-itll-take-a-fight/2019/08/18/d74c64c8-c062-11e9-b873-63ace636af08_story.html.

5 Yuki Noguchi, "New Round of Tariffs Takes A Bigger Bite of Consumers' Budget," NPR, May 10, 2019, https://www.npr.org/2019/05/10/721921317/new-round-of-tariffs-take-a-bigger-bite-of-consumers-budget.

6 Tyler Moran, "Tariffs Hit Poor Americans Hardest," Peterson Institute for International Economics, July 31, 2014, https://www.piie.com/blogs/trade-investment-policy-watch/tariffs-hit-poor-americans-hardest?utm_source=Bruegel%20Updates&utm_campaign=651aba2df0-Blogs%20review%20%2022/1/2017&utm_medium=email&utm_term=0_eb026b984a-651aba2df0-278510293.

7 Daniel J. Ikenson, "Trade on Trial, Again," Cato Institute, May/June 2016, CATO Policy Report, https://www.cato.org/policy-report/mayjune-2016/trade-trial-again.

8 Furman, "US Tariffs Are an Arbitrary and Regressive Tax."

9 Moran, "Tariffs Hit Poor Americans Hardest."

10 "N250294: The Tariff Classification of a Men's Knit Jacket from China," U.S. Customs and Border Protection Securing America's Borders, March 11, 2014, https://rulings.cbp.gov/ruling/N250294.

11 Ryan Nabil and Vincent H. Smith, "Ryan Nabil and Vincent H. Smith: $20 Billion In Farm Subsidies Doesn't Reach the Poor, Leaves Them Hungry," *La Crosse Tribune*, January 20, 2017, Commentary, https://lacrossetribune.com/news/opinion/editorial/columnists/ryan-nabil-and-vincent-h-smith-billion-in-farm-subsidies/article_f7df0bf4-d6ce-58ae-94c4-5cb596a44989.html.

12 "Harmonized Tariff Schedule (2019 Revision 12)," https://hts.usitc.gov/?query=orange%20juice.

13 "Customs Rulings Online Search System: Elizabeth Orzol," U.S. Customs and Border Protection Securing America's Borders, https://rulings.cbp.gov/search?term=Elizabeth%20Orzol&collection=ALL&sortBy=RELEVANCE&pageSize=30&page=1.

14 Marc Bain, "Your Sneakers Are A Case Study in Why Trump's America-First Trade Policy Is Nonsense," *Quartz*, December 20, 2016, https://qz.com/859628/your-nike-sneakers-are-a-case-study-in-why-trumps-protectionist-america-first-trade-policy-is-nonsense/.

15 Bain, "Your Sneakers Are A Case Study in Why Trump's America-First Trade Policy Is Nonsense."

16 "Americans Paid $7 Billion More For Shoes at Retail Than Needed in 2018," Footwear Distributors and Retailers of America, Tariff Reduction Initiatives, https://fdra.org/key-issues-and-advocacy/legislative-initiatives/.

17 SR, "US Tires: Tariff Expirations Will Not Hurt Bridgestone," *Selective Rationality*, October 2, 2012, http://selectiverationality.com/us-tires-tariff-expirations-will-not-hurt-bridgestone/.

18 Bruce Davis, "Tire Makers Invest $10 Billion In Expansions, Improvements," *Rubber & Plastic News*, September 13, 2016, https://www.rubbernews.com/article/20160913/NEWS/309059996/tire-makers-invest-10-billion-in-expansions-improvements.

19 Don Lee, "Limited Success of Chinese Tire Tariffs Shows Why Donald Trump's Trade Prescription May Not Work," *Los Angeles Times*, July 24, 2016, Business, https://www.latimes.com/business/la-fi-tariffs-trade-analysis-20160724-snap-story.html.

20 Ana Swanson, "Why A Weird Legal Dispute About Whether the Snuggie Is A Blanket Actually Matters A Lot," *The Washington Post*, March 6, 2017, Economic Policy, Analysis, https://www.washingtonpost.com/news/wonk/wp/2017/03/06/why-a-weird-legal-dispute-about-whether-the-snuggie-is-a-blanket-actually-matters-a-lot/.

21 Swanson, "Why A Weird Legal Dispute About Whether the Snuggie Is A Blanket Actually Matters A Lot."

22 Szu Ping Chan, "When's a Van a Van and When's it a Car?" BBC News, October 18, 2018, Business, https://www.bbc.com/news/business-45875405.

23 Todd. C Frankel, "The Strange Case of Ford's Attempt to Avoid the 'Chicken Tax'," *The Washington Post*, July 6, 2018, Business, https://www.bbc.com/news/business-45875405 https://www.washingtonpost.com/business/economy/the-strange-case-of-fords-attempt-to-avoid-thechicken-tax/2018/07/06/643624fa-796a-11e8-8df3-007495a78738_story.html.

24 David Boaz, "The Hidden Costs of Tariffs," Cato Institute, July 9, 2018, https://www.cato.org/blog/hidden-costs-tariffs.

25 C.R. "Protectionism Doesn't Pay: America's Department of Commerce Imposes a Tariff of 292% on Bombardier's C-Series Jets," *The Economist*, December 20, 2017, Gulliver, https://www.economist.com/gulliver/2017/12/20/americas-department-of-commerce-imposes-a-tariff-of-292-on-bombardiers-c-series-jets.

26 Leslie Josephs, "Boeing Loses Trade Case Over Bombardier Passenger Jets," CNBC, January 26, 2018, https://www.cnbc.com/2018/01/26/boeing-loses-trade-case-over-bombardier-passenger-jets.html.

27 Timothy Aeppel, "Whirlpool's Washer War Is Balancing Act for Trump," Reuters, October 4, 2017, https://www.reuters.com/article/us-trump-effect-trade-washers/whirlpools-washer-war-is-balancing-act-for-trump-idUSKCN1C91EL.

28 George Will, "Washington Post: Whirlpool, Lobbyists Putting Tariffs on Spin Cycle," *Waco Tribune-Herald*, December 16, 2017, https://www.wacotrib.com/townnews/commerce/george-will-washington-post-whirlpool-lobbyists-putting-tariffs-on-spin/article_6182df28-9ebb-5db5-93e6-56c4ad51205f.html.

29 "Marc R. Bitzer Executive Compensation," Salary.com, https://www1.salary.com/Marc-R-Bitzer-Salary-Bonus-Stock-Options-for-WHIRLPOOL-CORP.html.

30 "President's Decision on Solar Tariffs is a Loss for America," Solar Energies Industries Association (press release), January 22, 2018, https://seia.org/news/presidents-decision-solar-tariffs-loss-america.

[31] Steve Holland and Ginger Gibson, "Trump to Impose Steep Tariffs on Steel, Aluminum; Stokes Trade War Fears," Reuters, March 1, 2018, https://www.reuters.com/article/us-usa-trade-trump/trump-to-impose-steep-tariffs-on-steel-aluminum-stoking-trade-war-talk-idUSKCN1GD4ZW.

[32] Holland, "Trump to Impose Steep Tariffs on Steel, Aluminum; Stokes Trade War Fears."

[33] Dave Bryant, "Trump's China Tariffs - The List of Products Affected and What You Can Do," ECOMCREW, updated August 23, 2019, https://www.ecomcrew.com/trumps-china-tariffs/.

[34] Darin Von Ruden (President, Wisconsin Farmers Union, Eau Claire), interview by Lisa Conyers, November 2018.

[35] Emily Moon, "The Trump Administration Will Pay Farmers $16 Billion For Its Trade War," *Pacific Standard*, July 26, 2019, https://psmag.com/news/the-trump-administration-will-pay-farmers-16-billion-for-its-trade-war.

[36] Greg Gunthrope (Indiana Farmer), remarks at Indiana Farm Bureau Event, November 2018.

[37] Rachel Siegel, "Senators Urge USDA to Stop Trump Farm Bailout Money from Going to Foreign-Owned Companies," *The Washington Post*, March 30, 2019, Economic Policy, https://www.washingtonpost.com/us-policy/2019/05/30/senators-urge-usda-stop-trump-farm-bailout-money-going-foreign-owned-companies/.

[38] Jeff Stein, "Two U.S. Senators Applying for Bailout Money for Farmers Under White House Program," *The Washington Post*, September 28, 2018, Business, https://www.washingtonpost.com/business/2018/09/28/sen-charles-grassley-apply-bailout-money-farmers-under-white-house-program/.

[39] "Chuck Grassley," *Open Secrets*, 2015, https://www.opensecrets.org/personal-finances/net-worth?cid=N00001758; Simone Pathé and Bridget Bowman, "Wealth of Congress: 14 Vulnerable Incumbents Are Worth At Least $1 Million," *Roll Call*, February 27, 2018, Politics, https://www.rollcall.com/news/politics/wealth-congress-vulnerable-incumbents-worth-least-1-million.

[40] Milton Friedman, "Landon Lecture Series on Public Issues," Kansas State University, April 27, 1978, https://www.k-state.edu/landon/speakers/milton-friedman/transcript.html.

[41] Paul Krugman, "Tariff Tantrums and Recession Risks," *The New York Times*, August 7, 2019, Opinion, https://www.nytimes.com/2019/08/07/opinion/tariff-tantrums-and-recession-risks.html.

[42] The Editorial Board, "The Trade-War Growth Slowdown," *Wall Street Journal*, July 26, 2019, Opinion, https://www.wsj.com/articles/the-trade-war-growth-slowdown-11564182695?mod=hp_opin_pos_2.

The Sky-High Price of Big League Dreams: State Subsidies for Stadiums, Movies, and Mickey Mouse

A favorite debate over Fourth of July barbecues is whether football has replaced baseball as our national pastime…[But] America's true pastime has become sports subsidies, despite economists' nearly unanimous belief that they are a terrible deal for taxpayers.

—Michael Farren

The readiness of government officials to provide lucrative benefits to wealthy individuals and organizations is sometimes difficult to explain. But in many cases, the motivation is obvious—though it's often badly misguided. When economic times are tough and communities are hurting, it's understandable that state and municipal governments compete zealously to extend financial favors—often little more than bribes—to media corporations, athletic teams, movie makers, and others that they believe will bring jobs to their communities.

Unfortunately, most often these financial handouts produce only heavy losses for local taxpayers.

In their efforts to attract business activities that are considered desirable, states and localities grant tax holidays and abatements, provide valuable land at no cost, issue taxpayer-backed bonds, and sometimes make outright grants to businesses they want to attract. Giant companies that don't really need the help are usually the ones receiving it; as the *New York Times* noted in 2018, "tax incentives tend to flow overwhelmingly to big, established companies, rather than to the local start-ups that research has shown are a more significant source of job growth."[1]

Ordinary taxpayers pay a high price for this misguided generosity. When a major business or athletic team pays no taxes, state and municipal coffers get drained and others end up with the bill. The beneficiaries of these financial favors invariably predict, even promise, that they will bring jobs and other financial (and taxable) activities to the communities providing the largesse. Almost invariably, these rosy predictions come up short.

Let's consider a few examples of the kinds of ultra-wealthy entertainment-centered businesses that are profiting from taxpayer-funded payouts.

Millions for Sports Moguls: Stadium Mania at Taxpayer Expense

One of the most widespread forms of public subsidy for wealthy companies involves the use of taxpayer monies to help build sports stadiums—which generate revenues that usually benefit only the wealthy team owners, not the surrounding communities.

In 2018, Washington D.C.'s new professional soccer stadium, Audi Field, opened in southeast D.C. The $400 million stadium is the most expensive professional soccer stadium ever built in America.[2] Meanwhile, the franchise that will be housed in the stadium, called DC United, is valued at $500 million, despite the fact that it finished dead last in the league in 2016.[3] Its primary owner, Indonesian businessman (and former owner of Philadelphia's professional basketball team, the 76ers) is Erick

Thohir, whose family manages a $2 billion Thai energy consortium, among other investments.[4]

Although D.C. United paid to build the stadium, the city government agreed to purchase the land, worth $150 million. It's a dubious deal for a cash-strapped municipality with an above-average poverty rate of 18.6 percent. Notes the D.C. Fiscal Policy Institute, "Every dollar… for DC United is a dollar not going into the city's coffers that could be used for education, public safety, health care, or other services."[5]

During the negotiations, the league touted the jobs the project would bring to the city, including at the corporate offices. But by early 2018, even before the stadium opened, those jobs already appeared to be vanishing. DC United announced plans to build a second stadium in Loudoun County, Virginia, for its B team; included in that deal is a move of DC United's corporate offices out of Washington and into Virginia. Virginia taxpayers will be on the hook for $15 million in development funds for the stadium and offices.[6] The jobs that were promised to DC taxpayers are the very same jobs DC United later promised Virginia taxpayers in order to entice them to pay for their B team's stadium.

Boondoggles like this one are sadly common when stadium mania strikes. Even seasoned observers were shocked at the deal the Oakland Raiders (formerly the San Francisco Raiders and LA Raiders) wangled out of the public coffers in Las Vegas in order to move the team to that city. The new $2 billion stadium, scheduled to open in 2020, is the most expensive in football history.[7] Nevada is issuing tax-exempt bonds backed by a hotel room tax to raise the $750 million the state has committed to the project. Bank of America is lending the team $600 million towards their share of the stadium costs.[8] The team will pay no rent on the property; the state will provide it free of charge. The city also announced plans to spend an additional $200 million, to be financed through an additional gas tax, to improve the freeway around the stadium.[9] Estimated value of all the subsidies provided by the taxpayers: $750 million. Mark Davis, owner of the Raiders, has a net worth of $500 million.

The Raiders deal is not unique. Figure 3-1 is a table showing all the NFL's stadium projects (including new construction and renovations) since 1997. Public funding varies from 0 percent (for MetLife Stadium) to 100 percent (for Tampa's Raymond James Stadium).[10]

Meanwhile, CBS Sports reported in 2018 that seventeen NFL team owners are billionaires.[11]

NFL players and owners, as you might expect, take a positive view of the use of public funds for professional sports facilities. Notes NFL Hall of Famer and owner-hopeful Curtis Martin, "Look, cities *love* their teams! Team spirit is so important to local areas and can really bring communities together and make people bond over the excitement of supporting a team! And there is economic development with sports teams, all the employees at the stadium, restaurants, and so on." When pressed to reflect on the fiscal burden on cities, Martin's tone remained upbeat. "I don't know so much about that, but I know it is expensive to build a stadium, so if the cities want to help out, that's great."[12]

Private and Public Investment in NFL Stadium Construction Costs, 1997-2015, in Millions							
Stadium	Team	Year Opened	Total Project Cost	Private Funding		Public Funding	
				Total Private	% of Total	Total Public	% of Total
San Francisco 49ers	San Francisco 49ers	2015	$987	$873	88%	$114	12%
MetLife Stadium	New York Giants/Jets	2010	$1,600	$1,600	100%	$0	0%
Cowboys Stadium	Dallas Cowboys	2009	$1,194	$750	63%	$444	37%
Lucas Oil Stadium	Indianapolis Colts	2008	$720	$100	14%	$620	86%
University of Phoenix Stadium	Arizona Cardinals	2006	$455	$147	32%	$308	68%
Lincoln Financial Field	Philadelphia Eagles	2003	$518	$330	64%	$188	36%
Soldier Field	Chicago Bears	2003	$587	$200	34%	$387	66%
Lambeau Field	Green Bay Packers	2003	$295	$126	43%	$169	57%
Gillette Stadium	New England Patriots	2002	$412	$340	83%	$72	17%
Ford Field	Detroit Lions	2002	$440	$330	75%	$110	25%
Reliant Stadium	Houston Texans	2002	$474	$185	39%	$289	61%
CenturyLink Field	Seattle Seahawks	2002	$461	$161	35%	$300	65%
Heinz Field	Pittsburgh Steelers	2001	$281	$109	39%	$172	61%
Sports Authority Field	Denver Broncos	2001	$401	$112	28%	$289	72%
Paul Brown Stadium	Cincinnati Bengals	2000	$450	$25	6%	$425	94%
LP Field	Tennessee Titans	1999	$292	$85	29%	$207	71%
Cleveland Browns Stadium	Cleveland Browns	1999	$271	$71	26%	$200	74%
M&T Bank Stadium	Baltimore Ravens	1998	$226	$22	10%	$204	90%
Raymond James Stadium	Tampa Bay Buccaneers	1998	$194	$0	0%	$194	100%
FedEx Field	Washington Redskins	1997	$251	$180	72%	$71	28%
TOTAL Funding Amounts			$10,508	$5,746		$4,761	
Average Percentage of Total					55%		45%

Figure 3-1: Private and public investment in NFL stadium construction costs, 1997-2015.
Source: Brookings, September 2016

Such deals are not limited to the big boys of the NFL and other major sports leagues. Consider the Hartford Connecticut Yard Goats, a double-A minor league baseball team, and their new $71 million, publicly-funded Dunkin' Donuts ballpark in Hartford.[13] The Yard Goats' owner, Josh Solomon, is a real estate developer and co-founder of the DSF Group, which has invested more than $2.5 billion in real estate since 2000. Yet rather than finding investors to build his team a stadium, Solomon managed to convince the city of Hartford to foot the bill.

As with many stadium projects, rosy projections of future tax revenues were proffered based not on the gate receipts, but from the supposed peripheral developments that are presumed to follow stadium construction.[14] In Hartford, that has not happened, for two reasons. First, the project is mired in lawsuits with the original developers, who were fired partway through the project. The replacement contractor had his hands full simply completing the project. Second, the project is in an undesirable neighborhood in Hartford, so investors are not willing to take the risks of building there. With suits and countersuits flying between the previous developer and the developer who finished the project, there is not likely to be a solution before Hartford runs out of money.

A 2017 *Wall Street Journal* article summarized the economic impact of the project:

> Hartford, a city of about 124,000 residents, that is facing a fiscal crisis and a high poverty rate, is on the hook for $68.6 million in bonds issued to cover most of the construction of Dunkin' Donuts Park.
>
> Mayor Luke Bronin…said the ballpark alone will never generate enough money to pay back the debt… Mr. Bronin plans to borrow $20 million in bonds in the coming weeks to cover a shortfall in the city's budget, and next year the city is already projecting a $65 million deficit.[15]

In a visit to the ballpark for the opening games of the 2018 season, we saw stands filled with a sea of white faces—in a city that is 70 percent black and has a poverty rate of 32 percent. Noted one fan, "Look around.

Do you see any black faces? Only working the concession stands. This stadium wasn't built for the residents of Hartford, even though they are the ones paying for it. The plan was always to bring this stadium and team here and draw in wealthy white people from the surrounding affluent areas. We are within an easy driving distance from several [affluent neighborhoods], and that's who is buying tickets to these games." [16]

As to those peripheral economic activities, one resident noted, "no one is going to build anything else near the stadium because the neighborhood is too unsafe. No one would buy a nice condo here."

Another story illustrates the impact that an extreme case of stadium mania can have. In 2011, the Phoenix Coyotes, one of the few professional hockey teams in the American Southwest, were in financial trouble and in danger of being moved out of their home base in Glendale, Arizona. The city of Glendale reacted in panic, proposing to issue somewhere between $200 and $300 million in taxpayer bonds to keep the Coyotes in the Jobing.com Arena where they played.

The Goldwater Institute in Phoenix had long been opposed to the use of taxpayer funds to subsidize corporations or engage in other forms of crony capitalism. That included sports stadiums, and Goldwater raised the alarm. The institute's leadership, headed by CEO Darcy Olsen, demanded that the city of Glendale provide documents covering subsidies to the Coyotes, which, the institute averred, would be illegal in the light of the "Gift Clause" in Arizona's state constitution, which reads: "Neither the state, nor any county, city, town, municipality, or other subdivision of the state shall ever give or loan its credit in the aid of any individual, association, or corporation."

"This is a time of fiscal austerity," Olsen asserted, "and taxpayers are supposed to buy a hockey team for a multimillionaire?" [17]

When the Goldwater Institute threatened to sue if Glendale went ahead with the taxpayer subsidy, all hell broke loose. Arizona Senator John McCain, generally an anti-pork champion, went on TV opposing the troublemakers at Goldwater. City officials talked darkly about suing the institute. Calls poured into the institute accusing Olsen and Goldwater with trying to destroy Glendale's life's blood. Olsen was inundated with personal threats against her life and safety. She could not believe the venom. Olsen lived in a rural home outside Phoenix. At the height of the donnybrook, she walked out of her home one evening carrying her adopted infant son and came upon the carcass of a rabbit, its head neatly sliced from its body, trailing blood in her pathway. "They invaded my personal space," she says. "My personal life, and my baby's."[18]

Backroom negotiations went on for months. Deals were struck. Eventually, the level of taxpayer subsidy came way down, and threats of lawsuits were dropped. The Coyotes are now the Arizona Coyotes, and the stadium has been renamed Gila River Arena.

In many cases, the building of a sports facility is just one element in a grand "revitalization" plan designed to spur economic development in a struggling city. While such plans can sometimes be effective, too often they degenerate into corporate giveaways that do little to improve the local economy.

Fort Wayne, Indiana, is a modest city of 264,400, perched at the confluence of the Maumee, St. Joseph, and St. Mary's Rivers. On a recent visit, we could see that urban renewal was underway. Several new buildings were in evidence, and signs boasted of a soon-to-be developed riverfront trail. The story behind this program is a typical one.

In the fall of 2017, the Fort Wayne City Council considered funding a sports arena, a boutique hotel, and the creation of a tax-free district outside of town for developers who will benefit from infrastructure installed by the public.[19] The question is, who's paying for it all? City Councilman Jason Arp keeps asking that question at every council meeting. He's most concerned about a 2017 deal with the Model Group, a local development firm, for a mixed-use commercial and residential development downtown. Writing in the *Indiana Policy Review*, Arp describes the project in biting terms:

> When completed, this project will have used $10 million of local money, $7 million of state money, and $14 million in federal money to build apartments at $280,000 apiece (where the average home price is $100,000) that will rent for as much as $1,100 a month (two-thirds more than the average rent in the city). It will include thousands of square feet of commercial

property to be offered at subsidized rates to compete with properties that are already struggling with occupancy.

All told, taxpayers will have paid three times what it will have been worth to construct this project, then have given it away to investors who will have no skin in the game while putting competitive pressure on surrounding property owners with their own money at stake.[20]

Indiana Construction News reported in the summer of 2019 that the project, now projected to cost $34 million, will be completed by the fall of the year.[21] It remains to be seen whether the citizens of Fort Wayne will experience any benefits commensurate with their investment—but past experience suggests that such a result is unlikely.

While most of the funding for sports stadiums takes place at the state and local level, federal taxpayers get nicked, too. "All together," notes a 2017 report from the Brookings Institution, "the federal government has subsidized newly constructed or majorly renovated professional sports stadiums to the tune of $3.2 billion federal taxpayer dollars since 2000. But because high-income bond holders receive a windfall gain for holding municipal bonds, the resulting loss in total revenue to the federal government is even larger at $3.7 billion."[22]

DC journalist Chris Heller, writing for the *Pacific Standard* in 2015, adds:

> Over the past 15 years, more than $12 billion in public money has been spent on privately owned stadiums. Between 1991 and 2010, 101 new stadiums were opened across the country; nearly all those projects were funded by taxpayers. The loans most often used to pay for stadium construction—a variety of tax-exempt municipal bonds—will cost the federal government at least $4 billion in taxpayer subsidies to bondholders... Economists almost universally agree that publicly financed stadiums are bad investments, yet cities and states still race to the chance to unload the cash.[23]

Heller's observation about the findings of economists is well-founded. "Sports stadiums typically aren't a good tool for economic development," says Victor Matheson, an economist at the College of the Holy Cross. He suggests that cities contemplating such a venture "take whatever number the sports promoter says, and move the decimal one place to the left. Divide it by ten, and that's a pretty good estimate of the actual economic impact."[24]

Researchers at the St. Louis Federal Reserve Bank reached a similar conclusion in a 2017 paper: "Estimations of the economic impact of sports stadiums are exaggerated because they fail to recognize opportunity costs...Rather than subsidizing sports stadiums, governments could finance other projects such as infrastructure or education that have the potential to increase productivity and promote economic growth."[25]

Sometimes local governments are tempted to subsidize sports because of the perceived prestige associated with having a pro franchise, along with the assumption that public support is essential to making a big project like stadium construction possible. Yet *Forbes* magazine keeps a list of the wealthiest professional team owners. It shows that the top ten are worth between $6 billion and $34 billion each. Aren't such affluent individuals, and the organizations they run, capable of raising private money to fund their sports businesses?

The answer is yes. Example: The San Diego 49ers hosted Super Bowl 50 in 2016 in a privately funded stadium. Noted the *San Francisco Chronicle*, "As host of Super Bowl 50, the San Francisco 49ers will get a chance to show off their $1.3 billion stadium, with all of its state-of-the-art technology, stacks of luxury suites and gourmet food stands...the Super Bowl venue is showing the National Football League something else: It really *is* possible to finance a new venue without a huge taxpayer subsidy."[26] The cost of building Levi's Stadium was paid by the 49ers franchise and the NFL. All operating costs are being covered by revenue, and taxpayers will not be on the hook for any future costs.[27]

Sports entrepreneur E. Stanley Kroenke is also showing the way. He owns Kroenke Sports & Entertainment, which controls seven major sports franchises in the U.S. and the UK. Now he is building a new stadium complex in Inglewood, California, which will serve the former St. Louis Rams and the former San Diego Chargers (both NFL teams now call Los Angeles home). The $5 billion stadium is part of a massive three hundred-acre mixed-use complex known as the LA Stadium & Entertainment District at Hollywood Park—twice the size of the Vatican and three times the size of Disneyland—that is scheduled to open in 2020. It will include office buildings, housing, shops, and restaurants— and it's all being built not with taxpayer dollars, but with private money, including $1.6 billion from Kroenke's personal wealth. Notes Stanford University economist Stanley Noll, "This is a really good deal [from a public-policy standpoint] compared to virtually any football stadium that has been built in the last thirty years."[28] Undoubtedly, the taxpayers of Los Angeles agree.

Lights, Camera...Handouts

The world loves American movies and television shows. Hollywood grosses $10 billion annually in the U.S., while yearly global box office revenue for American movies nears $38 billion. This sounds like an industry that should be self-supporting. Yet its profit margins are fattened by American taxpayers, who provide over $1.4 billion in annual subsidies to filmmakers.[29]

Two-thirds of U.S. states lure filmmakers with tax rebates, tax credits, and outright grants. These taxpayer expenditures are normally justified by claims that filmmaking will bring jobs and provide money for the local economy. The prestige of having your state's locations and scenery featured in a popular film plays a role, too—yet, as with sports franchises, the concrete economic benefits generally prove to be elusive.

The practice of subsidizing moviemaking with taxpayer funds is relatively new. In 2003, Governor Gary Johnson made New Mexico one of the first states to use tax incentives to entice filmmakers. Today, the state offers some of the nation's most generous film subsidies, including a 25 percent tax credit for film shoots, a 30 percent tax credit for TV show shoots, plus a 5 percent rebate for resident crew wages if the filming is shot over at least 10 days at qualified facilities (or 15 days if the budget is over $30 million). These movie-luring investments are nearly always economic flops. A 2014 *Albuquerque Journal* article reported that film production in the state had "provided thousands of jobs and generated $1.5 billion in total economic output [from 2010-2014], but film production activity—both movies and TV shows—generated an estimated 43 cents in tax revenue for every incentive dollar spent by the state between 2010-2014."[30] So the state lost more than half its investment in movie-making subsidies.

Despite this, some New Mexicans remain convinced of the benefits. Jim Wisnewski, one of Albuquerque's more colorful casting agents, had nothing but praise for the role of film and television subsidies in his state:

> I say bring it on, it's great for New Mexico. Throw that state money at Hollywood—bring 'em in. When they come, they have to spend money in the state, renting cars and hotels, eating at restaurants, and that's all revenue for us, isn't it? In fact, I'm proposing a studio be built on the border between New Mexico and Colorado so that those guys can take the thirty percent tax rebate from New Mexico and the twenty percent tax rebate from Colorado. They could get back fifty percent of their taxes that way.[31]

Hawaii's tropical islands have been featured in dozens of TV shows, including the wildly successful series *Lost*, which was filmed in the state from 2004 to 2010.[32] The islands are generous to film producers, granting over a billion dollars in tax credits during 2000-2010. The *Lost* series alone benefitted from $32 million in tax breaks.[33] However, Good Jobs First, an online tracking database of state spending, notes that "Although the series is estimated to have spent $228 million in Hawaii between 2006 and 2009, critics question whether the state needed to subsidize a show that was wildly successful and that needed a tropical setting that could not be found in most areas of the country."[34]

The Center for Budget and Policy Priorities reviewed a number of studies commissioned by states with film subsidies to determine the impact of the subsidies. The most damning statistics are those showing the return on investment per dollar spent. The results included a return of only seven cents per dollar in Connecticut, eleven cents in Michigan, and thirteen cents in Louisiana. One of the reviewers concludes, "states would be better served by eliminating, or at least shrinking, film subsidies and using the freed-up revenue to maintain vital public services and pursue more cost-effective development strategies, such as investment in education, job training, and infrastructure."[35]

The Manhattan Institute reported in 2017:

> Tax deals have become so pervasive that projects ranging from massive summer blockbusters to the cheesiest TV reality shows get them. In 2015, all eight Oscar-nominated films, including the ultimate winner, "Birdman," received state tax breaks. Sometimes the money goes to movies that would almost certainly be made in a state anyway. A 2014 best-picture nominee, "The Wolf of Wall Street," is a tale of New York's finance world, made by a director, Martin Scorsese, long based in New York; nonetheless, the production won $30 million in incentives to film in…New York![36]

Some states are beginning to see the downside to these investments. In 2015, Chris Hudson and Donald Bryson wrote in the *Wall Street Journal* that "Michigan and New Jersey ended their handouts earlier this summer, while Louisiana capped its subsidies—albeit after doling out more than $1 billion in the past five years. Arizona, Idaho, Indiana, and Missouri have also either rolled back or shut down their programs in recent years."[37] And in 2015, when Florida Governor Rick Scott signed that year's budget, film subsidies in that state were eliminated for at least two years.

Subsidizing Mickey Mouse

Disney is an iconic American company that combines two kinds of glamour—the allure of moviemaking and that of theme parks. Both are supposed to generate massive economic activity in the states where they take place. That reasoning has been used to justify enormous taxpayer handouts over the years—despite the fact that the Walt Disney Corporation holds assets worth over $92 billion, has a stock market value of $152 billion, and returned $2.3 billion to investors in 2017 alone. Bob Iger, Chairman and CEO, earns $45 million a year.

The corporation's U.S.-based assets include the Disney theme parks in Anaheim, California, and Orlando, Florida, both of which benefit from massive property tax breaks and special financing deals. In a 2017 exposé, the *Los Angeles Times* described in detail what Disney has gained from some of the billion dollars in deals they've negotiated from the city of Anaheim:

- In 1996, the city of Anaheim spent $108 million to build Disney's parking garage, which earns tens of millions in parking fee revenue per year for Disney. The city's take: one dollar a year in leasing fees.
- In 2015, the city agreed to a deal with Disney that shields them from the city's entertainment tax for the next forty-five years.
- In 2016, the city gave Disney a $650 million tax rebate for a luxury hotel they are building near the theme park.[38]

This in a city with a high (17 percent) poverty rate and an unemployment rate well above the national average. Tax-paying property owners are footing the bill for the public services that Disney isn't paying for. As Jose Moreno, one of Anaheim's newest city council members and a Disney critic, wryly noted during his campaign, "We've invested billions, really, in the children of tourists. We'd now like to really turn our investments toward making sure we take care of the children of Anaheim."[39]

To get these hefty financial favors, Disney has used combined doses of bullying and lobbying, notes the *LA Times*:

Disney has negotiated these pacts with a carrot-and-stick approach—one that has often included the company's threat of directing its investment dollars elsewhere… The company masterfully works the political system. Support for various deals benefiting Disney has come from Anaheim City Council members who have received generous campaign contributions through a byzantine network of political action committees funded by the company.[40]

In 2016 alone, Disney spent $122 million on lobbying in Anaheim. They're also wielding their political clout in Florida, where they are currently involved in several lawsuits against the state property tax assessment office, arguing for lower assessments in order to lower their property tax bills—this from the same corporation that saves $1.5 million in Florida taxes by renting cows and putting them on small greenbelts in order to get an agricultural exemption on some of their land.[41]

In response to the 2017 *Los Angeles Times* reports, Disney announced they would ban the newspaper from all future Disney film pre-release events and other press events. (Disney later bowed to vehement film industry blowback and lifted the ban.)[42] The blatant effort to use company clout to silence their critics may not have worked, but Disney's lobbying efforts continue to bear fruit.

Pro sports, moviemaking, and theme parks are all high-visibility activities that generate local pride for the communities that host them. It's not surprising that political leaders savor the headlines they can earn by attracting these businesses to their hometowns, counties, or states. But the evidence shows that the concrete payoffs supposed to derive from taxpayer subsidies to entertainment businesses, measured in dollars and cents, most often fail to materialize. It's time for government leaders, and the voters who hire them, to insist on accountability when they consider doling out public dollars in support of private industry, rather than being blinded by the superficial allure of sports and show biz.

1   Ben Casselman, "Promising Billions to Amazon: Is It a Good Deal for Cities?" *The New York Times*, January 26, 2018, https://www.nytimes.com/2018/01/26/business/economy/amazon-finalists-incentives.html.

2   Adele Chapin, "7 Cool Design Facts to Know About DC United's Audi Field," *Curbed*, July 20, 2018, https://dc.curbed.com/2018/7/20/17595234/dc-united-audi-field-design.

3   Michael J. de la Merced and Andrew Ross Sorkin, "Owners of D.C. United Soccer Team Are Said to Consider Selling," *The New York Times*, July 30, 2017, https://www.nytimes.com/2017/07/30/business/dealbook/dc-united-soccer-owners-potential-sale.html.

4   Ben Bromley, "Is Erick Thohir a Billionaire? A Look at What We Know About His Finances and His Ownership of D.C. United," *SB Nation*, May 19, 2014, https://www.blackandredunited.com/opinion/2014/5/19/5731378/erick-thohir-billionaire-dc-united-stadium-inter-milan.

5   Editorial Board, "Give the D.C. United Stadium Plan's Tax Breaks a Final Review," *The Washington Post*, November 28, 2014, https://www.washingtonpost.com/opinions/give-the-dc-united-stadium-plans-tax-breaks-a-final-review/2014/11/28/483d97be-75a5-11e4-a755-e32227229e7b_story.html?utm_term=.9a8b85c7f54f.

6   Neil deMause, "DC United Asks for More Money and Public Parkland for Second Stadium Before First One Has Even Opened," *Field of Schemes*, December 27, 2017, http://www.fieldofschemes.com/2017/12/27/13282/dc-united-asks-for-more-money-and-public-parkland-for-second-stadium-before-first-one-has-even-opened/.

7   Richard N. Velotta, "Exact Cost of Raiders' Las Vegas Stadium Still Unknown," *Las Vegas Review-Journal*, June 12, 2017, https://www.reviewjournal.com/business/stadium/exact-cost-of-raiders-las-vegas-stadium-still-unknown/.

8   Adam Candee, "Raiders Stadium By The Numbers: What to Expect At The New Jewel Just Off The Strip," *Las Vegas Sun*, November 27, 2017, https://lasvegassun.com/news/2017/nov/27/raiders-stadium-by-the-numbers/.

9   Art Marroquin, "Studies to Start for Freeway Improvements Near Raiders Stadium Site," *Las Vegas Review-Journal*, October 9, 2017, https://www.reviewjournal.com/local/local-las-vegas/studies-to-start-for-freeway-improvements-near-raiders-stadium-site/.

10 "NFL Stadium Funding Information," CBS Minnesota, December 2, 2011, https://cbsminnesota.files.wordpress.com/2011/12/nfl-funding-summary-12-2-11.pdf.

11 Will Brinson, "Here's How Many NFL Owners Are Worth More Than a Billion Dollars," CBSSports.com, March 2, 2016, https://www.cbssports.com/nfl/news/heres-how-many-nfl-owners-are-worth-more-than-a-billion-dollars/.

12 Curtis Martin (NFL Hall of Famer), interview by Lisa Conyers, January 2018.

13 Michael McAndrews, "Yard Goats Owner Josh Solomon: 'Real Estate Is in My Blood'," *Hartford Magazine*, July 01, 2017, https://www.courant.com/hartford-magazine/hc-hm-josh-solomon-yard-goats-20170701-story.html.

14 Jeffrey Dorfman, "Publicly Financed Sports Stadiums Are A Game That Taxpayers Lose," *Forbes*, January 31, 2015, https://www.forbes.com/sites/jeffreydorfman/2015/01/31/publicly-financed-sports-stadiums-are-a-game-that-taxpayers-lose/#7e0da5c64f07.

15 Joseph De Avila, "New Ballpark Adds to Hartford's Financial Strain," *Wall Street Journal*, April 11, 2017, https://www.wsj.com/articles/new-ballpark-adds-to-hartfords-financial-strain-1491912002.

16 Yard Goat Fan, interview by Lisa Conyers, April 2018.

[17] John J. Miller, "Taxpayers Take the Puck," *National Review*, May 24, 2012, https://www.nationalreview.com/magazine/2012/06/11/taxpayers-take-puck/.

[18] Darcy Olsen (CEO The Goldwater Institute), interview with Phil Harvey, October 2017.

[19] Chris Darby, "Plan in Works to Expand Industrial Park, Widen Hillegas Road," Wane.com, November 8, 2017, https://www.wane.com/news/local-news/plan-in-works-to-expand-industrial-park-widen-hillegas-road/; Zach Bernard, "'Boutique Hotel' Plans for Downtown Fort Wayne Revealed," 89.1 WBOI NPR News and Diverse Music, November 7, 2017, https://www.wboi.org/post/boutique-hotel-plans-downtown-fort-wayne-revealed#stream/0.

[20] Jason Arp, "Anatomy of a Regional Cities Project, a Bad One," *Indianapolis Review*, July 26, 2017, http://inpolicy.org/2017/07/anatomy-of-an-eco-deco-project-a-bad-one/.

[21] Adriana Valentina, "Model Group to Build a 'Unique' Restaurant in Fort Wayne," *Indiana Construction News*, April 22, 2019, https://www.indianaconstructionnews.com/2019/04/22/model-group-to-build-a-unique-restaurant-in-fort-wayne/.

[22] Alexander K. Gold, Austin J. Drukker, and Ted Gayer, "Why the Federal Government Should Stop Spending Billions on Private Sports Stadiums," Brookings Institution, September 8, 2016, https://www.brookings.edu/research/why-the-federal-government-should-stop-spending-billions-on-private-sports-stadiums/.

[23] Chris Heller, "The Impossible Fight Against America's Stadiums," *Pacific Standard*, September 2, 2015, Economics, https://psmag.com/economics/the-shady-money-behind-americas-sports-stadiums.

[24] Pat Garofalo and Travis Waldron, "If You Build It, They Might Not Come: The Risky Economics of Sports Stadiums," *The Atlantic*, September 7, 2012, Business, https://www.theatlantic.com/business/archive/2012/09/if-you-build-it-they-might-not-come-the-risky-economics-of-sports-stadiums/260900/.

[25] Scott A. Wolla, "The Economics of Subsidizing Sports Stadiums," Economic Research; *Federal Reserve Bank of St. Louis*, May 2017, https://research.stlouisfed.org/publications/page1-econ/2017-05-01/the-economics-of-subsidizing-sports-stadiums.

[26] "Levi's Stadium is a Model for Privately Financed Venues," *San Francisco Chronicle*, February 5, 2016, Opinion/Editorials, https://www.sfchronicle.com/opinion/editorials/article/Levi-s-Stadium-is-a-model-for-privately-6808683.php.

[27] Anonymous, "Is the Levi's Stadium Going to Pay Off for Santa Clara? They Seem to Have Started on a Good Path with Sponsorship Revenues, But What Does the ROI Look Like?" Quora, September 18, 2016, https://www.quora.com/Is-the-Levis-stadium-going-to-pay-off-for-Santa-Clara-They-seem-to-have-started-on-a-good-path-with-sponsorship-revenues-but-what-does-the-ROI-look-like.

[28] Liz Clarke, "The Rams' $5 Billion Stadium Complex Is Bigger Than Disneyland. It Might Be Perfect For L.A.," *The Washington Post*, January 26, 2019, Sports, https://www.washingtonpost.com/sports/the-rams-5-billion-stadium-is-bigger-than-disneyland-it-might-be-perfect-for-la/2019/01/26/7c393898-20c3-11e9-8e21-59a09ff1e2a1_story.html?utm_term=.20122e7d9664.

[29] Jared Meyer, "No Matter Who Wins at the Oscars, Taxpayers Lose on Film Subsidies," *Reason*, February 26, 2016, https://reason.com/2016/02/26/no-matter-who-wins-at-the-oscars-taxpaye/.

[30] Dan Boyd, "New Mexico Film Impact Estimated at $1.5 Billion," *Albuquerque Journal*, July 23, 2014, https://www.abqjournal.com/433752/new-mexico-film-impact-estimated-at-15-billion.html.

[31] Jim Wisnewski (Albuquerque Casting Agent), interview by Lisa Conyers, April 2018.

[32] *"Lost,"* Wikipedia (TV Series), https://en.wikipedia.org/wiki/Lost_(TV_series).

[33] "Accountable USA - Hawaii," Good Jobs First, Major Subsidy Deals, https://www.goodjobsfirst.org/states/hawaii.

[34] "Accountable USA — Hawaii."

[35] Robert Tannenwald, "State Film Subsidies: Not Much Bang for Too Many Bucks," Center on Budget and Policy Priorities, December 9, 2010, https://www.cbpp.org/sites/default/files/atoms/files/11-17-10sfp.pdf.

[36] Steven Malanga, "When Will States Get Smart and Stop Subsidizing Movies?" *Los Angeles Times*, August 13, 2017, https://www.latimes.com/opinion/op-ed/la-oe-malanga-hollywood-subsidies-20170813-story.html.

[37] Chris Hudson and Donald Bryson, "Yelling 'Cut!' for Moviemaking Tax Breaks," *Wall Street Journal*, September 18, 2015, https://www.wsj.com/articles/yelling-cut-for-moviemaking-tax-breaks-1442613935.

[38] Daniel Miller, "Is Disney Paying Its Share in Anaheim?" *LA Times*, September 24, 2017, https://www.latimes.com/projects/la-fi-disney-anaheim-deals/.

[39] Miller, "Is Disney Paying Its Share in Anaheim?"

[40] Daniel Miller, "How One Election Changed Disneyland's Relationship with Its Hometown," *LA Times*, September 26, 2017, https://www.latimes.com/projects/la-fi-disney-anaheim-city-council/.

[41] Mike Schneider, "Mickey Vs. the Tax Man: Disney, Universal Fight Tax Bills," *US News*, March 23, 2017, https://www.usnews.com/news/best-states/florida/articles/2017-03-23/disney-universal-battle-tax-bill-for-florida-theme-parks/: Jordan Weissmann, "America's Dumbest Tax Loophole: The Florida Rent-a-Cow Scam," *The Atlantic*, April 17, 2012, https://www.theatlantic.com/business/archive/2012/04/americas-dumbest-tax-loophole-the-florida-rent-a-cow-scam/255874/.

[42] Sydney Ember and Brooks Barnes, "Disney Ends Ban on *Los Angeles Times* Amid Fierce Backlash," *The New York Times*, November 7, 2017, https://www.nytimes.com/2017/11/07/business/disney-la-times.html.

4.

Land of the Free?
That's Not What the Zoning Laws Say

Zoning…has become a tool of exclusion and protectionism that benefits the rich over the poor, the old over the young, and landlords over renters.

—Scott Byer

Exclusionary zoning practices allow the upper middle class to live in enclaves. Gated communities, in effect, even if the gates are not visible.

—Richard Reeves

Peter Berkowitz has wrestled with a dilemma that millions of other Americans face. Out-of-control housing costs. A successful freelance illustrator whose work has appeared in *The New Yorker,* Berkowitz sought in vain for an affordable home in the San Francisco area, where the median rent for a one-bedroom apartment is an eye-popping $3,670 a month. He came up with a clever solution: a $1,300 wooden box, eight feet long by four and a half feet tall, containing a twin bed and a fold-up desk, tucked in a corner of a friend's living room. "I really don't feel like I've taken a hit in terms of my quality of life," Berkowitz said. "I don't really notice I live in the pod anymore." [1]

Word got around. People started asking Berkowitz to build them boxes of their own—until the city of San Francisco got wind of it. They slapped him with injunctions, saying the structures violated building codes. "There are fire safety realities," said William Strawn, legislative and public affairs manager for the building inspection office. [2]

Berkowitz's home-in-a-pod solution may seem amusing, but America's housing problem is no joke. Homelessness, overcrowded apartments, unconscionable commutes, and lost work opportunities are just some of the consequences suffered by millions of individuals and families who simply can't find affordable, convenient places to live. What makes the problem doubly infuriating is that it's caused not simply by the inexorable forces of supply and demand, but in large measure by misguided government policies that protect real estate values for some—especially the wealthy—while harming the rest.

The Perverse Effects of Zoning Rules

Zoning and other land use restrictions constitute one of the more unnoticed, low-profile ways that government policies steer wealth to the wealthy. There are several ways that this happens.

First, zoning rules which restrict density or make building compliance codes costly and cumbersome typically result in fewer homes and housing units being built. This in turn increases the need and the demand for housing and makes the housing that does exist more expensive, producing ever-increasing value for existing owners. The result, particularly in coastal cities, is a lot of wealthy enclaves that ordinary people cannot afford.

Relatedly, zoning and the resulting shortage of housing leads to long commutes for those who can't afford housing near city centers, and in some cases, the loss of opportunity for those who would like to work where the best jobs are but cannot afford to live there. Tyler Cowen, a professor of economics at George Mason University, notes that high

WELFARE FOR THE RICH

housing costs have discouraged movement by workers to such cities and tend to keep them in lower-productivity jobs in less affluent parts of the country.[3] "Lower-skilled workers," notes Vanessa Brown Calder, a policy analyst at the Cato Institute, "cannot afford the high housing costs in heavily regulated cities, and so they get stuck in lower cost areas that have fewer job opportunities. Thus, land use zoning is contributing to a sort of geographical segregation by income. Many studies find that zoning is a regressive policy because the costs fall disproportionately on low-income households."[4]

Thanks to zoning laws, many low-skilled workers near cities face a punishing commute. The Pratt Center for Community Development and the Rockefeller Foundation report that over 750,000 New Yorkers now commute more than two hours a day each way. These trips are necessitated by high and rising rents in the city resulting from the overall dearth of housing. Priced out of the housing market, the poor move out, into the surrounding boroughs, only to find their commutes stretching longer and longer. Minorities get hit hardest. A 2018 study shows that nationally, blacks spend 25 percent more time commuting than whites, Hispanics 12 percent more. [5]

The economic impact extends beyond those most immediately affected. In a 2017 study, University of Chicago economics professors Chang Tai Hsieh and Enrique Moretti concluded that productivity drops when workers can't get housing near where they work, which causes U.S. productivity overall to suffer.[6] Workers who can't afford to live in major cities are pushed into less challenging, less lucrative jobs in smaller towns with more affordable property values and rentals. The result is a loss of human talent, which should be applied where it is needed most. The authors found that this phenomenon lowered aggregate U.S. growth by more than 50 percent from 1964-2009.

In effect, zoning laws in many communities have become tools for economic and social exclusion. In her 2017 book, *Snob Zones,* author Lisa Provost writes:

> In the broadest sense, zoning authority is a useful planning tool for safely and efficiently separating land uses for the good of the community. It prevents a

slaughterhouse from opening up shop next to a school. It keeps developers from jamming in houses on every available vacant lot. But there is a point at which controls on growth and development cross the line to unnecessary, purely self-interested exclusion.[7]

Libertarian legal scholar Ilya Somin adds that, in the case of zoning,

[E]conomists and property law experts across the political spectrum agree that government restrictions on building massively drive up the cost of housing for the poor and lower middle class, in many major cities. In addition to increasing housing prices, zoning also prevents many lower-income people from moving to areas with greater job opportunities. By artificially inflating the price of housing, zoning enriches (mostly already affluent) current property owners, and politically connected developers. But it inflicts vast harm on poorer people seeking opportunity.[8]

And Elizabeth Winkler, a journalist and expert on the subject of property rights and zoning, observes that "Segregation is buttressed by local laws and ordinances that exclude poor and working-class people from moving into certain communities, keeping those areas primarily the domain of the white and wealthy."[9]

Another significant and ironic side effect of the lopsided housing market shaped by zoning is the increasing demand for federal government housing subsidies for low-income Americans, frequently coming from the high-priced, heavily zoned areas. The result is that federal taxpayers foot the bill to provide housing for low-income people in areas that have otherwise been zoned out of reach for them. Because even middle-income families can't afford housing in many cities, they are deemed poor enough to be eligible for federal housing assistance. Says Brown Calder, "Relatively more federal housing aid flows to states with more restrictive zoning and land-use rules and higher housing costs. Federal aid thus creates a disincentive for the state to solve their own housing affordability problems by reducing regulation."[10]

Like many harmful government programs, zoning rules operate today in ways that were never foreseen by their creators. The original intent of zoning was to protect environmental areas, separate industrial and commercial areas from housing, and improve overall living conditions. The first city zoning law in the country was passed in New York City in 1916 to address public outcry over the height of the first tall building in Manhattan, which rose to forty-two stories.[11] Many citizens complained about the expected loss of light and air at street level, and borough president George McAneny spearheaded the creation of the first zoning committee in the city. The committee passed the 1913 Zoning Resolution. which limited the height of skyscrapers to "a height no more than two and a half times the width of the street on which they front."[12]

Since that time, zoning laws have proliferated. In Massachusetts, for example, the number of communities subject to various zoning provisions rose by fifty percent to seventy percent between 1975 and 2004. The real-world impact has been destructive. In 2009, Edward Glaeser and Byron Ward published a study in the *Journal of Urban Economics* in which they compared the number of zoning laws in Massachusetts to the number of new housing units built. "In this paper," they conclude, "we catalog the barriers to new construction...[including] minimum lot size, wetlands and septic rules. These barriers have all increased over time... Each extra rule reduces new construction by about 10 percent." Thus, the more rules there are, the less new housing is added, and the price of existing homes climbs upward. Yet the number of rules steadily increases.[13]

In January 2018, Massachusetts Governor Charlie Baker vowed to tackle this issue. "It's been decades since the state's produced enough housing to keep up with demand," he said. "A limited supply creates overheated demand and rising prices. Young people, seniors, young, working and middle-class families can't afford to rent or buy a home in Massachusetts."[14] The years to come will reveal whether Governor Baker is able to stem the ever-rising tide of zoning rules.

The Most Expensive City in America

One way of seeing exactly how zoning regulations harm middle-class and working-class citizens is to take a close look at one city that exemplifies the interlocking problems such rules cause. We'll use the same city featured in the anecdote that started this chapter—San Francisco.

Between 2005 and 2015, San Francisco added 114,000 new jobs. However, during that time, the city permitted only 8,000 new housing units.[15] In California overall, 80,000 homes a year have been built in the last decade—100,000 units below what's needed to keep pace with population growth, according to a study by the California Department of Housing and Urban Development.[16] This has been the result of some of the country's most stringent zoning laws, which prevent density increases in most areas and include limiting the height of buildings in downtown San Francisco to twenty-two floors. Exceptions require a lengthy and onerous permitting process which few have chosen to tackle.

In the San Francisco Bay Area, housing costs have skyrocketed. In 2017, San Jose's *Mercury-News* reported, "Here's one more dubious distinction for San Jose and San Francisco: The two metro areas are the runaway national leaders in the amount of household income needed to buy a house...a $216,181 household salary is required to buy a median-priced house in the San Jose Metro Area."[17] Housing this costly has forced the Department of Housing and Urban Development (HUD), the federal agency responsible for setting income limits for low-income housing assistance, to raise the official definition of "poverty" to unheard-of levels. Reports *The Mercury News*, "In San Francisco and San Mateo counties, a family of four with an income of $105,350 per year is considered 'low income.' A $65,800 annual income is considered 'very low' for a family the same size, and $39,500 is 'extremely low.' The median income for those areas is $115,300." What this means is that a family living on $105,350 in the Bay Area is poor enough to qualify for federal housing assistance normally reserved for people living below the federal poverty line (roughly $26,000 for a family of four).

Nationwide, HUD spends $50 billion each year, most of it to make housing affordable to low-income citizens.[18] This program is designed to allow low-income people to pay their rent with a reasonable fraction of their income, and provides tax-payer funded rent vouchers to cover any difference.[19] This creates a perverse incentive for local governments to avoid dealing with the housing crisis, leaving it to the federal government to solve the problem by subsidizing rents with HUD funds from the nation's taxpayers.

Unfortunately, this large pool of "the poor" who end up qualifying for the program in over-heated housing markets like San Francisco, often find the competition for housing vouchers far larger than the available HUD funds can accommodate. Thus, a costly government program that creates destructive incentives often fails even to achieve its purported purpose.

Further fueling the proliferation of zoning restrictions is the phenomenon of upper-middle-class and wealthy citizens using their political clout to protect their own communities from "undesirable" forms of development—a form of activism often referred to as Not in My Back Yard (NIMBY). Of course, the definition of "undesirable" is often highly self-serving. In the ritzy Noe Valley neighborhood of San Francisco, for example, where the average home sells for $1 to $2 million, parties planning to build duplexes face NIMBY wrath. Notes one journalist,

> Someone will buy a tiny, rundown, single-family home for a mere $1.5 million, then replace or add on to make it a gigantic single-family home or duplex that sells for $4.5 million. Neighbors who also own multimillion dollar homes, but refuse to admit that they're rich, are furious. "We need to stop this loss of affordable housing," they somehow manage to say with a straight face, as though a tiny home on expensive land selling for $1.5 million is remotely affordable.[20]

Enrico Moretti, an economics professor at the University of California, points out in 2018 article in the *New York Times* the odd combination of progressive politics and regressive zoning laws that limit housing for the poor and middle class in the country's most liberal state:

One way to think about it is that the enormous increase in wealth generated by the tech boom is largely captured by homeowners in the urban core who bought before the boom. By fighting new market-rate housing, Nimbys and Bay Area progressives are de facto making the housing shortage worse. Ironically, given residents' typically progressive political leanings, this has regressive consequences, because it helps rich insiders at the expense of everyone else.[21]

And sometimes keeping out undesirable parties is just part of the process. Says Ryan Avent in his book, *The Gated City*, "Often enough, exclusion is an explicit goal. In urban neighborhoods, residents wish to limit multi-unit buildings in order to keep poorer or younger residents out, fearing crime or nuisance."[22] A few California natives we talked to reflected this view.

"Look, I own a house in Santa Barbara," one man told us. "I rent the hell out of it, and I live off of the rent. It seems like no matter how much I raise it, I still find someone to pay the asking price, because the shortage of housing is so dire, people have to pay whatever I charge. Why would I want more housing to be built near me? It's just fine with me if we keep this shortage going." Neatly overlooking his own role in abetting homelessness, he added, "We need to get this homeless situation under control."[23]

Another longtime San Francisco homeowner, asked about the NIMBY sentiment in her upscale neighborhood, defended her stance: "It isn't really my problem, is it? I have owned my home for decades, and I want my neighborhood to stay just the way it is. I support anything that keeps things just the way they are for me."[24]

With the enthusiastic support of NIMBY advocates, city planners continue to routinely refuse to permit the building of most multi-family units or other more affordable housing.[25] A revealing footnote on San Francisco housing comes from a 2018 study that showed that new housing could be significantly increased if current residential buildings added a single additional story—well within zoning regulations. But there is a special rule to prevent that. City Ordinance 162-16 forbids adding additional dwelling units (ADUs) through building-height increases.[26]

A 2017 study charts the permit activity (building permits granted) and the increase in home values in the past decade in San Francisco compared to Austin, Texas, a city of one million. Austin issued over 14,000 permits per year between 1980 and 2016, and its average post-recession home value went up by 30 percent. The San Francisco Bay area, with a roughly equivalent population, issued a paltry 3,221 annual permits during the same period, and housing values increased 63 percent.[27]

In a surreal turn of events, San Jose, a high-tech corridor neighbor to San Francisco, in 2016 turned down a building permit for an office building downtown, not because of zoning issues, but because it would bring in *too many jobs*. The city planners noted that this would "exacerbate the region's housing shortage."[28] If more jobs are created in their city, there will be no place to put the workers. No one apparently suggested that it might be time to push back against the anti-development zoning regulations. Let the jobs go elsewhere.

Shane Phillips, writing on the website Market Urbanism, provides this stark assessment:

> We have a system in which…affluent residents in our cities each own a hugely valuable capital asset—their land and the home that [sits upon it]—which is appreciating at nearly double-digit rates each year, while everyone else just gets to pay more for rent, forever… There is a wealth inequality crisis afoot, and liberal cities are its greatest perpetrator. San Francisco is the vanguard of this movement—the most liberal city in the U.S., and one in which it is nearly impossible to afford unless you are very rich (enough to afford $3,000/month rents or $1 million homes) or very poor (and therefore eligible for a small number of subsidized housing units).[29]

New York Times columnist David Brooks underlined the economic consequences of such exclusionary zoning in a 2017 essay:

> Well-educated people tend to live in places like Portland, New York, and San Francisco, that have housing and construction rules that keep the poor and less educated away from places with good schools and good job opportunities. These rules have a devastating effect on economic growth nationwide. Research by economists Chang-Tai Hsieh and Enrico Moretti suggest that zoning restrictions in the nation's 220 top metro areas lowered aggregate U.S. growth by more than 50 percent from 1964 to 2009. The restrictions also have a crucial role in widening inequality.[30]

Of course, skyrocketing housing prices also exacerbate homelessness. Not only are the poor unable to afford housing, but rising rents and housing values "have made it far more difficult for local governments to afford housing options for those without homes."[31] According to *The Economist*, homelessness in California rose by 14 percent between 2016 and 2017, compared to 1 percent nationally. "Nearly a quarter of the nation's homeless population lives in California—about 134,000 people who often have carved out patches of curb, riverbed, public park or town square to live."[32]

The social impact of zoning rules is not a brand-new problem. As far back as 1920, two dissenting judges in a Minnesota case sensed the class implications of zoning restrictions: "Back of all suggestion of aesthetic considerations," they wrote, "is the disinclination of the exclusive district to have in its midst those who dwell in apartments. It matters not how mentally fit, or how morally correct, or how decorous in conduct they are, they are unwelcome." The law "in effect segregates the people into classes founded on invidious distinctions," allowing one class to "exclude from their selected neighborhood members of the other classes."[33]

A century later, the problem highlighted by those Minnesota judges is worse than ever.

Empty Apartments?

One ironic side-effect of stringent zoning is that a lot of prime living space in expensive cities like New York is empty much of the time. This is because the wealthy owners of such units don't spend a lot of time in them. If you are wealthy enough to afford a midtown Manhattan apartment, you're wealthy enough to live elsewhere.

"In a three-block stretch of Midtown, from East 56th Street to East 59th Street," reports the *New York Times*, "between Fifth Avenue and Park Avenue, 57 percent, or 285 of 496 apartments, including co-ops and condos, are vacant at least 10 months a year. From East 59th Street to East 63rd Street, 628 of 1,261 homes, or almost 50 percent, are vacant the majority of the time." [34]

A tragic waste of incredibly valuable real estate? In the eyes of some, this is considered a desirable state of affairs. State Senator Liz Krueger, whose district includes midtown Manhattan, notes, "I met with a developer who is building one of those billionaire buildings on 57th Street and he told me, 'Don't worry, you won't need any more services, because the buyers won't be sending their kids to school here, there won't be traffic.'"[35] Okay—but removing more apartments from the marketplace just drives up the price of the remaining units even higher, meaning that the teachers who work in those New York City public schools can only dream about being able to live in the neighborhoods where they teach.

The nation's capital is another rival for the title of most housing-challenged city in America. Spring Valley, in northwest Washington, D.C., is the wealthiest area in the city, where, under so-called R1A zoning, (which applies to any "Low-Density Single-Family Residential District"), each housing lot must be 7500 square feet or more. A typical household in this neighborhood spends $3,182 per month on housing, and the median home assessment is $1.65 million. As a local housing blogger noted in 2012, "In a city where the residents just told the mayor that affordable housing is their top concern, is it acceptable to set aside so much land exclusively for families that can afford almost a half-million dollars in land?"[36]

David Whitehead, Housing Program Organizer at Greater Greater Washington, a Washington, D.C. based non-profit organization that focuses on housing, transportation, and public policy, notes that zoning restrictions and NIMBY pressure make all building permits in desirable neighborhoods a battle. "You're a lot better at winning zoning and land use battles if you have access to power, money, resources, legal help, and lots of time...those tools are most often used effectively by certain neighborhoods [to exclude low-income buyers.]"

A Misguided Remedy—and a More Promising Alternative

Whenever rental housing gets scarce and expensive, the cry goes out for rent control. But studies show that increasing the percentage of units in a community with legally controlled rents almost always makes housing shortages worse. Notes the *Economist*:

> ...rent control is likely to make California's housing problem even worse. A team of economists at Stanford University recently studied a 1994 ballot initiative in San Francisco that brought in rent protections for small multi-family housing built before 1980. The policy inspired landlords affected by it to convert their units into condos or redevelop their buildings, reducing their supply of rental housing by 15% and pushing up rents by 5% across the city. Paul Habibi, a professor at the Anderson School of Management at the University of California, Los Angeles, who invests in a mix of rent-controlled and non-rent-controlled property in the city, also points out that rent control does not necessarily benefit those most in need. "It seems sort of perverse that you can end up with a banker making $400,000 in a rent-controlled unit, while a plumber is forced to pay market rates."[37]

It would make more sense to build some housing.

A Ray of Hope?

Of course, building more housing means overcoming the NIMBY activists and the other powerful forces that benefit from today's dysfunctional zoning rules. That's politically difficult—but it can happen.

For example, many residents of San Francisco have joined in support of some new initiatives for change. In 2016, the city approved a streamlined permitting process for secondary "mother-in-law units." Also known as "accessory dwelling units," these are separate living spaces built on the same lot as existing properties. They are often built to house aging parents who move close to their grown children late in life. Since the rules were simplified, applications to build such units have skyrocketed. The popularity of "tiny houses"—mini-houses in the two hundred- to five hundred-square-foot range that are self-contained and portable—has fueled the same trend toward greater flexibility in housing. These trends alone will not meet the demand for tens of thousands of new housing units, but they are a step in the right direction.

Even more promising are the results obtained when cities make a determined effort to relax zoning rules across the board. Houston, Texas, is America's quintessential un-zoned city. Along with Dallas and Austin, Houston is characterized by rapid growth in population and housing prices that continue to be affordable.

Houston has no zoning rules at all, a fact confirmed without apologies on their planning department website.[38] While some complain about the hodge-podge nature of construction that results, many consider the laissez-fair approach to building a breath of fresh air in an increasingly regulated economy.

The result for people seeking to buy a home is noticeable. With an average Houston home selling for $50,000 below the national average, the city is ranked the fourth most affordable city in the country.[39] A report issued by U-Haul, the moving and storage company, revealed that Houston was the number one destination people moved to in 2017.[40]

Affordable housing attracts new residents and fuels economic growth. To make it happen, citizens need to insist on reasonable zoning rules rather than tolerating a system that exacerbates inequality and provides economic benefits to those who need them least.

1   Yanan Wang, "Man Moves to San Francisco, Pays $400 a Month to Sleep in Wooden Box in Friends' Living Room," *The Washington Post*, March 29, 2016, https://www.washingtonpost.com/news/morning-mix/wp/2016/03/29/man-moves-to-san-francisco-pays-400-a-month-to-sleep-in-wooden-box-inside-friends-living-room/?utm_term=.2ed9ef57b152.

2   Fiona Lee, "After Going Viral, Outer Sunset 'Pod Guy' Selling Custom Pods," Hoodline, August 4, 2016, https://hoodline.com/2016/04/after-going-viral-outer-sunset-pod-guy-selling-custom-pods.

3   Heidi Glenn, "America's 'Complacent Class': How Self-Segregation Is Leading to Stagnation," NPR, March 2, 2017, https://www.npr.org/2017/03/02/517915510/americas-complacent-class-how-self-segregation-is-leading-to-stagnation; David Schleicher, "Stuck! The Law and Economics of Residential Stability" (The Yale Law Journal, Vol. 127, 2017), 78, https://papers.ssrn.com/sol3/papers.cfm?abstract_id=2896309.

4   Vanessa Brown Calder, "Zoning, Land-Use Planning, and Housing Affordability," Cato Institute (October 18, 2017): 5, https://www.cato.org/publications/policy-analysis/zoning-land-use-planning-housing-affordability.

5   Jim Dwyer, "Pushing New Yorkers Beyond the End of the Line," *The New York Times*, November 28, 2017, https://www.nytimes.com/2017/11/28/nyregion/new-york-subway-funding-real-estate.html; University of Chicago, "Longer Commutes Disadvantage African-American Workers," *ScienceDaily*, February 15, 2014, https://www.sciencedaily.com/releases/2014/02/140215122416.htm.

6   Chang-Tai Hsieh and Enrico Moretti, "Housing Constraints and Spatial Misallocation," *American Economic Journal: Macroeconomics 2019* 11, no. 2, (April 2019): 1, doi:10.3386/w21154.

7   Lisa Prevost, *Snob Zones: Fear, Prejudice, and Real Estate* (Boston: Beacon Press, May 7, 2013).

8   Ilya Somin and The Volokh Conspiracy, "Political Ignorance and The Captured Economy," *The Washington Post*, November 16, 2017, https://www.washingtonpost.com/news/volokh-conspiracy/wp/2017/11/16/political-ignorance-and-the-captured-economy/?utm_term=.839269372b47.

9   Elizabeth Winkler, "'Snob Zoning' Is Racial Housing Segregation by Another Name," *The Washington Post*, September 25, 2017, https://www.washingtonpost.com/news/wonk/wp/2017/09/25/snob-zoning-is-racial-housing-segregation-by-another-name/?utm_term=.95229dc09383.

10 Calder, "Zoning, Land-Use Planning, and Housing Affordability," 1.

11 Amanda Erickson, "The Birth of Zoning Codes, A History," CityLab, June 19, 2012, https://www.citylab.com/equity/2012/06/birth-zoning-codes-history/2275/.

12 "City Fixes Limit on Tall Buildings," *The New York Times* (July 26, 1916): 1, https://timesmachine.nytimes.com/timesmachine/1916/07/26/issue.html.

13 Edward L. Glaeser and Bryce A. Ward, "The Causes and Consequences of Land Use Regulation: Evidence from Greater Boston," *The Journal of Urban Economics* 65, no. 3 (May 2009): 265, 266, 278, doi: https://doi.org/10.1016/j.jue.2008.06.003.

14 Shira Schoenberg, "Gov. Charlie Baker Tries to Address Housing 'Crisis' in Massachusetts," Masslive.com, January 30, 2018, http://www.masslive.com/politics/index.ssf/2018/01/gov_charlie_baker_tries_to_add.html.

[15] Chris Roberts, "New Record Rents in SF: $3,410 For 1 Bedroom," NBC Bay Area, February 04, 2015, https://www.nbcbayarea.com/news/local/Record-Rents-in-San-Francisco-290737151.html.

[16] Tanza Loudenback, "Crazy-High Rent, Record-low Homeownership, and Overcrowding: California Has a Plan to Solve the Housing Crisis, but Not Without a Fight," *Business Insider*, March 12, 2017, http://www.businessinsider.com/granny-flat-law-solution-california-affordable-housing-shortage-2017-3.

[17] Richard Scheinin, "$216,181: That's the Household Income Needed to Buy a House in San Jose Metro Area, Report Says," *The Mercury News*, November 21, 2017, http://www.mercurynews.com/2017/11/20/216181-thats-the-household-income-needed-to-buy-a-house-in-san-jose-metro-area-report-says/.

[18] Peter Lawrence, "Congress Agrees to Historic Funding for HUD in Fiscal Year 2018 Omnibus Spending Bill," HUD Resource Center, March 22, 2018, https://www.novoco.com/notes-from-novogradac/congress-agrees-historic-funding-hud-fiscal-year-2018-omnibus-spending-bill.

[19] Scheinin, "$216,181: That's the Household Income Needed to Buy a House."

[20] Scott Feeney, "To Stop Monster Homes, Legalize Apartments," *San Francisco Examiner*, October 29, 2017, Opinion, https://www.sfexaminer.com/opinion/to-stop-monster-homes-legalize-apartments/.

[21] Enrico Moretti, "Fires Aren't the Only Threat to the California Dream," *The New York Times*, November 3, 2017, https://www.nytimes.com/2017/11/03/opinion/california-fires-housing.html?searchResultPosition=1.

[22] Ryan Avent, *The Gated City* (Amazon Digital Services LLC, Kindle Single, August 31, 2001): Chapter 6.

[23] Santa Barbara homeowner, interview by Lisa Conyers October 2018, name withheld on request.

[24] San Francisco homeowner, interview by Lisa Conyers October 2018, name withheld on request.

[25] Julie Litman, "Some Developers 'Terrified' Of Entering San Francisco's Development Process, But City Is Working to Improve It," Bisnow, April 15, 2018, https://www.bisnow.com/san-francisco/news/construction-development/san-francisco-policy-87227.

[26] Asheem Mamoowala, "Are San Francisco Buildings as Tall as They Could Be," Mapbox (blog), October 23, 2017, https://blog.mapbox.com/are-san-francisco-buildings-as-tall-as-they-could-be-77ecc4a3d32a.

[27] Ralph McLaughlin, "Who Will Win the Homebuilding Race of 2017?" Trulia Research, August 16, 2017, https://www.trulia.com/blog/trends/homebuilding/.

[28] Matthew Yglesias, "Silicon Valley's Profound Housing Crisis, in One Sentence," Vox, June 07, 2016, https://www.vox.com/2016/6/7/11877378/silicon-valley-housing-crisis.

[29] Shane Phillips, "The Disconnect Between Liberal Aspirations and Liberal Housing Policy Is Killing Coastal U.S. Cities," *Market Urbanism*, January 27, 2017, http://marketurbanism.com/2017/01/27/the-disconnect-between-liberal-aspirations-and-liberal-housing-policy-is-killing-coastal-u-s-cities/.

[30] David Brooks, "How We Are Ruining America," *The New York Times*, July 11, 2017, https://www.nytimes.com/2017/07/11/opinion/how-we-are-ruining-america.html.

[31] Scott Wilson, "As Gentrification Escalates in Calif., People Wonder: Where Can the Homeless Go?" *The Washington Post*, May 6, 2018, https://www.washingtonpost.com/national/as-gentrification-escalates-in-calif-people-wonder-where-can-the-homeless-

go/2018/05/06/d2b1018a-4a43-11e8-9072-f6d4bc32f223_story.html?utm_term=
.286fbd7e06f8.

[32] "The Wrong Remedy: Faced with a Housing Crisis, California Could Further Restrict Supply,"
The Economist, May 12, 2018, https://www.economist.com/united-states/2018/05/10/
faced-with-a-housing-crisis-california-could-further-restrict-supply.

[33] Timothy Sandefur, *The Permission Society: How the Ruling Class Turns Our Freedoms into
Privileges and What We Can Do About It*, (New York: Encounter Books, 2016):136.

[34] Julie Satow, "Pied-à-Neighborhood," *The New York Times*, October 24, 2014, https://
www.nytimes.com/2014/10/26/realestate/pieds-terre-owners-dominate-some-new-york-
buildings.html.

[35] Satow, "Pied-à-Neighborhood."

[36] Anonymous, "How the Other Half Lives," R.U. Seriousing Me? (blog), April 5th, 2012,
http://www.ruseriousingme.com/2012/04/how-other-half-lives.html.

[37] "The Wrong Remedy: Faced with a Housing Crisis, California Could Further
Restrict Supply."

[38] Sylvester Turner, "Official City of Houston Zoning Letter," City of Houston,
January 1, 2019, http://www.houstontx.gov/planning/Forms/devregs/2019-coh-no-
zoning-letter.pdf.

[39] "America's Most Affordable Cities," *Forbes*, accessed October 22, 2019, https://www.
forbes.com/pictures/mhj45hkhe/4-houston-tx/#6b3eadb2ba01.

[40] Natalie Daher, "Here Are the Top Cities Where U-Haul Says People Are Packing up and
Moving," CNBC Make It, May 27, 2017, https://www.cnbc.com/2017/05/27/houston-
chicago-among-top-destination-cities-for-movers-u-haul-says.html.

Thumbs on the Scale: How Big Businesses Tilt the Rules in Their Favor

Regulations grow at the same rate as weeds.

—Norman Ralph Augustine

We Americans live in a rigorously regulated society. The food we eat, the cars we drive, the toilets and showers in our homes—are all covered by an astonishing variety of rules, a lot of them promulgated by unelected officials. The result is an ever-growing morass of rules that can trip up even the most ambitious start-up or entrepreneur, while simultaneously providing advantages for major corporations and the well-connected.

In a 2015 report titled *The Fourth Branch and Underground Regulation*, the National Federation of Independent Business laid out the alarming scope of the regulatory state, which they call the fourth branch of government:

...the "Fourth Branch" is growing at a monstrous rate, entangled in every aspect of our lives...[this] reflects the reality that federal agencies are issuing increasingly more rules, including rules of broader scope and reach...The great irony is that the Framers designed our system to prevent factions from imposing new laws in the absence of broad-based social consensus; however, with the rise of the Fourth Branch, public policy is increasingly set by *unelected bureaucrats*, under the political direction of only the president [emphasis in original].[1]

Notes George Washington School of Law's Professor of Constitutional Law, Jonathan Turley, "Today, the vast majority of 'laws' governing the United States are not passed by Congress, but are issued as regulations, crafted largely by thousands of unnamed, unreachable bureaucrats."[2] Ryan Young at the Competitive Enterprise Institute echoes this point, noting that regulations have become in many ways more important than lawmaking. In 2015, for example, there were thirty binding regulations issued for every law passed by Congress.[3] The regulatory state has become a kind of shadow government, one that is often steered by well-connected insiders at the expense of the little guy.

As we'll discuss, the growth in the number of new federal regulations took a very welcome downward turn in 2017. However, virtually all of the previously accumulated regulations are still with us.

Until 2017, the flow of new federal regulations was predictable and voluminous (Figure 5-1). In 2016, for example, an average of seventy-four new regulations were introduced every week.[4] The *Federal Register*, which records all federal regulations, is now over 97,110 pages, a 19 percent increase since 2010. Regulatory agencies issued 3,853 new regulations in 2016, a 13 percent increase over 2015.[5] Should the government employees who issue those regulations have so much power over our lives?

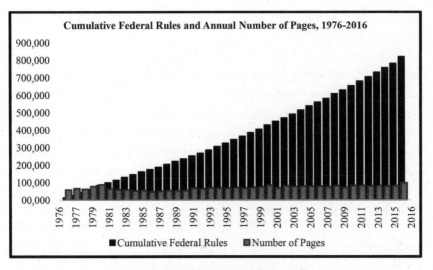

Figure 5-1: Cumulative federal rules since 1976.
Source: *Federal Register*

How Regulations Favor the Big and the Wealthy

Regulations are often well-intentioned, but frequently produce unintended consequences that outweigh any social benefits. In particular, business regulations often end up harming small businesses and working people, benefiting big companies and those who are already wealthy and well-connected.

The fate of home knitters in Vermont in the 1980s, many of whom had earned extra income while staying at home to mind children or perform other family obligations, serves as a classic illustration of this point. In an effort to protect the rights of these workers, President Reagan's Labor Secretary Raymond Donovan proposed to remove a Department of Labor regulation that, under the Fair Labor Standards Act of 1938, had forbidden work at home for knitted outerwear, and many other handmade items.[6] However, a federal appeals court in a case brought by the International Ladies Garment Workers Union reinstated that restriction. The court ruled that it would be too difficult to police the Labor Act's minimum wage provisions and its restrictions on child labor and working hours if this kind of home manufacturing was allowed. In effect, the government said you may want to work at home, but we won't let you earn money doing it.

The result, predictably, was the loss of thousands of jobs, especially in rural areas where employment opportunities were scarce. As reported by the *New York Times*, "[I]n hundreds of homes in the Green Mountains of Vermont, the atmosphere turned glum."[7] Sixty-three-year-old Virginia Gray was outraged. "Tell them to do their work down in Washington and leave us alone," she said. "Our knitting is our living."[8] The lost jobs shifted overseas, and today the production of knitted hats and gloves once made by hand by Americans in their homes has been turned over to factories abroad that service companies like L.L. Bean, REI, and Orvis.

More recently, in October 2015, the same Fair Labor Standards Act was applied to home care for the elderly and disabled, moving an increasing share of the home health care business to the biggest companies and forcing small ones out of business. Major home health care companies like Amedisys (2016 revenue: $1.4 billion), Apria ($2.5 billion), and Amer-Homepatient ($280 million) were the winners.

The losers were small start-ups like HomeHero, which provided home health care employees on contract. HomeHero workers were paid wages 25 percent higher than most other workers in the field, but without overtime pay or other benefits. The combination allowed HomeHero to provide home health care for 30 to 40 percent less than the industry average.[9] When the Department of Labor upheld a federal regulation that prohibited home care employers from hiring workers as contractors and required instead that workers be paid as employees with overtime and benefits, HomeHero was devastated. According to company CEO Kyle Hill, "The additional costs of payroll taxes, overtime, paid sick leave, minimum wage regulations, benefits and health insurance, unemployment tax, workers comp insurance, and potential for lawsuits in a highly litigious industry put us in heavy handcuffs."[10] The company was forced to go out of business.

Patients suffered in other ways, too. In response to the imposition of this rule, some caregiver agencies began rotating multiple caregivers in and out of homes to avoid overtime obligations, with especially serious effects on dementia patients. Caregivers saw their working hours and wages reduced, and seniors were no longer able to get the 24/7 care they needed.[11]

The net result is that only companies that are big enough and well enough financed to follow the letter of the law are able to continue operating, and their services are increasingly costly. A 2017 *Investment News* article notes that the median monthly cost for a home health aide is about $4,100.[12] As home health care gets more expensive, millions more members of today's working families will be forced to become full-time nurses for their parents.

Another way regulation favors the big and wealthy is through the imposition of stringent testing standards on businesses. In 2008, hundreds of home toymakers were confronted with the Consumer Product Safety Commission's Consumer Product Safety Improvement Act (CPSIA), which was signed into law by President Bush that year. Designed to protect consumers from substandard and potentially dangerous toys and other children's items being imported from abroad, the act sets specific standards for a variety of products made for children aged 12 and younger. However, the third-party testing required under the act, which checks for dangerous conditions like the presence of lead, is too costly for most small manufacturers even if their toys are perfectly safe.

This didn't happen by accident. The big toymakers, including Mattel (2016 sales: $5.5 billion) and Hasbro ($5 billion) had backed the new regulations, which they knew would deter competition from small producers.[13] According to Open Secrets, an organization that tracks lobbying expenditures, Mattel more than quadrupled its lobbying budget in the two years leading up to the adoption of CPSIA.[14]

"Once again, here's a situation where it's the small business that suffers the most," noted Kathryn Howard, an environmental and consumer expert with the Rochester Institute of Technology, in a 2009 *Christian Science Monitor* article. "Mattel can easily afford to test every one of their Barbie dolls. The smaller guys [can't afford it]."[15]

Cecilia Leibovitz, a distributor of small batch specialty children's toys, details the nature of the problem. "What we sell tends to include a lot of home-based activity—,retired grandfather supplementing his Social Security income making pine trucks…a lot of young mothers, too. There are small shops where they've got a handful of people. Sewing rooms or wood shops with six to eight people."[16] Thousands of such shops were forced out of business by the CPSIA, costing many home workers their livelihoods.[17]

Occupational Licensing

One of the sneakiest ways to pilfer from the taxpayer is through the use of occupational licensing to limit the entry of newcomers to existing occupations thereby raising the cost of licensed services. The Institute for Justice (IJ), which provides legal assistance to those trying to gain access to protected professions, and works to change unjustified occupational licensing rules nationwide, notes that "in most states, it takes 12 times longer to get a license to cut hair as a cosmetologist than to get a license to administer life-saving care as an emergency medical technician. Moreover, most occupations are unlicensed somewhere, suggesting they can be safely practiced without a state license."[18]

Licensing rules affect many Americans; the *National Conference of State Legislatures* reported in 2019 that over the last sixty years, the number of jobs requiring an occupational license, or government approval to practice a profession, has grown from about 1 in 20 to almost 1 in 4.[19] The Brookings Institution places that number even higher, estimating that 30 percent of occupational services require a license, and observing that "Occupational licensing can also be costly to consumers, who may pay as much as 15 percent more for services when an occupation is licensed."[20] Californians suffer the highest rate in the country, with 76 out of 102 low-income professions requiring a license including door repairers, painters, tree trimmers, and gaming dealers.[21]

In 2018 the Institute for Justice successfully argued a case before the Supreme Court on behalf of African American hair braiders in Mississippi, who had been forced to become licensed hairdressers in order to simply braid hair. Those demanding such training? Salons, beauty schools, and those already licensed, who felt threatened. Mississippi and many other states had passed laws in the 1930s demanding that hair braiders pay their way into the profession by going to cosmetology schools which required many months of work, substantial fees, and training, none of which involved braiding. IJ's victory liberated home hair braiders, but thousands of similar licensing laws continue in effect in every state in the country for a wide variety of other professions. A couple of outlandish examples:

> *Fortune telling.* Interested in telling fortunes? Well, in Annapolis, and many other jurisdictions in Maryland, this requires a license, a fee, and a background check. The application from the city of Annapolis requires a $50 fee and the submittal of an application which requires the applicant to provide any arrest history, even for misdemeanors, and a five-year history of residency, as well as a statement of moral character. The police department then "reviews the application, certifying that in the chief's opinion the applicant is of good moral character and that the granting of the license will not affect the public health and safety."[22] Failure to comply is a misdemeanor. It is hard to imagine any threat to public health or safety which is reduced by such intrusive meddling.
>
> *Manure spreading.* Farmers routinely use manure as fertilizer. In many states, including Iowa, Indiana, and Vermont, spreading manure onto cropland requires a license.[23] In Iowa, an application, a test, and a one hundred dollar licensing fee is required every three years. In Indiana, an application, a test (is there an accepted technique?), and an annual fee of forty-five dollars is required, unless you also spread pesticides, in which case you can use that license. Vermont requires registration, training, and a thirty dollar annual fee for spreading manure. This is a time-honored and tested farming practice, but in today's over-regulated world, you cannot even fertilize your fields without permission from the state.

Worth noting: Licensing also restricts worker mobility. Entrepreneurs who manage to obtain a license to practice their chosen profession in one state may have to start over if they move to another. In 2019, only three states honored professional licenses from other states.

> *Art Therapy.* Sadly, the drive to expand licensing to new professions continues. In August of 2019 we went to Massachusetts to learn why the state legislature was considering a bill to require art therapists to submit to a licensing requirement. Art therapy is basically the use of art as a counseling tool, a way of allowing people to express themselves and process their feelings non-verbally. Bill S141 would require art therapists to obtain a master's or doctor's degree in art therapy or an associated field, undergo two years of supervised experience, and pass an examination as determined by a nationally certified agency.

Katie Pelletier, Chapter President of the New England Art Therapy Association, is one of the art therapists heading up this licensing effort. "When people do art therapy, they are tapping into deep psychological issues, and if not done correctly you can really harm a person," she asserted. But art therapy just means using art as a way to communicate with people. What about kindergarten art class? we pondered. "Well, they probably shouldn't be doing it," she said. "Art is powerful stuff, and it needs to be handled with care." Maybe so, but what would licensing add? In fact, it turns out that the main motive for this licensing drive has more to do with financial and prestige advantages to practitioners than any added value to clients. "The best thing will be the ability to bill insurance for our services and be treated as mental health professionals," Pelletier said. "We are just as important to mental health as psychologists and psychiatrists are, and this way we can bill for services and gain recognition and protect our field." [24]

Existing practice in the many uses of art to help people renders the licensing argument spurious. Elizabeth Gordon, Art Program Manager at Boston Children's Hospital, described to us the successes of the unlicensed use of art therapy there.[25] "At the Children's Hospital we don't have art therapists, we have therapeutic artists," she said. "They do art with the patients, writing projects, play music to them. It has been a huge success—the patients really respond to art of all kinds." Licensing this kind of valuable work would only serve to make it more expensive and more difficult to obtain.

Fortunately, the absurdity and high costs of so many occupational licensing requirements have begun to stimulate a backlash. In 2018, the governors of Louisiana, Nebraska, and Oklahoma signed bills curtailing occupational licensing and requiring reviews of current licensing rules in their states. In 2019, the governors of Idaho and Ohio both signed similar bills.

While these are welcome steps toward protecting and expanding the right to earn a living, there are still many hundreds of license requirements for professions that don't need and shouldn't have them. IJ has tackled such requirements for flower arrangers, wooden casket makers, interior decorators, teeth whiteners and horse massagers. Licensing boards that insist on supervising such activities are sounding increasingly disconnected and patronizing.

Regulatory Costs

We've discussed the harmful impacts of the Labor Standards Act and the Consumer Product Safety Improvement Act. These represent only a tiny fraction of the tens of thousands of regulations governing economic activity. Others include the Occupational Safety and Health Administration (OSHA) safety requirements, the Equal Employment Opportunity Commission non-discrimination standards, Environmental Protection Administration (EPA) rules, the Farm Credit Administration's farm guidelines, the Office of Energy and Renewable Energy compliance rules, and dozens of others. These regulations add up to a huge economic burden that falls most heavily on individuals and businesses least able to bear it.

In 2019, the Competitive Enterprise Institute published its "Ten Thousand Commandments," an annual report on the federal regulatory state. In it, they note that the costs of regulatory compliance and intervention are equivalent to a cost of nearly $15,000 per U.S. household per year. The Heritage Foundation and the National Association of Manufacturers (NAM) have estimated that total costs of regulation are in the range of $2 trillion annually—about 10 percent of U.S. GDP. Further, the NAM finds that "small manufacturers face more than three times the burden of the average [larger] U.S. business."[26] Broken down by the cost of the regulations per employee, based on the size of the business, the regulatory burden is shown in Figure 5-2. The smaller the business, the higher the cost of the regulatory burden. Unsurprisingly, in some cases, the larger companies lobby to put those regulations in place and keep them there, knowing that their smaller competitors will suffer more than they will.[27]

| Type of Regulation | Cost Per Employee for All Business Types | | | |
	All Firms	< 50 Employees	50-99 Employees	100+ Employees
All Federal Regulations	$9,991	$11,724	$10,664	$9,083
Economic	$6,381	$5,662	$7,464	$6,728
Environmental	$1,889	$3,574	$1,338	$1,014
Tax Compliance	$960	$1,518	$1,053	$694
OSHHS	$761	$970	$809	$647

Figure 5-2: Regulatory costs in small, medium, and large firms, 2012.
Source: National Association of Manufacturers, September 2014

Many experts point to the excessive regulatory burden as the reason for the slowing rate of growth in the number of small business start-ups in America. Writes former BB&T Bank chairman John Allison, "Large companies' ability to absorb these [regulatory] costs relative to small businesses gives them a significant competitive advantage. By hindering small business growth, overregulation results in a less dynamic and innovative economy."[28] John Dearie, Executive Vice President at the Financial Services Forum and co-author of *Where the Jobs Are: Entrepreneurship and the Soul of the American Economy*, discussed this issue in a 2014 Chamber of Commerce article:

> At roundtables we conducted with entrepreneurs…I
> heard a number of major themes: …regulatory

burden, complexity, and uncertainty is undermining entrepreneurs' ability to successfully launch new businesses, expand, and create jobs... "Identifying, understanding, and complying with all these regulations is a huge loss of productivity... It's as if the politicians and regulators in Washington want me to fail—and spend all their time thinking up new ways to ensure that I do," said Sharon Delay, founder of Adjunct Solutions in Westerville, Ohio. "Quit throwing ridiculous roadblocks in front of me! You either want me to be the engine of the economy or you don't!" [29]

Greg H., owner/manager of Xtremeline Sports, a water sports equipment manufacturer based in San Pedro, California, brought this point home to us in a personal way when we talked with him in November 2018. "When I started my business as a young kid thirty-three years ago, it was purely a seat-of-my-pants operation," he said. "I was cranking out so much work so fast, learning so fast, getting so much product out the door. Now there are so many regulations out there I can't keep up with them."

We asked Greg about the future of start-ups. "There is no way a person today could start a business of any kind without an army of people just to do the paperwork associated with running a business," he told us. "And even when you try your best, you're still tripping over some rule or another, and there you are having to explain yourself to some agency. I'm done. My customers will be buying cheap knockoffs on Amazon, and I'm out of business." [30] By the end of the year, Greg closed his doors for good.

Some regulations are just dumb. Do we need the government dictating the size of olives? Requiring certain techniques for potato handling? Defining an appropriate "serving size" for foods? It is a federal crime to sell Swiss cheese that has no holes. So is marketing frozen cherry tarts in interstate commerce if their diameter exceeds four inches (penalty: up to one year in prison/$1,000). And look out for fruit cocktail. There are criminal sanctions for selling that item if it contains too many peaches (no more than 50 percent), or too few cherries. [31]

While these laws seem ridiculous, they are symptomatic of the over-regulation and over-criminalization of American life. There are thousands of federal crimes, for example, which, like many regulations, are arcane and little known. One educated guess in 2013 put the number of federal crimes at 4,000, and there are 300,000 federal regulations that can be enforced in criminal court.[32]

How do these developments shift resources from the less wealthy to the more wealthy? They destroy jobs that millions of low-income Americans would like to have, hobble entrepreneurial start-ups, and give an advantage to wealthier entities that can afford the high-priced legal help needed to stay on the right side of the law.

How Labor Regulations Can Hurt Workers

Another example of regulatory overreach that hurts working people is the Davis-Bacon Act of 1931, which covers employment law related to wages on all federal and some state construction projects. The act requires that "prevailing wages" be paid for mechanics and laborers on all federal construction jobs. Some states have added their own "Little Bacon" laws, applying the same rule to state-sponsored projects. Hailed as a protection for workers, the act has morphed into a costly burden on the American taxpayer, because the U.S. Department of Labor—the agency responsible for setting the prevailing wage scale for each project—uses local union wages as the benchmark despite that only a small percentage of workers in the private sector belong to unions.[33] Thus, wages on government contracts are inflated to the union wage level, regardless of the current supply and demand for labor in the subject area (Figure 5-3).

While it is impossible to state exactly what any construction project would have cost had it not been constrained by Davis-Bacon, it is clear that the act significantly increases costs, and at the same time, reduces employment opportunities in the construction industry. In 2014, scholars at the Illinois Policy Institute evaluated the impact of the state's little Davis-Bacon Bill on local construction projects over the previous ten-year period. They found a job-rationing effect associated with the law.

They also found a 7.9 percent increase in construction sector employment in states where these laws were repealed. That would translate to more than 14,000 additional construction-sector jobs in Illinois.[34]

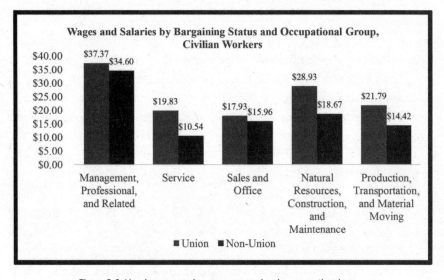

Figure 5-3: Hourly wages, union versus nonunion, by occupational group.
Source: *Monthly Labor Review*, April 2013

Of course, the workers who get the union-level Davis-Bacon wages benefit from that. But a larger number must go without work altogether.

Rules like those imposed by Davis-Bacon play a role in preventing many projects from even being launched. In 2017, President Trump proposed a trillion-dollar infrastructure bill, which, if implemented, would also be constrained by the Davis-Bacon Act regulations, costing taxpayers hundreds of millions of dollars. Tim Worstall, writing in *Forbes* in 2016, explained the trade-off: "Civil engineers tell us that there's a backlog of $3.2 trillion of infrastructure fixing that needs to be done. Would we like to do that by spending $2.56 trillion, with $640 billion left over to reduce the deficit, put a Man on Mars, or alleviate poverty...Or would we prefer to use union pay scales and spend $3.2 trillion?"[35]

To date, no ambitious infrastructure program has made any headway in Congress. The additional costs mandated by Davis-Bacon help to make such projects unaffordable.

The Costs of Environmental Regulations

Environmental regulations impact mostly middle-class Americans—home and property owners rather than the rich or the poor. But they illustrate how intrusive and destructive the regulatory state has become, and how severely the enforcers of regulations can undermine Americans' lives—in their very homes and livelihoods.

The case of Sackett vs the Environmental Protection Agency (EPA) reveals government arrogance at the extreme. In 2008, Mike and Chantell Sackett bought a building lot for their dream home near Priest Lake in Idaho. They got all the necessary building permits and began to prepare the land for construction by adding gravel for the home's foundation. On the third day of this seemingly routine activity, agents from the EPA and the Army Corps of Engineers entered the property and told the Sacketts' employees to stop work. They claimed that the lot contained wetlands protected under the Clean Water Act.[36]

The Sacketts were at first disbelieving, because their property was a completely land-locked lot within an existing subdivision where other homes were already occupied. Chantell asked the agents for some proof that their property contained a wetland. The agents said they didn't need any proof, but they pointed her to the National Fish and Wildlife Wetlands Inventory, a map that shows wetlands locations. The Sacketts consulted the map, which showed that their lot in fact was *not* on an existing wetland. Confronted, the agent told Chantell that "the map is not always correct."

Chantell responded, "You're going to stop me from working on my property that we paid for because of a wetland inventory that isn't always correct? How does that work?"[37]

Undeterred, the EPA issued a Compliance Order which instructed the Sacketts to stop their construction and restore the property to its "original state." The order even told them what type of shrubbery to plant on the site, and exactly where to plant it. If they failed to comply with the order, they were subject to $37,500 in fines *per day.*

The Cato Institute's Ilya Shapiro describes the implications of that order:

The Sacketts were, understandably, shocked…They asked for a hearing—and that was when they learned that he Compliance Order process does not entitle them to a hearing. They must either comply with the Order immediately to avoid the fines, or play chicken with the EPA—waiting until the EPA decides to file an "enforcement action." At that time, they would be allowed to present their arguments that the land is not actually a "wetland." But of course, by that time, the fines would have accumulated to hundreds of thousands or millions of dollars.

Worse, these Compliance Orders are issued by a single EPA bureaucrat, on the basis of "any evidence." That's the language of the statute itself—and federal courts have interpreted "any evidence" to mean even an anonymous phone call or a newspaper story.

And a Compliance Order doesn't just demand that you obey EPA's orders or face fines—ignoring a Compliance Order is a separately punishable offense against federal law, aside from the liability for any environmental damage. In other words, you can face penalties for violating the Clean Water Act *and also* for ignoring a Compliance Order. Worse still, ignoring a Compliance Order can serve as the basis of a finding of "willfulness," and thus the basis of criminal charges.[38]

Unable to get a hearing, the Sacketts tried to negotiate with the EPA agents. They even hired wetland specialists—hydrologists and soil scientists—who confirmed that they could find no evidence of a wetland on the Sacketts' property. That didn't matter. The EPA claimed that they couldn't be challenged in court or any other way because the Compliance Order had not yet been enforced. "You can't win," says Mike Sackett. "They've got you in a corner."[39]

Their lawyer, Damien Schiff of the Pacific Legal Foundation (PLF), was dumbfounded. "The chutzpah, the arrogance [of the EPA] is almost unimaginable," he said.

There's a happy ending and a not-so-happy ending to this episode. Managed by the PLF, the Sacketts' case ended up in the Supreme Court, where all nine justices ruled that the Sacketts had a constitutional right to challenge the EPA's Compliance Order in court. This was a resounding victory for property owners' right to challenge arbitrary government regulators' decisions about wetlands. However, the court did not rule on the EPA's classification of the Sacketts' property as a wetland. That fight goes on. In 2019, the Priest Lake building lot was still vacant as the Sacketts continued their battle with the EPA.[40]

A tributary of EPA wetlands regulations is the Waters of the United States (WOTUS) rule issued by the Corps of Engineers and the Environmental Protection Agency in 2015. That rule expands federal jurisdiction under the Clean Water Act to almost all standing or flowing water in the country and over major swaths of land surrounding those waters.[41]

To Annette Sweeney, a cattle farmer in Hardin County, Iowa, WOTUS "felt like the government's hands on her throat." Reported the *Washington Post* in 2017:

> Was some bureaucrat now going to show up and police her puddles and tiniest ditches of water? She said that is what happened several years ago: A federal conservation official told Sweeney she had a half-acre of wetland in the middle of a 160-acre field. Wetlands are protected habitats for migrating birds and other wildlife and are important for healthy soil and water.
>
> "Suddenly this piece of land that we had been farming for 70 years was federally protected, and we had to stop everything," said Sweeney, who was born on the farm and raised two boys there.
>
> In the end, Sweeney had to pay $5,000 to preserve a small parcel elsewhere so she could continue farming her own property. The experience contributed to a feeling that "we were smothered" by the federal government, Sweeney said.[42]

The rules and the enforcement agents were robbing the Sweeneys of their ability to decide for themselves how their farm should be run. "It was like telling us how to raise our children," said her husband, Dave.

People like the Sacketts and the Sweeneys are not well-connected in Washington. They do not have lobbyists promoting their interests at the EPA. All they can do is importune government agencies on their own behalf.

The Heavy Burden of Agricultural Regulations

As we've explained, many farmers benefit from unjustified government subsidies. But not all farmers are rich, or even subsidized. However, all farmers confront a staggering array of regulations that are especially burdensome on small independent growers who don't have the assets—especially the administrative depth—of the mega-farms. Manuel Cunha, head of the Nisei Farmers League and a farmer in central California, shared a list of the regulatory agencies he has to interact with in order to operate his farm (Figure 5-4).

"I fall under eighty-five different regulatory rules just to grow my crops." Cunha told us. "How can I keep up with all that *and* do my work?"[43]

California farmer Doug Benick was emphatic in his assessment of the impact of regulations on his business:

> Stop with the regulations. They're killing me. It's impossible to keep up with all the rules we are expected to follow…air pollution rules, water use rules—don't get me started on water use rules here in drought-stricken central California. We aren't allowed to use our own water for farming. It pours right through our county, out to the populations on the coast…the rules are so cumbersome, and they come at us from so many angles, it's exhausting.[44]

- **U.S. Gov't**
- Dept. of Labor
  - Employment Standards Administration
    - Wage & Hour Division (Fair Labor Standards Act (FLSA) and Migrant and Seasonal Workers Protection Act (MSWPA)
  - OSHA
  - H-2A (very difficult to implement)
  - Regulations preventing people under the age of 18 from working
- Dept. Homeland Security
  - Immigration & Customs Enforcement (ICE)
    - · E-Verify
    - · I-9
    - · Enforcement of immigration laws
- Dept. of Treasury
  - Internal Revenue Service - accrual vs. cash accounting
  - Alcohol & Tobacco Tax and Trade Bureau
- Dept. of Transportation- hauling of commerce
- Dept. of Health & Human Services
  - Food & Drug Administration- food safety regulations
- Dept. of the Interior
  - Bureau of Land Management- grazing requirements
  - Bureau of Reclamation- federal water allocations
    - · Army Corps of Engineers
  - Fish & Wildlife Service- endangered species
  - US Forest Service- harvesting of timber
- Dept. of Agriculture
  - Agricultural Marketing Service
  - Agricultural Research Service
  - Animal & Plant Health Inspection Service
  - Farm Service Agency
  - Food Safety & Inspection Service
  - National Agricultural Statistics Service- surveys
  - Natural resources Conservation Status
  - Federal Crop Insurance Corporation
- Dept. of Commerce
  - National Marine Fisheries Service- Delta pumping
- Equal Employment Opportunity Commission- discrimination and harassment training
- Environmental Protection Agency
  - Air Quality
  - Pesticide registration and use
  - Water quality
  - Spill Prevention Control- petroleum products (state too)
  - Fugitive Dust
  - Diesel and gasoline emissions
- National Labor Relations Board
- Social Security Administration- No Match letters to employers which requires response by employer

Figure 5-4: U.S. government regulatory agencies impacting agricultural industries.
Source: Manuel Cunha, August 2018

Roger Pistorisi, a local rancher, agreed:

Look at the rule about overtime. We now have to pay overtime for any hours our workers are on the job over forty hours. This is *agriculture*! When the crops come in, everyone wants to work those long hours. Everyone!

When I was a younger man, my brother and I would share a tractor and we never turned that thing off. He'd work twelve hours, get off the tractor, I'd work twelve hours, get off the tractor and give it back to him. But now if we farmers have to pay time and a half for any hour over the weekly forty, we will just hire more people and keep them under the forty hours a week, and all our crews will be mad. They want the extra hours, and they didn't ask for overtime pay.[45]

As for the immigration laws under scrutiny in 2018, all these farmers agreed, "The president is wrong on this one. You cannot get rid of all the Mexicans we have in this country, or we will run out of food so fast, grocery store shelves will be empty, and there will be riots in the streets. Do what you need to do to make them legal, don't build a wall to keep them out! That's ridiculous."

Fruit and vegetable farmers seem to bear a particularly heavy burden when it comes to the daily grind of regulatory compliance. A 2018 *New York Times* article profiled apple farmers near Albany, New York, and their experiences with the regulatory regime. The Indian Ladder Farm is run by a fifth-generation member of the Ten Eyck family, and sells apples, apple pies, cider, and donuts. In the fall, visitors come to learn about apple farming, school children come for field trips, and the forty employees of the farm stay busy from dawn to dusk. Unfortunately, this is also when regulators from various state and federal agencies choose to come and inspect, and the time it takes to comply with their requests is onerous.

Noted the *Times* reporter:

> [The] Ten Eyck family, which owns the farm, along with the staff devoted about forty hours to serving the investigators. "It is terribly disruptive," said Peter G. Ten Eyck II, 79, who runs the farm. "And the dimension that doesn't get mentioned is the psychological hit: They are there to find something wrong with you. And then they are going to fine you...If it isn't pest poisons and

pesticides, then it is food safety," said Mr. Ten Eyck, describing how one rule maker seemingly tries to outdo the next. "And they come in waves."[46]

In 2014, after trying to sell apples to Whole Foods and learning that the company has its own layer of bureaucracy and regulations, Ten Eyck decided to stop selling his apples anywhere but on the farm and at local grocers. "All I'm trying to do is grow so that my grandchild can pick an apple off a tree and take a bite out of it and be O.K. That's where I want to be."

The Costs of Transport Regulations

The 1920 Jones Act (sometimes also known as the Merchant Marine Act), is a sweeping piece of legislation that regulates the shipping industry. It stipulates that all goods traveling between U.S. ports must be shipped on U.S.-built ships owned by U.S. nationals and crewed by U.S. citizens or sailors. This is an expensive combination. Although Alaska, Hawai'i, and Puerto Rico suffer mightily under these provisions, they aren't the only ones affected. Shipping oil from the Gulf Coast to the Northeast, for example, would cost $1.20 a barrel if producers were able to use foreign-flagged vessels, as opposed to the four dollars it costs on all-American vessels.[47]

Noted David Hackett, president of Stillwater Associates, a transportation energy consulting company in a 2015 *Business Insider* interview:

> [The Jones Act is] inefficient and it distorts the market. It makes life more expensive for people living on islands like Puerto Rico, Guam, Hawaii and those in Alaska. The U.S. East Coast imports 500,000 barrels of gasoline a day from overseas, while the Gulf Coast exports nearly that same amount to foreign buyers. A primary reason the Gulf Coast does not simply send its gasoline to the East Coast is because of the Jones Act, which makes it prohibitively expensive.[48]

A 2013 New York Federal Reserve study underlined the cost issue: "It costs an estimated $3,063 to ship a twenty-foot container of household and commercial goods from the East Coast of the United States to Puerto Rico; the same shipment costs $1,504 to nearby Santo Domingo (Dominican Republic) and $1,687 to Kingston (Jamaica)—destinations that are not subject to Jones Act restrictions."[49]

The principal beneficiaries of this Americans-only policy are Kirby Marine of Houston, Texas, which gets about 35 percent of the business created under the Jones Act; Maersk, an international conglomerate headquartered in Reston, Virginia, which operates both international and all-U.S. vessels; and Matsons and Pasha Hawaii, the latter two companies operating primarily between Hawaii and the U.S. mainland. These are wealthy companies that don't seem to need federal help. In 2016, for example, Kirby Marine earned $141 million and paid its CEO $3.5 million. [50]

The workers who service the U.S.-based ships also benefit. Average salaries among the members of the Seafarers Union International are in the $70,000 per year range, with captains earning over $100,000 annually. These wages are inflated by the requirement to use American employees. Mega-yacht ships' captain Delos Gurney—who has thirty years' experience as a private captain—dryly observes, "I retired because as an American captain I command too high a salary. Why would anyone flag their ship in America and be forced to hire Americans like me, when they can flag their boats elsewhere and get captains and crew for half the price?" [51]

One argument often touted by Jones Act supporters is that American-built ships and crews are safer. But recent scholarship contradicts that claim. The Cato Institute's Thomas Greene points out that American shipping companies are slow to purchase new American-made ships because they are very expensive. As a result, "the U.S. merchant marine fleet has become older and less safe…It is doubtful that the original sponsors or the current defenders of the Jones Act intended to create conditions that would increase the dangers faced by American seamen, but that has been the result."[52]

Hawaiian cattle farmers get hit twice by the Jones Act. They must import feedstock from the mainland on Matson's or Pasha Hawaii's vessels (the only U.S. vessels that cover these routes) and then ship their cattle or beef to their mainland markets, paying two or three times the market price for transport, coming and going. While Matson rakes in the subsidized profits, Hawaiian farmers struggle and consumers pay more for food. [53]

Another feature of the Jones Act includes the provision of subsidized loans to shipbuilders building vessels for American flagging. Former Navy Secretary John F. Lehman, having founded a private equity firm after leaving the Navy, headed up a notable boondoggle in this category when he landed two guaranteed loans worth $140 million from the United States Maritime Administration (MARAD) to build a high-speed ferry service for the Hawaiian inter-island market. After the boats were built, the ferry service was denied operating permits due to environmental concerns. Hawaiian taxpayers footed the bill for the $40 million in harbor improvements and infrastructure needed to berth the boats. American taxpayers ended up paying $138 million for two boats, and Hawaiian taxpayers paid dearly for harbor improvements that sit idle.[54] Lehman Holding Company, in 2019, has assets valued at $3.1 billion. [55]

When disaster strikes, the distortions caused by the Jones Act become particularly egregious, On September 10, 2017, Puerto Rico was devastated by Hurricane Maria, the most powerful hurricane to hit the island in 85 years. Everything from food, medicine, and water to emergency shelter and generators was in short supply.[56] Constrained by the Jones Act, relief from the mainland had to wait for American-flagged vessels which could not meet the emergency demand. U.S. relief supplies were delayed for eight days until the president issued a waiver so that international shipping companies could chip in.[57] And then, under fierce lobbying from the maritime industry, that waiver was allowed to expire ten days later.[58]

The Jones Act has its supporters, of course. Responding to a blog exchange on the act initiated by the Cato Institute's David Boaz, one reader in Hawaii stressed the role of the maritime industry there. "America's maritime industry is vital to Hawaii, accounting for thousands of jobs. A strong maritime industry is critical to accessing the goods families need to lead productive lives. That's why I support the Jones Act."

Yet another participant in the exchange pointed out how Jones Act supporters tend to keep a low profile. "I once did a talk show for Hawai'i Public Radio. We wanted to look at the Jones Act and it was easy to find opponents to come on the air, but we couldn't get a single pro-Jones Act guest. They don't want to debate. Public radio fairness rules made us cancel the show."[59] If the Jones Act really served any vitally important purpose, its supporters would probably be less shy about standing up for it in public.

California—Poster Child for Regulatory Overkill at the State Level

California is almost certainly the most regulated state in the nation. Its citizens have been subjected to some pretty wacky (and often harmful) rules. A good many of these emanate from Proposition 65, a voter initiative that California residents approved in 1986. The initiative called on state agencies to better inform citizens about "chemicals that cause cancer, birth defects, or other reproductive harm." While some good may have come of this, the fallout from Prop 65 has been damaging, and at times, ludicrous.

State authorities took Prop 65's mandate to mean that they should warn citizens about even the slightest risks of exposure to substances that might cause cancer, even in minuscule amounts that are, in practice, perfectly safe. The result has been that everyone in California who enters a restaurant, a supermarket, or a food convenience store must pass by a printed warning, conspicuously posted at the entry to all such establishments, that "Certain foods and beverages sold or served here can expose you to chemicals including acrylamide in many fried or baked foods, and mercury in fish, which are known to the State of California to cause cancer and birth defects or other reproductive harm."[60] Presumably all forty million California citizens, and the many others who visit there each year, have gotten over the anxiety caused by these signs, since the alternative, it would seem, is to give up eating.

Drilling further into the arcana of cancer warnings, we learned on a visit to a boat supply store in Long Beach that plastic anchor chain markers—items that boat owners use to mark the length of their anchor chains so they can anchor safely—are no longer available for sale in California. Again, Prop 65 is to blame. The store manager explained that the chain markers are made with some of the hundreds of different chemicals covered under the law. "It just costs too much to go through the hassle of finding a way to print the warning on to products, to say nothing of the cost for testing. Boat items are pretty unique, and our suppliers don't sell a lot of what they make. This is just too much of a hassle." [61]

Further, these rules have led to lawsuits. It is up to the manufacturer or producer to test for all potentially carcinogenic chemicals. Enforcement is by civil complaint from consumers, which has led to some savvy consumers and aggressive attorneys making a living from catching out manufacturers or producers who haven't tested for all known chemicals.[62] This clogs the courts, enriches unethical trolls, and makes countless products more expensive.

Prop 65 has its supporters. James Wheaton, president of the Environmental Law Center and a proponent of Prop 65, says "Proposition 65 has been a very effective policy…If the law pushes companies to make their products safer, the public is the winner."[63]

But defense attorney Lisa Halko disagrees:

> It should be a health and communication issue, not a legal issue. Why would we think that a bunch of lawyers, however well-meaning, know best how to communicate risks and benefits? [T]he problem is that the law allows anybody to bring a case by finding a listed chemical in a product, even if it is present in an amount 1,000 times below the "no observable effect" level. The defendant can prove the level is meaninglessly low—but that is extremely expensive to do in court. Defendants end up settling with the plaintiff even when they are not liable, to avoid the expense of litigation. [64]

The cost of these lawsuits is significant. Between 2010 and 2017, defendant producers and manufacturers spent over $180 million defending themselves, and that doesn't include the fees and penalties they incurred along the way. The fine now is $2,500 per day for any uncorrected violation.[65] The result is that Californians pay too much for a lot of things and must simply do without other products that those of us in the other 49 states can buy and enjoy.

Rolling Back the Regulatory Tide

One of President Trump's first moves in office was to cut back on federal regulations. As a result, the number of new federal regulations slowed to a crawl in 2017. *Politico*'s Danny Vinik observes:

> From Inauguration Day until the end of May [2017], just 15 regulations were approved by the Office of Information and Regulatory Affairs (OIRA), the White House department that reviews important new federal rules. That's by far the fewest among comparable periods since recordkeeping began in the 1990s: Ninety-three rules were approved during the same period in Barack Obama's administration, and 114 under George W. Bush.[66]

The president also issued an order requiring an agency to identify two regulations to eliminate for each new one it wants to issue. In addition, under the order, the economic costs of the two so-called deregulatory actions must equal or exceed the economic cost of the new regulation.[67]

The reduction in the rate of new regulations is good news. Note, however, that most of the old regulations remain in force. Under the terms of 1996 Congressional Review Act (CRA), rules promulgated in the last months of the Obama Administration were vulnerable to being repealed by the Trump administration. As of May 2018, sixteen of those regulations had been repealed. Internet neutrality rules were also overturned by vote of the Federal Communications Commission in 2018, which has independent authority. On the other hand, most of the important rules promulgated by the federal government under Obama were too old for CRA repeal, which means that any attempt to eliminate them must be justified by changed circumstances and be subject to judicial review.

Congress has the authority to exert significant control over the regulatory process, but in this, as in so many other areas, Congress has supinely allowed its powers to shift to the president. One effort to buck this trend is the Regulations from the Executive in Need of Scrutiny (REINS) Act, which requires that Congress approve all new major regulations. This act was introduced by Representative Doug Collins in early 2017, and passed the House, but not the Senate. In January 2019, Senator Rand Paul reintroduced the act for consideration, but as of this writing it had not come up for a vote in the Senate.

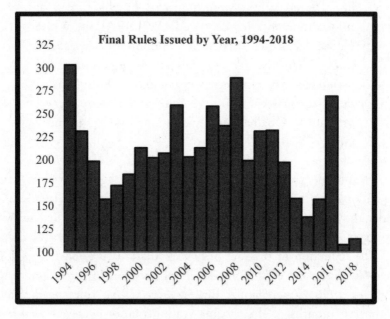

Figure 5-5: Economically significant final rules by presidential year.
Source: Office of Information and Regulatory Affairs

It will take time and steady pressure from the citizenry to force a real reduction in the regulatory burden borne by Americans. Hopefully, the slowdown in new regulations under President Trump is a first step in the right direction.

1 Karen R. Harned, Esq., "A Forward on Checks and Balances," The Fourth Branch & Underground Regulations, September 2015, https://www.nfib.com/pdfs/fourth-branch-underground-regulations-nfib.pdf.

2 The President's Constitutional Duty to Faithfully Execute the Laws: Hearing Before the Committee on the Judiciary House of Representatives, First Session, 113th Cong. 113-55 (December 3, 2013) (Oral Testimony and Prepared Statement of Jonathan Turley, Shapiro Professor of Public Interest Law, George Washington University), https://www.govinfo.gov/content/pkg/CHRG-113hhrg85762/html/CHRG-113hhrg85762.htm.

3 Ryan Young, "REINing in Regulatory Overreach," Competitive Enterprise Institute, November 15, 2016, https://cei.org/content/reining-regulatory-overreach.

4 Ryan Young, "This Week in Ridiculous Regulations: 2016 Wrap-Up," Competitive Enterprise Institute (blog), January 3, 2017, https://cei.org/blog/week-ridiculous-regulations-2016-wrap.

5 "Reg Stats," Columbian College of Arts & Sciences, https://regulatorystudies.columbian.gwu.edu/reg-stats.

6 Peter G. "Why Not Let Americans Work at Home?" The Heritage Foundation, January 30, 1984, Jobs and Labor, https://www.heritage.org/jobs-and-labor/report/why-not-let-americans-work-home.

7 Dudley Clendinen, "Court Ban on Work at Home Brings Gloom to Knitters in Rural Vermont," The New York Times, December 3, 1983, https://timesmachine.nytimes.com/timesmachine/1983/12/03/issue.html.

8 Clendinen, "Court Ban on Work at Home Brings Gloom to Knitters in Rural Vermont."

9 Kyle Hill, "There's No Magic in Venture-Backed Home Care," Medium, February 24, 2017, https://medium.com/@kaleazy/theres-no-magic-in-venture-backed-home-care-8f5389528279.

10 Kyle Hill (CEO, HomeHero), personal interview by Lisa Conyers, June 2017.

11 Hill, "There's No Magic in Venture-Backed Home Care."

12 Greg Iacurci, "Filial Law Puts Kids on the Hook for Parents' Health-Care Costs," Investment News, November 22, 2017, https://www.investmentnews.com/article/20171122/FREE/171129951/filial-laws-put-kids-on-the-hook-for-parents-health-care-costs.

13 Joe Weisenthal, "The New York Times Goes to Bat for Big Toymakers," Business Insider, February 19, 2009, https://www.businessinsider.com/the-new-york-times-goes-to-bat-for-big-toymakers-2009-2.

14 "Mattel, Inc." https://www.opensecrets.org/lobby/clientsum.php?id=D000000571&year=2008.

15 Yvonne Zipp, "A New Law Hurts Small Toy Stores and Toymakers." The Christian Science Monitor, January 9, 2009, https://www.csmonitor.com/The-Culture/The-Home-Forum/2009/0109/p25s23-hfgn.html.

16 Katherine Mangu-Ward, "Dangerous Toys, Strange Bedfellows," Reason, June/2009, Regulation, https://reason.com/2009/05/18/dangerous-toys-strange-bedfell?print.

17 "Understanding the True Cost of CPSIA Testing Requirements," Handmade Toy Alliance, October 1, 2009, http://handmadetoyalliance.blogspot.com/2009/09/understanding-true-costs-of-cpsia.html.

18 Dick M. Carpenter II, Ph.D., et al., "License to Work; A National Study of Burdens from Occupational Licensing, 2nd ed." Institute for Justice, 2019, https://ij.org/report/license-work-2/.

19 Suzanne Hultin, "The National Occupational Licensing Database; Executive Summary," National Conference of State Legislatures, June 19, 2019, http://www.ncsl.org/research/labor-and-employment/occupational-licensing-statute-database.aspx.

20 Brad Hershbein, David Boddy, and Melissa S. Kearney, "Nearly 30 Percent of Workers in the U.S. Need a License to Perform Their Job: It Is Time to Examine Occupational Licensing Practices," The Brookings Institute, January 27, 2015, https://www.brookings.edu/blog/up-front/2015/01/27/nearly-30-percent-of-workers-in-the-u-s-need-a-license-to-perform-their-job-it-is-time-to-examine-occupational-licensing-practices/.

21 Dick M. Carpenter II, Ph.D., et al., "License to Work; A National Study of Burdens from Occupational Licensing, 2nd ed. (California)," Institute for Justice, 2019, https://ij.org/report/license-work-2/ltw-state-profiles/ltw2-california.

22 "Fortune Telling License Application," City of Annapolis; Office of the City Clerk, https://www.annapolis.gov/DocumentCenter/View/860/Fortune-Telling-License-Application-PDF.

23 "Manure Applicator Certification," Iowa Department of Natural Resources, https://www.iowadnr.gov/Environmental-Protection/Land-Quality/Animal-Feeding-Operations/Applicator-Certification; "Becoming a Certified & Licensed Fertilizer Applicator," Office of Indiana State Chemist, https://www.oisc.purdue.edu/pesticide/how_do_i_fert.html; "Custom Manure Applicators," State of Vermont Agency of Agriculture, Food and Markets, https://agriculture.vermont.gov/custom-applicator; "Agency Fees," State of Vermont Agency of Agriculture, Food and Markets, https://agriculture.vermont.gov/license-and-registrations/agency-fees#33.

24 Katie Pelletier (Chapter President, New England Art Therapy Association), interview by Lisa Conyers, August 2019.

25 Elizabeth Gordon (Art Program Manager, Boston Children's Hospital) interview by Lisa Conyers, August 2019.

26 W. Mark Crain and Nicole V. Crain, "The Cost of Federal Regulation to the U.S. Economy, Manufacturing and Small Business," National Association of Manufacturers, September 10, 2014, https://www.nam.org/wp-content/uploads/2019/05/Federal-Regulation-Full-Study.pdf.

27 Sean Hackbarth, "How Excessive Regulations Stifle Small Businesses," U.S. Chamber of Commerce, May 29, 2014, https://www.uschamber.com/above-the-fold/how-excessive-regulations-stifle-small-businesses.

28 John Allison, "Red Tape Is Strangling the Recovery," U.S News & World Report, October 19, 2012, https://www.usnews.com/opinion/blogs/economic-intelligence/2012/10/19/lift-the-regulatory-burden-on-small-businesses.

29 Hackbarth, "How Excessive Regulations Stifle Small Businesses."

30 Greg H. (owner, Xtremeline Sports, San Pedro, California), interview by Lisa Conyers, November 2018.

31 Krissy Clark, "The Uncertain Hour," NPR (podcast), https://www.npr.org/templates/story/story.php?storyId=476015630.

32 "John Baker, "Revisiting the Explosive Growth of Federal Crimes," The Heritage Foundation, June 16, 2008, https://www.heritage.org/report/revisiting-the-explosive-growth-federal-crimes.

33 "Wage and Hour Division (WHD)," U.S. Department of Labor, https://www.dol.gov/whd/programs/dbra/faqs/calculat.htm.

[34] Orphe Divounguy, "Building Fairness and Opportunity: The Effects of Repealing Illinois' Prevailing Wage Law," Illinois Policy, ch 9, https://www.illinoispolicy.org/reports/building-fairness-and-opportunity-the-effects-of-repealing-illinois-prevailing-wage-law/.

[35] Tim Worstall, "Union Wages Increase Construction Costs By 20% - Abolish Davis Bacon," *Forbes*, August 31, 2016, https://www.forbes.com/sites/timworstall/2016/08/31/union-wages-increase-construction-costs-by-20-abolish-davis-bacon/#4ddb6541406e.

[36] "Sackett v. EPA: How One Couple's Battle against the Feds Might Protect Your Land," ReasonTV (YouTube), March 7, 2012, https://youtu.be/40iHXAOjJ3U.

[37] "Sackett v. EPA: How One Couple's Battle against the Feds Might Protect Your Land."

[38] Ilya Shapiro, "EPA Actions Should Be Subject to Judicial Review," Cato Institute, January 9, 2012, https://www.cato.org/blog/epa-actions-should-be-subject-judicial-review.

[39] Root, "Supreme Court Ruling Against EPA Inspires New Novel."

[40] Jessica Robinson, "A Unanimous Supreme Court Ruling, But Still No House for Idaho Couple," My News Network, October 2, 2013, https://www.nwnewsnetwork.org/post/unanimous-supreme-court-ruling-still-no-house-idaho-couple-0.

[41] Reed Hopper, "PLF Testifies on WOTUS Rule," Pacific Legal Foundation (blog), November 30, 2017, https://pacificlegal.org/plf-testifies-on-wotus-rule/.

[42] Mary Jordan and Kevin Sullivan, "'Smothered' and 'Shoved Aside' in Rural America," *The Washington Post*, December 29, 2017, https://www.washingtonpost.com/graphics/2017/national/iowa-farm-waters-trump/.

[43] Manuel Cunha (Head of Nisei Farmers League, Central CA Farmer), interview by Lisa Conyers, August 2018.

[44] Doug Benick (CA Farmer), interview by Lisa Conyers, August 2018.

[45] Roger Pistorisi (CA Rancher), interview by Lisa Conyers, August 2018.

[46] Steve Eder, "When Picking Apples on a Farm With 5,000 Rules, Watch Out For Ladders," *The New York Times*, December 27, 2017, https://www.nytimes.com/2017/12/27/business/picking-apples-on-a-farm-with-5000-rules-watch-out-for-the-ladders.html.

[47] The Editors, "How the Jones Act Blocks Natural Disaster Relief: View," *Bloomberg*, January 2, 2013, Opinion, https://www.bloomberg.com/opinion/articles/2013-01-01/how-a-disaster-called-the-jones-act-blocks-disaster-relief-view.

[48] Rory Carroll, "The US Shipping Industry is Putting a Multimillion Dollar Squeeze on Puerto Rico," *Business Insider*, July 9, 2015, https://www.businessinsider.com/r-us-shippers-push-back-in-battle-over-puerto-rico-import-costs-2015-7.

[49] Jaison Abel et al., "Report on the Competitiveness of Puerto Rico's Economy," Federal Reserve Bank of New York, June 29, 2012, https://www.newyorkfed.org/medialibrary/media/regional/PuertoRico/report.pdf.

[50] "Kirby Corporation Annual Report," Kirby Corporation, 2018, http://www.annualreports.com/HostedData/AnnualReports/PDF/NYSE_KEX_2018.pdf.

[51] Delos Gurney (American Ship Captain), interview by Lisa Conyers, June 2018.

[52] Thomas Grennes, "Does the Jones Act Endanger American Seamen?" *Regulation* (Fall 2017): 2, https://object.cato.org/sites/cato.org/files/serials/files/regulation/2017/9/regulation-v40n3-7_2.pdf.

[53] Stacy Yuen, "Keeping Up With The Jones Act," *Hawaii Business Magazine*, August 4, 2012, Government, https://www.hawaiibusiness.com/keeping-up-with-the-jones-act/.

[54] "Taxpayers Stuck with Unsold Ferries in Default," *Maui Tomorrow*, August 11, 2011, http://maui-tomorrow.org/superferry-an-economic-disaster-for-state-and-federal-taxpayers/.

[55] "Our Approach," J.F. Lehman & Company, https://www.jflpartners.com/approach.

[56] Chandrika Narayan, "'Apocalyptic' Devastation in Puerto Rico, and Little Help in Sight," CNN US, September 26, 2017, https://www.cnn.com/2017/09/25/us/hurricane-maria-puerto-rico/index.html.

[57] Niraj Chokshi, "Trump Waves Jones Act for Puerto Rico, Easing Hurricane Aid Supplies," *The New York Times*, September 28, 2017, https://www.nytimes.com/2017/09/28/us/jones-act-waived.html.

[58] . Mark Ruge, Sarah Beason, and Elle Stuart, "Fiscal Still Matters: How Social Media and Even Mainstream Media Publications Got It Wrong on the Jones Act and Puerto Rico," *The Maritime Executive*, February 25, 2018, https://www.maritime-executive.com/magazine/facts-still-matter.

[59] Steven Craven @OldPaddler replying to @David_Boaz @cpgrabow, "I once did a talk show for Hawai'i Public Radio. We wanted to look at the Jones Act and it was easy to find opponents to come on the air, but we couldn't get a single pro-Jones Act guest." Twitter, July 1, 2018, https://twitter.com/David_Boaz/status/1012459559804375040.

[60] "Restaurants: New Warning," *CA.gov*, August 30, 2016, Proposition 65, https://www.p65warnings.ca.gov/places/restaurants.

[61] Manager (CA Boat Supply Company), interview by Lisa Conyers, October 2018.

[62] Chris Chase, "Changes to California's Labeling Law Prop 65 to Take Effect by Month-End," *Seafood Source*, August 22, 2018, https://www.seafoodsource.com/news/foodservice-retail/changes-to-california-labeling-law-prop-65-taking-effect-by-month-end.

[63] Brendan Borrell, "Are Proposition 65 Warnings Healthful or Hurtful?" *Los Angeles Times*, November 2, 2009, https://www.latimes.com/health/la-he-pro-con2-2009nov02-story.html.

[64] Borrell, "Are Proposition 65 Warnings Healthful or Hurtful?"

[65] Breanne Kincaid, "2018 Proposition 65 State Impact Report," *Center for Accountability in Science*, June 2018, https://www.accountablescience.com/wp-content/uploads/2018/06/2018-Proposition-65-State-Impact-Report.pdf.

[66] Danny Vinik, "Under Trump, Regulation Slows to a Crawl," *Politico*, June 7, 2017, The Agenda, https://www.politico.com/agenda/story/2017/06/07/trump-regulation-slowdown-000446.

[67] Donald J. Trump, "Presidential Executive Order on Reducing Regulation and Controlling Regulatory Costs," The White House, January 30, 2017, https://www.whitehouse.gov/presidential-actions/presidential-executive-order-reducing-regulation-controlling-regulatory-costs/.

Energy: How America's Wealthiest Industry Gets Your Tax Dollars

> We subsidize a lot of different energy sources. We subsidize wind energy. We subsidize ethanol. We subsidize solar. We subsidize oil and gas…
>
> —Rick Perry, U.S. Energy Secretary, 2018

Americans have a love affair with energy. With just 5 percent of the world's population, we manage to eat up 25 percent of the world's energy supply every year. The energy sector of our economy—whose annual revenues topped $238 billion in 2018—has been the best performing sector of the S&P Index for many years.[1] Why does such a robust sector of our economy need billions of dollars every year in taxpayer-funded subsidies?

While many Americans know that renewable energy sources like wind and solar are supported with government assistance, it might surprise them to learn that the U.S. government continues to provide massive subsidies for the same energy sources we have long relied on: petroleum, natural gas, and coal.[2] A "grotesque bipartisan avalanche of welfare for the well-connected" was how Ed Crane, then president of the Cato Institute, and Carl Pope, president of the Sierra Club, characterized this flood of government largesse in 2002.[3] Little has changed since then.

Like so many government giveaways, energy subsidies have been patched, added to, and changed in so many ways over the years that they are nearly impossible to untangle. For example, in November 2016, the University of Texas at Austin published a report on federal support for electricity generation in which they assessed 116 federal programs that provide support to the energy sector with a total value of approximately $60 billion per year.[4] The report covered direct expenditures (such as cash grants and taxpayer-funded pilot programs), tax expenditures (targeted tax credits, tax deductions, and preferential tax rates), and government guarantees. (Loan guarantee arrangements are common in the energy industry; under such arrangements, the federal government promises to pay any loans that aren't paid by the company itself, which makes loans available at the lowest possible interest rates.)

The University of Texas report excluded state and local subsidies as well as programs targeted at consumers, such as those who purchase solar power systems for their homes under special government programs. So the $60 billion annual subsidy figure is almost certainly an understatement. But what is startling is the degree to which programs in the report are impossible to justify on any rational basis.

Nicholas Loris, an energy policy expert at the Heritage Foundation, offers the Department of Energy's Advanced Technology Vehicles Manufacturing program as an example. This loan and credit subsidy program, which amounted to $25 billion between 2007 and 2017, was intended to encourage fuel efficiency gains in the automotive industry. The low interest loans are used by the automotive companies to upgrade their plants so they can manufacture the newly designed cars.[5] For instance, as Loris notes, the program "issued more than $1 billion in loans to Nissan and Ford to retool their factories. This program is simply a transfer of wealth from taxpayers to these massive companies. These companies should have no trouble financing a project without government-backed loans if they find it is worth the investment."[6] We agree.

Prior to the 2016 election, the federal government decided to provide many new supports for the coal and nuclear industries. Each one constitutes a gift from the taxpayer to millionaires and billionaires, many of whom appear regularly on the Forbes list of the richest people in the world. Here are some examples:

- Richard Kinder, co-founder and CEO of Kinder-Morgan, Inc., an energy company specializing in pipelines, has a net worth of $7.5 billion.[7] Yet Kinder Morgan, Inc. received close to $500 million in subsidies from 2010 to 2017, including federal grants and tax credits, state and local loans, and bond financing, along with federal loans, loan guarantees and bailouts.[8]
- Jack Fusco is CEO of Cheniere Energy, a Louisiana-based energy company whose $1.7 billion in subsidies were featured on the Good Jobs First website as a "Megadeal"—a special designation for deals that are so big and complex they can't be easily categorized.[9] Yet Fusco himself received $21 million in compensation in 2018, which suggests that his company is scarcely hurting for funds.[10]
- R.A. Walker, CEO of Anadarko Petroleum, earned $15.2 million in 2018.[11] But his company, Texas-based Anadarko, has received $184 million in subsidies, including tax abatements for property taxes on their headquarters in Houston.[12]

It's not just Americans who are getting rich off the American taxpayer. Consider the case of Bernardus "Ben" van Beurden, the CEO of Royal Dutch Shell, an Anglo-Dutch company headquartered in the Netherlands. Van Beurden's annual compensation is $11 million. With revenue of $305 billion in 2017, Shell is ranked the sixth-largest company in the world. Their Pennsylvania Megadeal provides tax credits with an estimated value of $1.65 billion for an ethane cracker plant in Potter Township, thirty miles north of Pittsburgh. The facility, known as the Pennsylvania Petrochemicals Complex, will process ethane from shale gas. The deal was helped along by Pennsylvania Governor Tom Corbett, who in 2012 received over a million dollars in campaign contributions from the oil and gas industry.[13]

Oil and Gas Subsidies

The three largest American oil and gas companies are Exxon Mobil, Chevron, and ConocoPhillips. They are gigantic companies by any standard, and extremely wealthy—and all three benefit handsomely from taxpayer support.

Exxon Mobil is the tenth largest company in the world, with worldwide revenue of $237 billion in 2017. President Trump's first Secretary of State, Rex Tillerson, served as CEO until 2016, when he was replaced by Darren Woods, a veteran of Exxon Mobil's management team. Woods's compensation package in 2017 was $14 million. He ranked 34th on Forbes' "Most Powerful People in the World" list for 2017.[14] According to Americans for Tax Fairness, "In 2011, Louisiana taxpayers generously granted Exxon Mobil $120 million in tax abatement, through a ten-year 'industrial tax exemption,' which allowed them to avoid property taxes on their Baton Rouge refinery."[15]

Altogether, Exxon Mobil received close to $4 billion in subsidies between 2010 and 2017, according to the Good Jobs First subsidy tracker database. Not coincidentally, Exxon Mobil spent $193 million on lobbying between 2001 and 2015.[16]

Chevron is the world's second largest oil company; it ranks nineteenth on the *Fortune* 500 list of top American corporations with revenue of $142 billion in 2017. Chevron CEO Michael Wirth's 2017 compensation package was over $15 million, and his estimated net worth is between $30 and $50 million.[17] In 2016 alone, Chevron spent $5 million on campaign contributions and over $7 million on lobbyists.[18] This investment has paid off—since 2009, the company has received $115 million in subsidies and $2 billion in state and federal loans and guarantees, including a 2013 grant from Texas for $12 million, and a 2009 employee training reimbursement of over a million dollars from the state of California.[19] Most taxpayers in California and Texas are probably not aware that they are paying to subsidize Chevron.

ConocoPhillips had almost $30 billion in revenue in 2017. Their CEO, Ryan Lance, received compensation of $19 million in 2016. In 2011, then-CEO James Mulva famously called legislators who opposed continued energy subsidies "un-American," a sentiment echoed on the company's website.[20] Since 2010, ConocoPhillips and its subsidiary Phillips 66 have received $240 million in subsidies, federal loans, guarantees, and bailouts. Their subsidies include multimillion dollar tax abatements for properties in Texas, Louisiana, and New Mexico, as well as multiple grants from the state of Oklahoma.

These and other oil and gas companies benefit from a variety of subsidies, tax breaks, federal loan guarantees and state and local incentives, including:

- Royalty payment reductions on federal lands, allowing them to avoid paying for federal land they use.
- Domestic manufacturing deductions, essentially a reward for manufacturing in the United States.[21]
- Grants designed to lure their projects into a given state. These grants can be research grants, grants of free land on which to build facilities, and/or operations grants while they get up and running.
- Rebates on taxes, as well as tax abatements and deferments which allow them to either delay paying taxes or never pay them at all. These can include property taxes as well as state and local taxes on profits.
- Training grants and other employee-centered benefits, particularly in states where corporations promise to increase jobs in exchange for subsidies.

Many of these subsidies are not unique to the oil and gas industry, which has been an industry argument for keeping them. As *Forbes* columnist David Blackman put it, "the tax treatments in question are not…in any way outside of the mainstream of tax treatments commonly available to all U.S. industries…repeal [of oil and gas subsidies] would serve no legitimate public policy purpose, other than to unfairly discriminate via the tax code against one of the nation's most productive— albeit easily demonized—manufacturing industries."[22] In other words, if other industries are given unfair preferences, energy should get unfair preferences, too.

However, the oil and gas industry does get its own special privileges. One example is the deduction for intangible drilling costs (IDCs):

When an oil or gas well is drilled, several expenses may be deducted immediately. These expenses are deductible because they offer no salvage value whether or not the well is subsequently declared to be dry. Examples of these types of expenses would be labor, drilling rig time, drilling fluids, and so on. IDCs usually represent 60 to 80 percent of the well cost.[23]

Thus, oil and gas companies can drill wells and write off 60 to 80 percent of the cost, whether the well produces anything or not. While other businesses may expense against income some of the costs of new facilities or projects, those write-offs are limited. For gas and oil companies, the intangible drilling write-offs are much more generous.

In 2013, the Committee for a Responsible Federal Budget produced a report detailing this subsidy, and found that removing this unique tax benefit would have saved taxpayers $16 billion through 2023.[24] Opponents also point out that, given the state-of-the-art technology involved in oil and gas exploration today, there is no reasonable excuse to subsidize such projects. Supporters respond by arguing that oil and gas exploration won't happen if the risk isn't borne in large part by the government—a hard argument to swallow given the massive earnings in the oil and gas sector.

Another subsidy that primarily benefits oil and gas companies is the depletion allowance, which allows those with investments in oil and natural gas to write off annually either a portion of their initial capital investment or a percentage of their income from the investment. The way the allowance is calculated allows investors to recoup many times their initial investment, an attractive reason to take advantage of the allowance, and one heavily favored by investors.

Over the years, most recently in 2011, there have been attempts by Congress to pass legislation preventing the five biggest oil companies from using the depletion allowance to avoid taxes. The 2011 measure (which required a 60 percent majority to pass) failed after fierce lobbying from the industry. Journalist Russ Baker described the situation for *Business Insider*: "In the 52-to-48 vote, 3 Democrats joined 45 Republicans in opposing the bill, which was supported by the Obama administration and fiscal watchdog groups that saw the tax help for the oil industry as wasteful. Forty-eight Democrats, two independents and two Republicans backed it. It's not that [the depletion allowance] is wasteful. It's that it is welfare for the rich—giving an unnecessary advantage to those who already have every advantage."[25]

Louisiana, though still struggling to rebuild its economy since Hurricane Katrina (2005), gives a special tax break to certain oil and gas companies, called a "severance tax rebate," that allows them to get a refund of the 12.5 percent tax they'd otherwise pay on their earnings. The rebate, originally passed in the 1990s as a way to spur investment in the nascent fracking industry, is available only to those companies that are fracking; any earnings not generated from fracking are subject to the regular tax. By the end of 2017, Louisiana had given oil and gas companies fracking rebates worth $1.2 billion.

Jan Moller, executive director of the Louisiana Budget Project, says of the fracking rebate, "The usefulness of this credit is long gone. We're giving them an incentive to do what they would do without an incentive."[26] One company is especially happy the incentive stays in place—Goodrich Petroleum Corporation, a Houston-based oil company which has long been drilling in Tangipahoa Parish in southeast Louisiana. They are expecting whopping profit margins of 53 percent in 2018, in part thanks to the tax rebate.[27] One has to wonder why they need the cash-strapped Louisiana taxpayer's dollars to do their job.

Making matters worse, in 2018, the state government faced a "fiscal cliff," and managed to fend off insolvency only by increasing the state sales tax paid by all Louisiana consumers from 4 to 4.5 percent.[28] This now makes Louisianans among the most highly taxed consumers in the country, with a combined local tax rate of close to 9.5 percent. That tax hike could have been avoided by rescinding the fracking tax rebate, an unneeded subsidy to the largest and most profitable industry in the state.

We believe that lower taxes, especially when they have the effect of reducing government spending on bad programs, are good. But when tax breaks are targeted to specific industries, or especially, to particular companies, they constitute a form of corporate welfare that is unfair to nearly everyone, especially those companies (usually smaller or medium-sized companies) that must compete with the subsidized corporations. The big boys, thus favored, are often able to smother their smaller competitors and prevent new entrants from getting into their business at all. Such targeted tax breaks undermine the concept of free enterprise based on fair competition, and are therefore fundamentally destructive.

Trump's Energy Vision: Subsidies for Coal and Nuclear Power

In June 2018, Bloomberg News reported on a Department of Energy memo outlining the Trump administration's plan to compel the department to help keep coal and nuclear power plants open by invoking Section 202 of the Federal Power Act.[29] This act allows the Energy Secretary to keep American energy sources running during times of war.

According to *The Economist*, "Mr. Trump's latest proposal would direct regional grid operators to buy power from coal and nuclear plants, which have been struggling to compete with natural gas and renewable energy sources for years. The cost…would be borne by consumers, and could come to as much as $12 billion per year."[30] At a 2018 Senate hearing, one member of the Federal Energy Regulatory Commission noted that requiring utilities to buy from coal fired and nuclear power plants would raise the price of electricity by $500 per year for the average person who pays an electric bill.[31]

Reaction to the news was swift, bipartisan, and strongly negative. Mary Anne Hitt, director of Sierra Club's Beyond Coal campaign, said, "This is an outrageous ploy to force American taxpayers to bail out coal and nuclear executives who have made bad decisions…" Meanwhile, Todd Snitchler, market development group director for the American Petroleum Institute, complained, "The Administration's draft plan to provide government assistance to those coal and nuclear power plants that are struggling to be profitable under the guise of national security would be unprecedented and misguided."[32]

In late 2018, President Trump nominated his friend Bernard McNamee to head up the Energy Department's Department of Policy, which is the office tasked with finalizing any plans to implement coal and nuclear subsidies. As of this writing, the plans have been delayed, but industry analysts believe that the Federal Energy Regulatory

Commission's new pro-coal Commissioner, Neil Chatterjee, will try to push through some form of this legislation.[33]

Are there valid arguments to be made on behalf of the Trump plan to use federal subsidies to strengthen the coal and nuclear industries? Let's consider the facts.

Should King Coal Be Restored to His Throne?

Coal accounts for 14 percent of the energy used in America. However, its use was steadily declining until President Trump was elected in 2016, promising, among other things, to "bring back coal!"

In 2017, four states—Wyoming, West Virginia, Kentucky, and Illinois—provided the lion's share of the country's 665 million tons of coal used to generate electricity. Job losses and bankruptcies among coal companies have become increasingly common as the nation moves to cleaner, more sustainable sources of energy, primarily natural gas. Three big coal producers—Alpha Natural Resources, Contura, and Peabody—declared bankruptcy in 2016.[34] But by late 2018, they had all emerged from their bankruptcies, ready to resume business.

Even before Trump took office, the struggling coal industry had been increasingly reliant on government support. Here are some of the subsidies the coal industry received from 2008-2018:

- In 2008, McCracken County, Kentucky, granted Clean Coal Power Options, LLC, $500 million in tax rebates, a favor not granted to any other company. In return, Clean Coal promised to create 830 local jobs. If implemented according to plan, that comes to more than $600,000 per job created.[35]
- In 2011, Ector County, Texas, granted Summit Power $91 million in property tax abatements, amounting to ten years of 100 percent property tax relief, for a carbon capture coal gasification plant. These abatements were specific to Summit. In exchange, taxpayers were promised one hundred local jobs—an almost laughable trade-off.[36]

- In 2014, Marissa, Illinois, granted Prairie State Generating a cash subsidy of $6 million to build a coal combustions residuals repository (a storage facility to store the byproducts of coal production).
- In 2017, the Export-Import Bank gave preferential rate loans to Pennsylvania's XCoal Energy and Resources, plus $22 million in export guarantees. (The coal was to be exported to the Ukraine.)[37]

As we've seen, subsidies are common throughout the energy industry. But a case can be made that coal subsidies are the least justifiable of all the energy subsidies, because coal is the dirtiest major fuel used in energy production. Burning coal emits maximum amounts of CO2 and harmful particulate matter as well.[38] These problems, combined with other negative impacts of coal production and use, make the idea of supporting coal through taxpayer handouts even more questionable.

Here are more examples of government largesse lavished on the coal industry.

Alpha Natural Resources, headquartered in Tennessee, was once the largest publicly traded coal company in the United States. Between 2000 and 2018, it received $3.3 million in state and local subsidies.[39] After filing for bankruptcy in 2015, it reorganized and became a private company, with 2016 revenue of $3 billion.

During Alpha's bankruptcy proceedings, CEO Kevin Crutchfield wept on national television, describing his sadness over the loss of his employees' livelihood. Unbeknownst to those employees, Crutchfield was simultaneously arranging with the bankruptcy court to cut health and life insurance benefits for 1,200 of Alpha's non-union employees. At the same time, the company was taking steps to ensure that Crutchfield and the top fifteen executives at Alpha would share $12 million in bonuses.[40]

Missouri's Arch Coal (revenue: $2.32 billion in 2017), is America's second largest coal producer. Arch also declared bankruptcy in 2016, but emerged the same year, after leaving investors badly shortchanged.[41] Before the company's strategic bankruptcy and re-emergence, Arch Coal received close to $10 million in state and local subsidies. Ironically, this amount does not cover the cost of the 684 penalties they have incurred in the mining business during the same period, including over $8 million in environmental penalties, and another $8 million in workplace safety violations. Their bankruptcy has let them duck their responsibility for these fines.[42]

Arch Coal is best known for mountaintop removal mining, described in a 2016 PBS special as "…the practice of blasting off the tops of mountains…Coal mining companies dump the mountaintops into nearby valleys and streams…converting mountain landscapes covered in hardwood forests into fields of sparse grass."[43] In 2017, Arch Coal spent just under $500,000 on lobbying, and Arch CEO John Eaves earned a cool $10 million.[44]

Peabody is the largest private coal company in the world, with revenue of $5.6 billion in 2017. Peabody has benefitted from $275 million in state and federal subsidies, mostly since 2010.[45] The company may be best known for the rigidity of its climate-change-denial stance. Nick Surgey, with the Center for Media and Democracy, notes that "Peabody is the treasury for a very substantial part of the climate denial movement."[46] Peabody declared bankruptcy in 2016, but is since back in business. CEO Glenn Kellow earned $21 million in 2017.

Why do coal companies keep getting taxpayer help despite their dismal environmental and employment records? Supporters justify the subsidies on the grounds that coal jobs need protecting in a region of the country that is struggling economically. National security is also invoked because the U.S. is self-sufficient in coal. These and other arguments are touched on in a graphic published by the Rocky Mountain Coal Mining Institute on its website in 2018 (Figure 6-1).[47]

And of course, President Trump is a big fan of coal. Bloomberg News, in an article describing coal subsidies, noted that they are "a priority for some of the president's top supporters, including coal moguls Robert E. Murray and Joseph Craft of Alliance Resource Partners, who donated a million dollars to the president's inauguration."[48]

However, Trump's desire to use federal support to revive the coal industry isn't universally supported, even in coal country itself. Visiting the coal regions of Kentucky and Tennessee, we were repeatedly reminded of the long, sad history of Appalachian coal mining: black lung disease, mine explosions, children laboring in mines, mountaintop removal, environmental destruction, and the poisoning of waterways all remain vivid in residents' memories.

On a cold and cloudy November afternoon in 2018, we spoke with Gail Disney at the Coal Creek mining museum in Rocky Top, Tennessee, while perusing the museum displays chronicling the history of long-ago coal strikes and skirmishes between labor and management.

Gail, a frequent docent of the museum and a local historian with deep roots in the surrounding hills, put it this way: "I have kin who died of black lung. It's a terrible way to die. We got kin all over these hills who've passed from that disease. And others who died in the Coal Creek mining explosion, one of the worst mining disasters in coal country. Why in the world would you want to bring that back?"

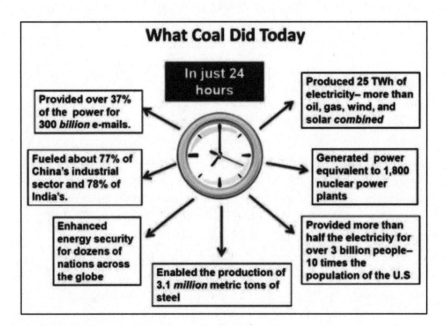

Figure 6-1: Infographic touting the benefits of coal published by an industry lobbying group.
Source: Courtesy of Professor Frank Clemente, Penn State

Gail showed us dioramas and artifacts from the coal mining years, including a tiny stuffed canary in a small cage, representing the canaries kept in the mines as bellwethers of impending danger. "Why can't we bring good jobs to this area," she went on, "which will help our kids and grandkids stay here? The young folk are moving out." [49]

Does Nuclear Energy Deserve Government Handouts?

There are solid arguments for encouraging the development and maintenance of nuclear power plants. Although nuclear power, which provides 19 percent of America's energy via sixty-six plants operating around the country, has often been vilified as unsafe (the Fukushima and Chernobyl disasters serving as poster children for this argument), the risks associated with nuclear power have so far, over six decades, been far fewer than those associated with traditional fuels.[50] Nuclear energy is clean energy, emitting no $CO2$ or other pollutants. Thus, subsidizing these plants is often justified on the grounds that nuclear energy is at least a partial answer to climate change. Another advantage of nuclear energy is that it is a baseload form of energy, which means it provides a steady stream of energy, unlike wind and solar, whose output fluctuates with the sun and wind.

Still, subsidizing the nuclear industry remains a mistake. Governments are notoriously bad at choosing the companies and plants to subsidize. As a result, energy markets become distorted, and taxpayers foot the bill for unknown returns.

Nevertheless, many states provide subsidies to the nuclear power industry. In 2018, New Jersey Governor Phil Murphy signed a bill that would subsidize the state's four aging nuclear power plants for the next ten years at a cost of $300 million a year. The bill provides a cost recovery program whereby nuclear plants will be reimbursed for a certain percentage of their operating costs. The owner of the plants, Public Services Enterprise Group (PSEG), is a publicly traded company, with revenue of $1.475 billion in 2017.

PSEG won the subsidies in New Jersey after threatening to close their plants if they didn't receive the subsidies, essentially holding 40 percent of New Jersey's electricity customers hostage.[51] Noted one local editorialist, "...this is a stacked deck...the PSEG goal here isn't coming up with a minimal amount that will keep the plants afloat. This is about

PHIL HARVEY AND LISA CONYERS

what owners *want* in their profit margins, recrafted as a need...a whopping $3 billion over 10 years out of ratepayer [New Jersey taxpayers] pockets to keep plant investors happy." In the 2016 election cycle, PSEG spent $1.8 million on lobbying and campaign contributions.

New York, Illinois, and Connecticut have adopted similar plans to protect their nuclear power plants.[52]

Nuclear power's baseload characteristic (no supply fluctuations) is why Phoenix, Arizona, home to the nation's largest nuclear power plant, the Palos Verdes plant, attracts companies that require enormous amounts of steady energy, particularly data centers—energy-intensive enterprises famous for consuming huge amounts of energy as they store, manage, disseminate, and process data at the high speeds essential to maintaining corporate competitiveness in the digital age.[53] Such centers are drawn to locations like Phoenix because of the subsidized nuclear power there, and to sites in at least eleven other states that provide mega-deal subsidies for nuclear power.

These nuclear subsidies include everything from a 40 percent reduction in the price the plants pay for water for their cooling towers, to grants to build and maintain facilities and to install pipes to carry the energy to consumers. There are also special tax treatments to reduce the amount of corporate taxes nuclear energy producers pay.[54]

IO Corporation is a company with a large data center nestled in a low-rise suburb outside Phoenix. When we visited the sparklingly clean interior of IO's state-of-the-art data center in 2017, the tour guide explained the benefits of nuclear energy. "We host thousands of cloud-based web businesses here," he said, as we toured the temperature and climate-controlled warehouses full of servers, which emit a low hum in their dimly lit cages. "We came to Phoenix because it is out of the path of major natural disasters," the guide went on. "Arizona has cheap land, and has very cheap energy, which we get from the nuclear power plant outside of town. Without a steady source of cheap electricity, we wouldn't be here."[55]

But while the energy might be cheap for IO and the many other data center owners whose centers dot the Phoenix landscape, it isn't cheap for the taxpayers funding the subsidies. The owners of the nuclear plants are the ones who benefit most from the grants and subsidies given to their industry. Twenty-nine percent of the Palos Verdes plant is owned by the Arizona Public Service Company, which is in turn owned by Pinnacle West Capital Corporation, a publicly traded company in the S&P 500 with assets of $18 billion.[56] According to Open Secrets' database of lobbying expenditures, Pinnacle West spent $2.6 million on political contributions in the 2018 election cycle, including a contribution of $1,650,000 to Arizona Grassroots Action, a super-PAC which supported Senator John McCain.[57] The late Senator McCain was a consistent staunch supporter of nuclear power and of providing subsidies for it.

Exelon is a major energy producer specializing in nuclear power. It had revenues of $34 billion in 2017. Its CEO, Christopher M. Crane, earned $13.4 million that year. In the 2016 election cycle, Exelon spent $16 million on contributions and lobbying, which has clearly paid off.[58] In New York, Exelon Corporation engineered a $7.6 billion bailout of its nuclear power plants in 2016, a bailout that landed squarely on the backs of taxpayers and became the blueprint for other state bailouts. Assemblyman Fred Thiele, Jr., who opposed the deal, fumed at the time, describing it as a "$7.6 billion bailout to keep open four aging and expensive upstate nuclear power plants. Make no mistake about it, this $7.6 billion subsidy is nothing more than a tax increase. It is one of the largest tax increases in recent history, and it will be buried in your electric bill."[59]

Exelon has also been supported by the taxpayers of New Jersey. In a shocking display of bravado, Michael Krancer, the lobbyist responsible for winning Exelon $5.7 billion in subsidies from that state, gave a presentation to an oil and gas industry conference in which he described Exelon Nuclear's experience in New York. According to Krancer, the cost to acquire the FitzPatrick nuclear site was $110 million. An additional $500 million was spent on capital expenditures, lobbying and public relations, for a return of a (whopping) twelve years of public subsidy, valued at up to $5.7 billion. Noted Krancer, this is a return on investment of *over 750 percent.*[60]

Observed a journalist in attendance:

> Krancer's presentation is notable for the frank language
> he uses to explain to potential clients how spending on
> lobbying and public relations translates into corporate

profit… The March 2017 presentation focuses on tactics
that the oil and gas industry can employ to overcome
popular opposition to extractive projects. [61]

The Nuclear Energy Institute is the industry's trade organization and
main lobbying representative in Washington D.C. It occupies dazzlingly
modern office space just off the city's famed K Street lobbyists' corridor.
Matthew Wald, the Senior Communications Advisor of the institute and
a former *New York Times* energy reporter, agreed to meet with Lisa in
November 2018. After passing through the lobby with a large blaring
TV screen, Lisa joined Wald in a guest interview area near the conference
room, where he defended the Institute's position on government subsidies. "Nuclear energy gets a lot less in subsidies than most other energy
industries," he said. "Throw us a bone for not producing pollution, at
the least. If America wants clean, reliable energy, and fuel security, part
of the solution is nuclear energy. As for safety, no one died at Fukushima.
Nuclear energy, especially with all the safeguards we have in place, is safe.
We are part of the solution."[62]

Wald is an effective advocate. Yet for all its pluses, nuclear energy
remains too expensive to compete with natural gas and other alternatives
on price. And if we live in a free market economy, shouldn't this be a
basic test that any industry ought to be able to pass?

One of the major stumbling blocks for nuclear energy—and a driver
of still more government subsidies—is that the cost of building new
nuclear plants is extremely high.

In July 2019, we visited TerraPower, a new nuclear energy venture that is being financed, in part, by one of the world's richest men,
Microsoft founder and philanthropist Bill Gates. TerraPower plans to
design a new kind of nuclear reactor that will be "walk-away safe," in
the words of Christian Blessing, the company's Director of Business
Development. TerraPower is nestled in a nondescript office park in the
Seattle suburb of Bellevue. A warren of offices clusters around the central
lab, where machines buzz and blink, analyzing the processes that will be
required to someday run their new reactor.

Gates's original plan was to complete the demonstration project
in China, but Trump's trade war put an end to that. Now TerraPower

has turned to Congress for help. In February 2019, Bill Gates went to Capitol Hill, where he announced that he would put a billion dollars into a TerraPower demonstration project here in America, and that he had another billionaire friend who would do the same. He was also asking for another billion from the American taxpayer to help finance this massive research and development effort.

We asked our hosts at TerraPower why federal support was needed. Marcia Burkey, Chief Financial Officer of TerraPower, explained, "There has never been a big project that hasn't been partially funded by the government. The government has to be involved."

We pushed back. Wouldn't government involvement slow down the work of the scientists and engineers who are developing the project?

"Yes," Burkey replied, "we could move a lot faster on this if we didn't have to answer to the government oversight commissions and reviewers that authorize our progress. That's just how government works." [63]

Maybe so. But we came away from our meeting feeling embarrassed at the thought of America's most generous billionaire philanthropist begging for a handout from Washington.

Subsidizing Renewable Energy—At What Cost?

In a world where climate change is a growing source of concern, subsidies to promote renewable energy are often justified, not unreasonably, as a way of accelerating America's move to a low-carbon future. But when the government chooses the industries it will invest in, a lot of things tend to go wrong. Private investors who put their own money at risk usually assess their investment targets with great care. After all, there's plenty of money to be made by investors who get it right. When government officials use taxpayers' money, they tend to be less careful and usually far less expert. For this reason, letting government pick winners and losers in the renewable energy game is generally a mistake. History suggests that the most durable advances in renewable energy will almost certainly come from unsubsidized private sector initiatives.

The story of solar technology provides a telling example.

Solar energy is not new. The first solar steam engine was displayed at the Universal Exposition in Paris in 1878.[64] During the energy crisis of the 1970s, interest in solar power rose dramatically, and the following decades have brought increasing use of solar technology. Under the Obama administration, this interest translated into massive taxpayer investments in solar energy. Unfortunately, a number of these investments went south, offering object lessons in the dangers that arise when governments intercede in free markets.

The most famous example is the solar energy company Solyndra, which in 2010 was granted $528 million in federal stimulus loans under the American Reinvestment and Recovery Act of 2009.[65] Two years later, battling increasing competition from Chinese competitors selling cheaper, simpler solar panels, Solyndra declared bankruptcy, leaving investors and taxpayers holding the bag.[66] Their CEO, the savvy former CEO of Intel, Brian Harrison, received $400,000 a year in executive compensation during his tenure with the company. During Congressional hearings concerning Solyndra's demise, he and other executives pleaded the Fifth Amendment in response to questioning.[67] The congressional hearings and bankruptcy did not stop Solyndra from handing out bonuses to Harrison and other senior staff, and negotiating with the federal government to have those bonuses paid before any funds were disbursed to the federal government to repay the failed loans. Investigative reporting from GreenTech Media revealed:

> Karen Alter, Senior Vice President of Marketing at Solyndra, received $55,000 on April 15, 2011, and $55,000 on July 8th. Ben Bierman picked up $60,000 on April 15th, and another $60,000 on July 8th to supplement his $276,000 salary. Bierman was EVP of Operations and Engineering and was presenting cheery, optimistic PowerPoint obfuscation sessions as late as July. Wilbur Stover, Solyndra's CFO had a $367,000 salary and also collected at least $120,000 in bonuses. He joined CEO Brian Harrison in pleading the Fifth Amendment while under congressional questioning.[68]

The *Washington Post* reported that efforts by private investors to get more money for the failing company included references to "what a Solyndra executive referred to as the Bank of Washington—his apparent term for U.S. taxpayers."[69] When Solyndra closed its doors, they gave no warning to their employees, and no final paychecks; employees were simply left unemployed, without health insurance, while their bosses walked away with their taxpayer-funded "Bank of Washington" bonuses.

Solyndra was not alone. SolarCity, now owned by Tesla, has also been reaping the benefits of federal subsidies for solar power, while reneging on their business responsibilities. In 2016, the company settled lengthy lawsuits filed by the federal government, accusing SolarCity of overstating the value of their subsidized systems.[70] The main subsidy in SolarCity's case was a government program whereby SolarCity was reimbursed for 30 percent of the cost of solar panel installations they installed in U.S. homes. In this case, SolarCity was found to have fraudulently overbilled for the cost of the systems.

It's ironic that one of the main beneficiaries of the federal benefits lavished on SolarCity was Elon Musk. The founder and primary investor in Tesla, SolarCity, SpaceX, and other ventures has a net worth of $23.5 billion.[71] According to the *Los Angeles Times*, by 2015 Musk's companies had benefitted from $5 billion in government subsidies and tax breaks, including from New York State, which is spending $750 million to build a solar panel factory which Solar City will lease for one dollar a year.[72] The company also will pay no New York property taxes for a decade, saving an estimated $260 million. Nevada has provided Tesla with $1.3 billion in incentives for a huge battery factory near Reno.

According to Musk biographer Ashlee Vance, "Musk has proved so adept at landing incentives that states now compete to give him money."[73]

Supporters of government aid to solar energy companies often tout the number of jobs created by their industry. But as Mark Perry, an analyst at the American Enterprise Institute wryly noted in 2017,

> ...today's most productive energy workers are in coal and natural gas, not solar. And there's only one reason that the solar workforce has been increasing so rapidly (25 percent gain last year) despite its dismal record

of worker productivity and minuscule share of U.S. electric power [2 percent]—government policies that have subsidized the solar industry nearly 350 times more than fossil fuels per unit of electricity production. Only in the fantasy world of the Beltway does it make sense to spend billions of taxpayer dollars to artificially support an energy source that is so labor-intensive that it requires a workforce 79 times greater per unit of energy produced than coal, and nearly 40 times greater than natural gas.[74]

Legal mandates are now emerging as a new way for government to force citizens to support solar energy. In May 2018, California became the first state to mandate solar panels for all new-home construction, beginning in 2020. This marks the successful culmination of a long effort by environmentalists hoping to move California, and the world, toward a renewable energy-based electric grid that is free from dependence on fossil fuels. A look at the numbers, however, is cause for circumspection. On average, the solar mandate is expected to increase the cost of every new home by $9,500, a fact which hasn't escaped those concerned about California's increasingly dire shortage of affordable housing.[75] Notes prominent scientist and political writer Alex Berezow, author of *The Little Black Book of Junk Science*:

> Perhaps the biggest problem with solar subsidies is that they are regressive; i.e., they disproportionately hurt the poor. How does a subsidy hurt somebody? Because only rich people can afford to slap solar panels on their houses. Not only do they get a tax break, but in California, they can sell their unused energy back to the grid at an above-market rate. The utilities, in turn, pass these costs on to everybody else. That means poor people using coal in Compton are literally paying for solar panels for rich people in Malibu. That's plain nuts.[76]

Other states are poised to follow California's lead. In Arizona, billionaire Tom Steyer is financing a ballot initiative to force Arizonans to increase their reliance on renewable energy sources to 50 percent by 2030. Tucson Electric Power, a major Arizona provider of electricity, estimates the cost of this initiative would raise its residential customers' electricity bills by more than $500 per year.[77]

Wind power is another form of renewable energy that has benefited from massive government support. Wind energy companies receive the same kinds of subsidies as other energy industries, including state and federal tax credits, federal loans and loan guarantees, and production tax credits (tax credits based on the amount of energy produced). In 2011, *Forbes* magazine published a glowing report on "green billionaires," people who had made their billions in solar and wind energy. "Being green and making money don't always go hand in hand," the magazine observed, "but these 10 billionaires have tapped global demand for solar and wind power and gotten very rich from it," noted the author.[78] What the author didn't mention was the role that subsidies played in their rise.

In Illinois, for example, a recent twenty-nine-dollar-per-year rate increase for electricity customers of Commonwealth Edison went to subsidize wind and solar power generation in that state.[79]

Customers, of course, are also taxpayers, so they are paying twice—once on their electric bills, and once at tax time, when some of their taxes are allocated to their local utilities.

In 2016, *National Review* took an in-depth look at wind energy subsidies. They reported:

> MidAmerican Energy Company, a subsidiary of Berkshire Hathaway [received] $1.5 billion [in wind subsidies]—and it's primed to collect lots more… the company announced plans to spend $3.6 billion on wind projects in Iowa…Berkshire's CEO, Warren Buffett, explained why his companies are in the wind business. "We get a tax credit if we build a lot of wind farms. That's the only reason to build them," he said. "They don't make sense without the tax credit."[80]

Warren Buffett, of course, is one of the richest men on the planet—yet another example of how government subsidies often go to those who need them the least.[81]

The subsidization of wind power can also lead to the selection of less-than-optimal business decisions—for example, regarding the sites for wind turbines. Driving up the east coast of the Hawaiian island of Oahu en route to the famed North Shore in 2018, we passed through the small town of Kahuku, home of the Kahuku High School. Looming over the school are seven wind turbines. At the schoolhouse entrance, the whoosh of the blades sets up a constant, distracting thrumming as they spin in the breeze.

Locals are not pleased. "It's not just an eyesore. It is way too close to residential areas and to the school," noted one of the employees of the Kahuku Superette, across the street from the high school.[82] The store is a favorite after-school haunt for the teens who flock there for snacks and their famous poke, made with raw tuna, green onions, ginger, and other spices. We spoke with several students, who expressed disgust with the behemoths on the hill. "They're ugly and noisy," said one senior, rolling her eyes. "This is country. Why did they put them here so close to our homes and schools? We get headaches from listening to the stupid things."[83]

Constance Lau is CEO of Hawaiian Electric, the publicly traded energy company that serves all the islands except Kauai. Lau earns $5.4 million a year, despite earning a grade of F on her job performance in serving ratepayers and investors from Glass, Lewis & Co., a proxy advisory firm that provides research data to Wall Street and institutional investors.[84] Hawaii Electric has received $12 million in federal grants and tax credits since 2007, and continues to expand into wind energy, including installations proposed offshore at Oahu's North Shore, home to some of the best surfing grounds in the world.

Electricity customers in Hawaii are impacted multiple times—once when they pay their electric bills, once when their state and local taxes go to support subsidized energy, and yet again when their primary source of income, tourism, is impacted by turbine installations in high-traffic tourist locations.

The energy business in all its forms is a foundation of modern industrial society. Decisions about the future of energy will have a profound impact on people living all over the planet, which is a valid reason for giving government representatives a seat at the table when those decisions are being made. But energy is also an enormously profitable business. There's no reason why big, wealthy, and powerful energy companies need to rely on government subsidies—especially when experience shows that, in the vast majority of cases, smart investments are much more likely to be made by technology and business experts operating in a free and open marketplace.

1 "Advanced Energy Now 2019 Market Report," Advanced Energy Economy, https://www.advancedenergynow.org/aen-2019-market-report?utm_campaign=Press%2FMedia%20Outreach&utm_source=hs_email&utm_medium=email&utm_content=72063212&_hsenc=p2ANqtz-9Q4tlOGFZp4GYx-oXwCse1EVqBnx2dnVp3pXFH1VYzP3tuHIxe27GBHC9VhBNreTAGQ5sJ-FT64e7zt3HPUpu9LPXXD5JooDBnt9HB_G8o6-0m95k&_hsmi=72063212.

2 "Direct Federal Financial Interventions and Subsidies in Energy in Fiscal Year 2016," U.S. Energy Information Administration, April 24, 2018, https://www.eia.gov/analysis/requests/subsidy/.

3 Edward H. Crane and Carl Pope, "Fueled by Pork," Cato Institute, July 30, 2002, https://www.cato.org/publications/commentary/fueled-pork.

4 Benjamin W. Griffiths, Gürcan Gülen, James S. Dyer, David Spence, and Carey W. King, "Federal Financial Support for Electricity Generation Technologies," White Paper, UTEI/2016, no. 11 (January 11, 2016).

5 "Advanced Technology Vehicles Manufacturing Loan Program," Wikipedia, https://en.wikipedia.org/wiki/Advanced_Technology_Vehicles_Manufacturing_Loan_Program.

6 Nicolas Loris and Bryan Cosby, "How 'Green' Energy Subsidies Transfer Wealth to the Rich," The Daily Signal, July 18, 2018, Energy/Commentary, https://www.dailysignal.com/2018/07/18/how-green-energy-subsidies-transfer-wealth-to-the-rich/.

7 "#67 Richard Kinder," Forbes, October 22, 2019, https://www.forbes.com/profile/richard-kinder/#49cc0beb2f62.

8 "Subsidy Tracker Parent Company Summary," Good Jobs First, Subsidy Tracker: Kinder Morgan, https://subsidytracker.goodjobsfirst.org/prog.php?parent=kinder-morgan.

9 "Subsidy Tracker Parent Company Summary," Good Jobs First, Subsidy Tracker: Cheniere Energy, https://subsidytracker.goodjobsfirst.org/prog.php?parent=cheniere-energy.

10 "Jack A. Fusco Executive Compensation," Salary.com, https://www1.salary.com/Jack-A-Fusco-Salary-Bonus-Stock-Options-for-CHENIERE-ENERGY-INC.html.

11 "R.A. Walker Executive Compensation," Salary.com, https://www1.salary.com/R-A-Walker-Salary-Bonus-Stock-Options-for-ANADARKO-PETROLEUM-CORP.html.

12 "Subsidy Tracker Parent Company Summary," Good Jobs First, Subsidy Tracker: Anadarko Petroleum, https://subsidytracker.goodjobsfirst.org/parent/anadarko-petroleum; "Subsidy Tracker Individual Entry," Good Jobs First, Subsidy Tracker: Anadarko Petroleum, https://subsidytracker.goodjobsfirst.org/subsidy-tracker/tx-anadarko-petroleum.

13 Jack Lawrence Luzkow, Monopoly Restored How the Super-Rich Robbed Main Street (Palgrave Macmillan, 2018), 41.

14 "Newcomers to the World's Most Powerful People List," Forbes, https://www.forbes.com/pictures/5af099a8a7ea436b547c830d/darren-woods-34/#32ce1d5d1fb7.

15 "Subsidy Tracker Individual Entry," Good Jobs First, Subsidy Tracker: Exxon Mobil, https://subsidytracker.goodjobsfirst.org/subsidy-tracker/la-exxonmobil.

16 "Subsidy Tracker Parent Company Summary," Good Jobs First, Subsidy Tracker: Exxon Mobil, https://subsidytracker.goodjobsfirst.org/prog.php?parent=exxon-mobil; "Exxon Mobil Corporate Tax Dodger," Institute for Policy Studies, Americans for Tax Fairness, https://americansfortaxfairness.org/files/Exon_PR_final.pdf.

17 Nat Berman, "10 Things You Didn't Know About Chevron CEO Michael Wirth," Money Inc, https://moneyinc.com/chevron-ceo-michael-wirth/.

[18] "Chevron," Center for Responsive Politics, https://www.opensecrets.org/orgs/summary.php?id=D000000015&cycle=2016.

[19] "Subsidy Tracker Parent Company Summary," Good Jobs First, Subsidy Tracker: Chevron, https://subsidytracker.goodjobsfirst.org/prog.php?parent=chevron.

[20] Ted Barnett, "ConocoPhillips Angers Senator by Declaring Tax Proposal 'Un-American'," Political Ticker...CNN Politics (blog), May 11, 2011, http://politicalticker.blogs.cnn.com/2011/05/11/conocophillips-angers-senator-by-declaring-tax-proposal-un-american/; ConocoPhillips, "ConocoPhillips Highlights Solid Results and Raises Concerns Over Un-American Tax Proposals at Annual Meeting of Shareholders," ConocoPhillips (news release), May 11, 2011, http://www.conocophillips.com/news-media/story/conocophillips-highlights-solid-results-and-raises-concerns-over-un-american-tax-proposals-at-annual-meeting-of-shareholders/.

[21] Len Tesoro, "Debunking Myths About Federal Oil & Gas Subsidies," *Forbes*, February 22, 2016, https://www.forbes.com/sites/drillinginfo/2016/02/22/debunking-myths-about-federal-oil-gas-subsidies/#2ed28cdd6e1c.

[22] David Blackmon, "Oil and Gas Tax Provisions Are Not Subsidies for 'Big Oil'," *Forbes*, January 2, 2013, https://www.forbes.com/sites/davidblackmon/2013/01/02/oil-gas-tax-provisions-are-not-subsidies-for-big-oil/#4952b88252e8.

[23] "Oil and Gas Tax Benefits," Western Capital, INC., http://www.oilandgasjointventures.com/tax-benefits.html.

[24] "The Tax Break-Down: Intangible Drilling Costs," The Committee for a Responsible Federal Budget (blog), October 17, 2013, http://www.crfb.org/blogs/tax-break-down-intangible-drilling-costs.

[25] Russ Baker, "What They Don't Tell You About Oil Industry Tax Breaks," *Business Insider*, May 23, 2011, https://www.businessinsider.com/what-they-dont-tell-you-about-oil-industry-tax-breaks-2011-5.

[26] Mark Ballard and Gordan Russell, "Giving Away Louisiana- Fracking Tax Incentives," *The Advocate* (blog), http://www.cleanwaterlandcoast.com/giving-away-louisiana-fracking-tax-incentives/.

[27] Mark Ballard and Gordon Russell, "Giving Away Louisiana- Fracking Tax Incentives," *The Advocate* (blog), December 4, 2014, https://www.theadvocate.com/baton_rouge/news/article_3958382c-1062-5702-81af-d793f62c9918.html.

[28] "How High Are Sales Taxes in Your State?" Tax Foundation, January 1, 2019, https://files.taxfoundation.org/20190130101615/LOST-Jan-2019-Final-03-e1548861386125.png.

[29] Jennifer A Dlouhy, "Trump Prepares Lifeline for Money-Losing Coal Plants," Bloomberg, May 31, 2018, https://www.bloomberg.com/news/articles/2018-06-01/trump-said-to-grant-lifeline-to-money-losing-coal-power-plants-jhv94ghl.

[30] The Data Team, "Donald Trump Hopes to Save America's Failing Coal-Fired Power Plants," *The Economist,* June 6, 2018, https://www.economist.com/graphic-detail/2018/06/06/donald-trump-hopes-to-save-americas-failing-coal-fired-power-plants; "Wyden Presses FERC: Trump Administration's Coal Bailout Will Raise American's Utility Rates," Ron Wyden United States Senator for Oregon (press release), June 12, 2018, https://www.wyden.senate.gov/news/press-releases/wyden-presses-ferc-trump-administrations-coal-bailout-will-raise-americans-utility-rates.

[31] The Data Team, "Donald Trump Hopes to Save America's Failing Coal-Fired Plants."

[32] Tom DiChristopher, "Trump Administration Moves to Keep Failing Coal and Nuclear Plants Open, Citing National Security," CNBC, June 1, 2018, https://www.cnbc.com/2018/06/01/trump-plan-bails-out-coal-and-nuclear-plants-for-national-security.html.

[33] Victor Reklaitis, "Trump's New FERC Chairman Could Give New Life to Plan to Help Coal and Nuclear Power Plants, Analysts Say," MarketWatch, October 26, 2018, https://www.marketwatch.com/story/trumps-new-ferc-chairman-could-give-new-life-to-plan-to-help-coal-and-nuclear-power-plants-analysts-say-2018-10-25.

[34] "The U.S. Coal Industry: Historical Trends and Recent Developments," EveryCRSReport.com, August 18, 2017, https://www.everycrsreport.com/reports/R44922.html.

[35] "Subsidy Tracker Individual Entry," Good Jobs First, Subsidy Tracker: Clean Coal Power Operations (KY) LLC, https://subsidytracker.goodjobsfirst.org/subsidy-tracker/ky-clean-coal-power-operations-ky-llc.

[36] "Subsidy Tracker Individual Entry," Good Jobs First, Subsidy Tracker: Summit Power Group, https://subsidytracker.goodjobsfirst.org/subsidy-tracker/tx-summit-power-group.

[37] Timothy Gardner, "U.S. Company XCoal Energy to Sell Steam Coal to Fuel-Strapped Ukraine," Reuters, July 31, 2017, https://www.reuters.com/article/us-usa-coal-ukraine/u-s-company-xcoal-energy-to-sell-steam-coal-to-fuel-strapped-ukraine-idUSKBN1AG22Q.

[38] "Coal and Air Pollution," Union of Concerned Scientists, December 19, 2017, https://www.ucsusa.org/resources/coal-and-air-pollution.

[39] "Subsidy Tracker Parent Company Summary," Good Jobs First, Subsidy Tracker: Alpha Natural Resources, https://subsidytracker.goodjobsfirst.org/prog.php?parent=alpha-natural-resources.

[40] Madeleine Sheehan Perkins, "The Coal Industry Is Collapsing, and Coal Workers Allege That Executives Are Making the Situation Worse," *Business Insider,* July 1, 2017, https://www.businessinsider.com/from-the-ashes-highlights-plight-of-coal-workers-2017-6.

[41] Tracy Rucinski, "Arch Coal Files for Bankruptcy, Hit by Mining Downturn," Reuters, January 10, 2016, https://www.reuters.com/article/us-arch-coal-restructuring-idUSKCN0UP0MR20160111.

[42] "Violation Tracker Parent Company Summary: Arch Coal," Good Jobs First, https://violationtracker.goodjobsfirst.org/parent/arch-coal; Rucinski, "Arch Coal Files for Bankruptcy, Hit by Mining Downturn."

[43] "Razing Appalachia," produced by Sasha Waters, PBS SoCal, 2003, Independent Film, 54:00, http://www.pbs.org/independentlens/razingappalachia/mtop.html.

[44] David Nicklaus, "Bonuses Bring Arch Coal CEO's Pay to $9.8 Million," *St. Louis Post-Dispatch*, March 21, 2018, https://www.stltoday.com/business/columns/david-nicklaus/bonuses-bring-arch-coal-ceo-s-pay-to-million/article_e95bc108-0da9-5962-b60a-e88f9c580c76.html.

[45] "Subsidy Tracker Parent Company Summary: Peabody Energy," Good Jobs First, https://subsidytracker.goodjobsfirst.org/prog.php?parent=peabody-energy.

[46] Suzanne Goldenberg and Helena Bengtsson, "Biggest US Coal Company Funded Dozens of Groups Questioning Climate Change," *The Guardian*, June 13, 2016, https://www.theguardian.com/environment/2016/jun/13/peabody-energy-coal-mining-climate-change-denial-funding.

[47] Judy Colgan (Rocky Mountain Coal Mining Institute), interview by Lisa Conyers, October 2019.

[48] Dlouhy, "Trump Prepares Lifeline for Money-Losing Coal Plants."

[49] Gail Disney, (Local Historian, Coal Creek Mining Museum Docent), interview by Lisa Conyers, November 2018, Rocky Top, Tennessee.

[50] "What Is U.S. Electricity Generation by Energy Source?" U.S. Energy Information *Administration*, https://www.eia.gov/tools/faqs/faq.php?id=427&t=3.

[51] "Editorial: Nuclear Subsidy Plan Bows to PSEG Demand," *My Central Jersey, USA Today Network,* April 6, 2018, Opinion, https://www.mycentraljersey.com/story/opinion/editorials/2018/04/06/editorial-nuclear-subsidy-plan-bows-pseg-demand/33609071.

[52] Scott DiSavino, Chris Reese, ed., and Diane Craft, ed., "New Jersey Governor Signs Nuclear Power Subsidy Bill into Law," Reuters, May 23, 2018, https://www.reuters.com/article/us-new-jersey-pseg-exelon-nuclear/new-jersey-governor-signs-nuclear-power-subsidy-bill-into-law-idUSKCN1IO2RL.

[53] "Data Center," https://www.techopedia.com/definition/349/data-center.

[54] Kevin Hengehold, "Subsidy or Investment: Arizona's Energy Future," *Arizona Community Press,* October 2, 2015, http://azcommunitypress.org/2013/10/02/subsidy-or-investment-arizonas-energy-future/.

[55] IO Corporation Tour Guide, interview by Lisa Conyers, 2017, Phoenix, Arizona.

[56] "About Us," Pinnacle West Capital Corporation, http://www.pinnaclewest.com/about-us/default.aspx.

[57] "Profile for 2018 Election Cycle," OpenSecrets.org, Pinnacle West Capital, Contributions, https://www.opensecrets.org/orgs/summary.php?id=D000000658&cycle=2018; "Profile for 2018 Election Cycle," OpenSecrets.org, Pinnacle West Capital, Top Recipients, https://www.opensecrets.org/orgs/summary.php?id=D000000658&cycle=2018.

[58] "Profile for the 2016 Election Cycle," OpenSecrets.org, Exelon Corp, https://www.opensecrets.org/orgs/summary.php?id=D000000368&cycle=2016.

[59] Karl Grossman, "Why 'One of the Largest Tax Increases in Recent History' is Buried in Your Electric Bill," *Riverhead Local,* June 17, 2018, https://riverheadlocal.com/2018/06/17/why-one-of-the-largest-tax-increases-in-recent-history-is-buried-in-your-electric-bill/.

[60] Michael L. Krancer, "UpstreamPA 2017 Conference," Silent Majority Strategies LLC, March 21, 2017, http://www.upstreampa.com/Presentations/Krancer.pdf.

[61] Rob Galbraith, "Exelon Lobbyist Bragged About Profitability of Cuomo's Nuclear Bailout," Eyes on the Ties, March 27, 2018, https://news.littlesis.org/2018/03/27/exelon-lobbyist-bragged-about-profitability-of-cuomos-nuclear-bailout/.

[62] Mathew Wald (Senior Communication Advisor, The Nuclear Energy Institute), interview by Lisa Conyers, November 2018, Washington DC.

[63] Christian Blessing and Marcia Buerkey, (Director of Business and Chief Financial Officer, TerraPower), interview by Lisa Conyers, July 2019, Bellevue, Seattle.

[64] Paul Collins, "The Beautiful Possibility," *Cabinet Magazine,* Spring 2002, Issue 6, http://www.cabinetmagazine.org/issues/6/beautifulpossibility.php.

[65] David R. Baker, "Feds Probe Solyndra's Upbeat July Report," *SF Gate,* September 13, 2011, https://www.sfgate.com/business/article/Feds-probe-Solyndra-s-upbeat-July-report-2309983.php.

[66] Joe Stephens and Carol D. Leonnig, "Solyndra: Politics Infused Obama Energy Programs," *The Washington Post,* December 25, 2011, https://www.washingtonpost.com/solyndra-politics-infused-obama-energy-programs/2011/12/14/gIQA4HllHP_story.html?utm_term=.0a3ddf42ae05.

[67] Eric Wesoff, "Solyndra CEO and CFO Pleading the Fifth: Part 2," *GreenTech Media,* September 21, 2011, https://www.greentechmedia.com/articles/read/solyndra-ceo-and-cfo-pleading-the-fifth#gs.qe5ez9.

[68] Eric Wesoff, "Executives Bonuses Kept Coming in 2011," *GreenTechMedia,* November 2, 2011, https://www.greentechmedia.com/articles/print/Solyndra-Executive-Bonuses-Kept-Coming-in-2011.

[69] Stephens, "Solyndra: Politics Infused Obama Energy Programs."

[70] Louis Hansen, "Solar City Agrees to Settle Government Fraud Claims," *The Mercury News*, September 22, 2017, https://www.mercurynews.com/2017/09/22/solarcity-agrees-to-settle-government-fraud-claims/.

[71] "#40: Elon R Musk: $23.5B," Bloomberg, October 22, 2019, https://www.bloomberg.com/billionaires/profiles/elon-r-musk/.

[72] Jerry Hirsch, "Elon Musk's Growing Empire Is Fueled by $4.9 Billion in Government Subsidies," *Los Angeles Times*, May 30, 2015, Business, http://www.latimes.com/business/la-fi-hy-musk-subsidies-20150531-story.html.

[73] Ashlee Vance, *Elon Musk Tesla, SpaceX, and the Quest for a Fantastic Future* (Harper Collins, 2015), Kindle, https://play.google.com/store/books/details/Ashlee_Vance_Elon_Musk?id=Yd99BAAAQBAJ.

[74] Mark J. Perry, "Inconvenient Energy Fact: It Takes 79 Solar Workers to Produce Same Amount of Electric Power as One Coal Worker," Carpe Diem AEI, May 3, 2017, https://www.aei.org/publication/inconvenient-energy-fact-it-takes-79-solar-workers-to-produce-same-amount-of-electric-power-as-one-coal-worker/.

[75] Jeff Daniels, "California Regulators Approve Plan to Mandate Solar Panels on New Home Construction," CNBC, May 9, 2018, https://www.cnbc.com/2018/05/09/california-approves-plan-to-mandate-solar-panels-on-new-homes.html.

[76] Alex Berezow, "Panel Power: Solar Advocates Openly Celebrate Crony Capitalism," American Council on Science and Health, May 9, 2018, https://www.acsh.org/news/2018/05/09/panel-power-solar-advocates-openly-celebrate-crony-capitalism-12941.

[77] Tim Benson, "Steyer's Renewable Mandate Would Punish Arizona's Poor," The Heartland Institute, October 3, 2018, https://www.heartland.org/news-opinion/news/steyers-renewable-mandate-would-punish-arizonas-poor.

[78] Kerry A. Dolan, "World's Richest Green Billionaires 2011," *Forbes*, April 19, 2011, https://www.forbes.com/sites/kerryadolan/2011/04/19/worlds-greenest-billionaires-2011/#2fbe05d749a5.

[79] Steve Daniels, "Charges for Green Power, Nuke Subsidies Hike Electric Bills," *Crain's Chicago Business*, June 14, 2017, https://www.chicagobusiness.com/article/20170614/NEWS11/170619959/comed-customers-paying-extra-starting-this-month-to-support-nuclear-renewable-power.

[80] Robert Bryce, "Wind-Energy Sector Gets $176 Billion Worth of Crony Capitalism," *National Review*, July 18, 2019, https://www.nationalreview.com/2016/06/wind-energy-subsidies-billions/

[81] "Warren Buffett," *Forbes*, https://www.forbes.com/profile/warren-buffett/#477e723c4639; Bryce, "Wind-Energy Sector Gets $176 Billion Worth of Crony Capitalism."

[82] Kahuku Superette Employee, interview by Lisa Conyers, June 2018, Oahu, Hawaii.

[83] Kahuku high school seniors, interview by Lisa Conyers, June 2018, Oahu, Hawaii.

[84] Rick Daysong, "Special Report: CEO Pay Soars, HEI Receives 'F' for Executive Pay," *HawaiiNewsNow*, April 25, 2013, updated July 11, 2013, https://www.hawaiinewsnow.com/story/22084152/ceo-pay-soars-hei-receives-f-for-executive-pay/.

7.

Grabbing the Taxpayers' Money— There's an App for That

Technological progress has merely provided us with more efficient means for going backwards.

—Aldous Huxley

B ack in the days of the robber barons, everyone knew their names: those infamous Vanderbilts, Carnegies, Rockefellers, and other industrialists who grew the economy and transformed the world— while accumulating enormous wealth and power for themselves.

Today, the names everyone knows are those of the high-tech business titans: Bill Gates (Microsoft), Mark Zuckerberg (Facebook), Jeff Bezos (Amazon), Elon Musk (Tesla), and many more. They, too, have transformed the world. Thanks to them, we're all connected, our lives organized around websites, apps, and smart devices that track our every move. And unlike the robber barons of old, today's high-tech titans have done it all on their own, through sheer creativity, genius, and determination—right?

Not so fast.

Despite their carefully honed public images as self-made entrepreneurs, the tech titans have joined other giant businesses in feeding at the public trough. According to research by Good Jobs First, from 2013 to 2018, giant tech companies including Amazon, Google, Facebook, and Microsoft received $9.3 billion in state and local subsidies.[1] Add federal support, especially in energy-related subsidies, and the total is much more.

Subsidies in 2018–2019 include boondoggles such as the 2018 Amazon "beauty contest" among a large group of cities competing to host a new Amazon headquarters. New York and Northern Virginia were eventually selected by Amazon for the honor of ponying up billions in taxpayer monies—tax incentives, rebates, and cash—as hosts of two new management facilities for the online retail giant. While Amazon has since pulled back on its commitment to New York in the wake of vehement protests by local citizens, the Virginia project remains on track, so the bulk of the subsidies will now be provided by taxpayers from that state. (We'll delve more deeply into this story later in the chapter.)

Deals like these are eagerly pursued by state and local politicians because of the jobs they promise to create and the image of prestige associated with booming high-tech businesses. But like the community-provided subsidies for other kinds of businesses, the state and local payments to attract tech companies seldom result in substantial economic benefits. Notes Greg LeRoy, President of Good Jobs First, these communities should resist the impulse to buy, with taxpayer dollars, the prestige they believe attaches to the big tech projects that have to be built whether subsidies are provided or not. "They gotta build these things," LeRoy says. "They're coming. Don't pay them to do what they're going to do anyway."[2]

Before we begin our review of some of the remarkable sweetheart deals the tech giants have extracted from taxpayers, a word about the financial status of these companies and their executives. According to the executive compensation research company Equilar, in 2018, no CEOs fared better than CEOs in the technology sector. Their salaries averaged $6.6 million, frequently supplemented with stock options. For example, with stock options included, Apple CEO Tim Cook's compensation in 2018 was $137 million.[3] Tech employees lower on the totem pole also did quite well; the average pay for tech workers was $82,500.[4]

It is hard to fathom why an industry that is prospering and paying its CEOs and employees so well needs to dip its hands into the taxpayer pocket in order to succeed. And yet in state after state, that is what they do. Here are some examples.

Private, For-Profit Data Centers That Your Tax Dollars Help to Build

Over the past decade, the tech giants have been on a building spree, expanding their cloud computing and data centers across the country. It's a sign of how healthy the information technology industry is—which makes one wonder why so many of these facilities are being substantially assisted by taxpayer gifts.

Like many of the other big tech companies, Apple has been lured to locate its data centers in states and communities offering a full range of costly subsidies. Iowa taxpayers, for example, pay a hefty price to host an Apple data center in their state. In 2017, the city of Waukee granted Apple's new center a 71 percent reduction in property taxes over the next twenty years, a deal valued at $188 million. In return, Apple suggested that fifty jobs would be created—an absurd cost of almost $4 million per job. Thus, 16,000 Iowans (the population of Waukee) are helping to pay for a $1.375 billion data center owned by the largest company in the world, and receiving little in return.[5]

The Waukee deal wasn't the first of its kind. In 2009, Apple built a $1 billion data center in Maiden, North Carolina. In that deal, Apple received $321 million in subsidies, a cost of $2 million per job created.[6] Those in the area have seen little in the way of improvements. Notes Tony Parker, owner of a local company called Temple Furniture, "Apple really doesn't mean a thing to this town." His son-in-law, Kelly McRee, agrees, commenting on the unfulfilled promise the company's arrival appeared to offer: "Apple was the apple of everybody's eye, but that's about it. It was something for everyone to ooh and aah over."[7] Overall, during 2009-2018, Apple benefitted from more than $700 million in subsidies from the states of California, Iowa, and North Carolina.

Google is another tech giant that has been getting help from state governments for its data centers. Perhaps understandably, the company executives, and presumably the legislators and council representatives who make the subsidy decisions, don't seem to want voters to know about it. Reported the *Washington Post* in 2019, "officials in Midlothian, Tex., a city near Dallas, approved more than $10 million in tax breaks for a huge, mysterious new development across from a shuttered Toys R Us warehouse." [8] That "mysterious" building turned out to be a Google data center.

Google has been experiencing massive growth for over a decade, but in many of the bidding wars over where the new facilities will be located, Google demands that negotiations be shrouded by non-disclosure agreements. These agreements prevent local taxpayers from learning the details and make it impossible for them to know, protest, or debate who will be using their land, their resources, and their tax dollars until the deals are already done. In the case of the Midlothian development, Travis Smith, managing editor of the local *Waxahachie Daily Light*, said, "I'm confident that had the community known this project was under the direction of Google, people would have spoken out, but we were never given the chance to speak. We didn't know that it was Google until after it passed."[9]

Smith's frustration is understandable. After all, Google's revenue in 2018 was $137 billion, and in 2019, Sergey Brin and Larry Page, co-founders of Google, were each worth over $50 billion.[10] Yet taxpayers from Texas and several other states have granted the company close to $861 million in subsidies since 2012. Oregon has been especially generous, providing nearly $7 billion in subsidies in the last few years to Google and other corporate giants headquartered there. (Not all are tech giants; shoe and sportswear giant Nike finagled $2 billion in tax breaks from the state.)[11]

Some of the communities lavishing gifts on Google can scarcely afford such generosity. In 2016, Google built a $600 million data center on the site of a retired coal mining plant in Jackson County, Alabama, near the Tennessee border. In return, the county provided Google with an investment credit of $50 million to offset income and utility tax liabilities, sales tax abatements of $20 million, and state property tax abatements of $11.08 million.[12] Yet Jackson County, with about 50,000 residents, has a poverty rate of over 16 percent, 25 percent higher than the national average.[13] Surely local funds might be better spent on assisting the county's low-income residents and taxpayers than on subsidizing a corporation as big and wealthy as Google.

Tech giant Microsoft is another beneficiary of taxpayer largesse. Bill Gates, the company's principal founder, has a net worth of $103 billion (2019), and in April 2019, Microsoft reached a market capitalization of $1 trillion.[14] Yet despite this enormous capital base—or perhaps because of it, and the political clout it provides—Microsoft has managed to rake in $424 million in taxpayer subsidies since 2012.

The sum includes a whopping $107 million for a new $1.1 billion, million-square-foot data center in the small town of West Des Moines, Iowa (population 65,000), Microsoft's second facility in the area.[15] The city is spending $87 million on infrastructure for the operation, and Microsoft has also received $20 million in state tax credits. In return, Microsoft promises to bring just eighty-four jobs to the area. In 2019, with this project still under construction, Microsoft began building a third data center nearby, this time receiving $4 million in state incentives in return for a promise of bringing in fifty-seven jobs.[16]

Now consider the political and economic context. In 2018, Iowa faced a $300 million budget shortfall worsened by corporate tax cuts enacted in 2013. Between 2013 and 2018, Iowans granted $430 million in tax cuts to Google and other tech companies, and according to the *Des Moines Register*, new tax credits granted in 2018 were set to eat up another $430 million—the biggest such business windfall in the state's history. Meanwhile, under pressure from the budget crisis, state lawmakers were considering cuts in spending on departments that oversee corrections, higher education, and public safety. Such cuts are particularly ironic given the fact that West Des Moines has been experiencing a disturbing surge in crime rates even as the new Microsoft projects continue to grow.

One more poster child for data center subsidies is social media behemoth Facebook, whose founder and CEO, Mark Zuckerberg, is worth $76 billion.[17] Facebook made $22 billion in 2018, and has a market capitalization of $583 billion (July 2019).[18] In building this wealth, the company has benefitted from over $330 million in government subsidies during 2010–2018.[19] In 2018, for example, Facebook received $150 million in a massive deal with the state of Utah to build a data center in Eagle Mountain, a small community outside of Provo.[20] Fifty jobs are promised, so Utah residents will be forking out $3 million in tax subsidies for each job created. In response to this news, one irate Utah resident wrote to the local *Deseret News*, "Only a politician or an economic development official can make giving millions to one of the world's richest companies—one that earned $12 billion in the first quarter of this year alone—sound like a great deal."[21]

In Fort Worth, Texas, Facebook is building another data center, and reaping $147 million in tax breaks in the process. Reviewing the 2019 Texas legislative session during which this deal was approved, Mitchell Schnurman, a business columnist for the *Dallas News*, wrote, "The cookie jar is full again in Texas. At a time when New York, Florida, and Washington, D.C. are pulling back on so-called corporate welfare, Texas lawmakers are staying the course."[22]

Other Lavish Deals for the Tech Elite

Taiwan-based Foxconn is a contract manufacturer that builds electronic products for Apple, Nintendo, Microsoft, and other brands. In 2018, Wisconsin Governor Scott Walker promised Foxconn up to $4.8 billion in subsidies in return for its building a new plant in the village of Mount Pleasant, Wisconsin. This would be the highest subsidy ever paid to a foreign corporation.[23]

Foxconn won its plush Wisconsin deal by promising to create 13,000 jobs for blue collar workers who had suffered through the rust belt's long economic decline. But as the plan proceeded, some hard facts began to emerge. Many of the 13,000 jobs would be "multiplier" jobs, not at Foxconn, but at local businesses that *might* benefit from the presence of the electronic giant—many of them beyond the borders of Wisconsin. Even when the multiplier effect is assumed to be valid, early estimates of the cost to taxpayers was between $350,000 and a million dollars per job.[24]

The deal was a lousy one for Wisconsin taxpayers in other ways. The state had already paid $300 million for infrastructure around the project.[25] In addition, a number of environmental rules were relaxed to accommodate the plant. Foxconn was granted access to seven million gallons of water a day from Lake Michigan, in what local environmentalists see as a betrayal of the Great Lakes Compact, an agreement meant to protect the Great Lakes Basin, which is home to one fifth of the world's fresh water. Then the state went further; it designated the entire project area "blighted," allowing the government to seize homes within the footprint under eminent domain.[26] Noted one homeowner, "We're just in their way. We're an annoyance. And that's just wrong, because they're not supposed to be representing the interest of a wealthy foreign corporation. They're supposed to be representing the interests of their constituents."[27]

Writing in the *New York Times Book Review* in March 2019, E. Tammy Kim noted that the costs go beyond the deal itself. Even as this massive giveaway of taxpayer dollars was being negotiated, "local schools and state universities were suffering from years of budget cuts, and inner-city communities had been hit by rising levels of incarceration and long-term unemployment…There is little evidence that Foxconn, even if it does a fraction of what it has promised, will create jobs, let alone good ones at family sustaining wages."[28]

Despite the one-sidedness of the deal, Foxconn couldn't even be counted on to live up to its modest obligations. In 2019, Foxconn suddenly announced it wouldn't be building the plant after all. Under pressure from President Trump, who'd boasted about the deal, the company backtracked—their plans for the plant have been dramatically downsized. As of mid-2019, no one in Wisconsin seems to know what will happen next, least of all the taxpayers footing the bill.[29]

Then there's Tesla, whose owner, Elon Musk, we wrote about in the chapter on energy. Musk has a net worth of $20 billion. Nonetheless, his high-tech auto and energy company, Tesla, Inc., and its subsidiary SolarCity have pocketed over $9 billion in subsidies, grants, loans, and tax abatements since 2009, according to reporting by the *Los Angeles Times.* The benefits include:

- $1.5 billion in federal subsidies for the installation of residential solar panel systems nationwide.
- $1.3 billion in tax incentives from the state of Nevada to build the Tesla battery factory near Reno.
- $750 million from the state of New York to build a solar panel factory; SolarCity's lease is $1/year, and it will pay no property taxes on the property for a decade.[30]
- $20 million in economic development grants from the state of Texas to build a launch facility in the state, along with local subsidies that reportedly include a fifteen-year property tax break from the local school district worth $3.1 million.[31]

How do these deals happen? The *Los Angeles Times* describes the negotiations that led to the Nevada factory:

> The $1.3 billion in benefits for Tesla's Nevada battery factory resulted from a year of hardball negotiations. Late in 2013, Tesla summoned economic development officials from seven states…Tesla executives explained their plan to build the biggest lithium-ion battery factory in the world—then asked the states to bid for the project…[Nevada] shored up the deal with an agreement to give Tesla $195 million in transferable tax credits, which the automaker could sell for upfront cash.[32]

Despite all this help (or very possibly because of it), Musk's companies continue to lose money, and may not reach profitability any time soon.

In a further bizarre turn, in 2017, Musk made headlines by suggesting that the government end its subsidies for electric cars. (Buyers currently get tax rebates from federal and state governments for buying all-electric vehicles.) It wasn't that Musk didn't want those subsidies, but he felt it was unfair that other car companies would benefit from the rebate even more than Tesla does. As one columnist noted, "Elon is now looking at it from the point of view of a winner, and he doesn't want to see other people win because they get government money. I do think there is a tendency of people, once they have succeeded, to want to pull the ladder up after them."[33] The losers are the taxpayers of Texas, Nevada, and New York State, whose legislators have given away the farm to a multibillionaire, leaving them to foot the bill in the form of increased property and other taxes.

Finally, let's return to the Amazon story with which we started this chapter. Worth $430 billion, Amazon is one of the boldest bidders for government favors among the tech giants, and in July 2019, its CEO, Jeff Bezos, bumped Bill Gates from the top of the list of the world's richest people, with a net worth of $91 billion.[34] Bezos owns 17 percent of Amazon, as well as other assets that include Whole Foods and the *Washington Post*. Yet according to Good Jobs First, Amazon has received over $1.1 billion in subsidies from state and local governments since 2000.

In 2017, Amazon announced plans for a second Amazon headquarters to match its home base in Seattle, and asked cities to bid on the chance to land the deal, which is expected to create 50,000 jobs. According to the request for bids prepared by Amazon and reported by *Salon*, Bezos asked bidders for offers that included some combination of property tax abatements, job creation credits, direct grants, sales tax refunds, land-acquisition assistance, and the other varieties of corporate welfare that governments have concocted to lure businesses.[35] Bidders were not permitted to disclose their offers to anyone.[36] However, New Jersey reportedly offered $7 billion in tax credits and incentives; California, $1 billion. Atlanta offered to build a town called Amazon, on 345 city acres, and to make Bezos its mayor for life. Other local officials weren't talking.[37]

Amazon announced two winning bidders in November 2018. They were Crystal City, Virginia, just across the Potomac from Washington, D.C., and Long Island City in the New York City borough of Queens. Virginia ponied up $573 million in cash, plus $23 million in other benefits, while New York had promised $1.525 billion in incentives, access to a heliport, and other subsidies.

Here is where the story took a rare and surprising turn. In New York, activism on the part of citizens and local leaders managed to derail the sweetheart deal. Stung by objections raised by New York residents and politicians, Amazon pulled out of the deal a few months after it was announced, leaving the partial deal for Virginia's Crystal City intact.

Presumably, Amazon is sticking to its promise of 25,000 jobs in the city and adjacent areas. But if past performance is any guide, the benefits to Virginia citizens will be modest compared to Virginia taxpayers' costs.

In the aftermath of this turnaround, New York's mayor Bill DeBlasio, who'd favored the deal, blasted Amazon, calling the company's decision to pull out "an abuse of corporate power."[38] But expert observers have a different view of what happened. In January 2018, over 200 economists and urban planners made themselves clear:

> Tax giveaways and business location incentives offered by local governments are often wasteful and counter-productive…Such incentives do not alter business location decisions as much as is often claimed…[and] they divert funds that could be put to better use under-writing public services such as schools, housing programs, job training, and transportation…This use of Amazon's market power to extract incentives from local and state governments is rent-seeking and anticompetitive…
>
> States, cities, and metropolitan regions should com-pete on the underlying strength of their communities—not on public handouts to private business.[39]

Knowledgeable observers tend to agree that New York was fortu-nate to lose the opportunity to host Amazon. Similarly, Generation Opportunity, an organization supported by energy billionaire Charles Koch—who is consistently critical of crony capitalism, though, as we've observed, not above enriching himself at the public trough occa-sionally—issued a statement saying, in part, "while small businesses and young entrepreneurs struggle, government cuts special deals with Amazon, a corporation that raked in $175 billion last year! Does this look like a company that needs taxpayer cash?"[40]

All the evidence suggests these critics are right. The direct costs of subsidies are sometimes only part of the price that communities pay for luring high-tech businesses. Amazon's headquarters in Seattle has brought, along with jobs, skyrocketing housing prices, gridlock on the roads, and a workforce struggling to cope with living costs that are now over 20 percent higher than most of the country.

The Ultimate Cost: Eroded Public Services

We're not big fans of high taxes. No individual or business should pay more in taxes than the law requires, and tax rates should be set as low as possible, consistent with public needs. But when states, cities, and counties use property tax exemptions and outright public subsidies to woo high-tech businesses, ordinary citizens often suffer. The foregone taxes leave public service budgets short, eventually leading to the long-term hollowing-out of local economies. The results include devastated school budgets, reduced funding for police and fire departments, neglected maintenance to parks and other civic infrastructure, and other forms of public decline.

JoAnn Adams, a retired teacher in Kentucky, explained all this in plain language in 2019, after yet another session of the Kentucky legislature ended with massive gifts to corporate interests and cuts to support for basic services:

> We want to give back and serve our communities. Whether we're teachers, firefighters, or police officers, we all want to make a positive impact...The Commonwealth of Kentucky is one of the largest spenders on corporate welfare. This is due to a combination of factors. The first is our tax code is so arcane that it's riddled with loopholes that corporations have been exploiting for decades. Secondly, at every turn, our lawmakers are giving away big tax breaks to corporations—just handing away our hard-earned tax dollars to companies who don't need it. In the heat of the pension and budget debate, lawmakers were looking to casually give away $60 million in tax breaks. Meanwhile, our schools and social services are fighting for every single dollar. [41]

The leaders of the big tech firms seem to recognize, at least on an unconscious level, that the taxpayer subsidies they receive are not justified. On those occasions when they make do without government favors, they are openly proud of it. In 2018, while Amazon was being wooed by New York City, Facebook weighed in, saying they had brought their operations to New York without receiving a handout. Noted Anthony Harrison, a spokesman for Facebook, in an interview with *Politico*, "We have not received any incentives from the state. We are very proud of our connection to New York City since we opened our first office in 2014."[42] Similarly, in 2019, the *Wall Street Journal* reported that Google has not applied for any subsidies or handouts for its large new campuses under construction in Manhattan.[43]

These two high-tech exceptions raise an obvious question: If Google and Facebook didn't need financial incentives to build in New York, why should Amazon? In fact, why should any companies in one of today's most powerful, profitable, and rapidly growing business sectors receive taxpayer handouts for any reason?

1   "Subsidy Tracker Parent Company Summary: Foxconn Technology Group (Hon Hai Precision Industry Company)," Good Jobs First, https://subsidytracker.goodjobsfirst.org/prog.php?parent=foxconn-technology-group-hon-hai-precisi.

2   Jeremy C. Owens, "Why Governments Are Giving Billions in Tax Breaks to Apple, Amazon and Other Tech Giants," MarketWatch, October 14, 2016, https://www.marketwatch.com/story/why-governments-are-giving-billions-in-tax-breaks-to-apple-amazon-and-other-tech-giants-2016-10-13.

3   Christian Zibreg, "Apple Gave Tim Cook a $12 Million Bonus as His Total 2018 Compensation Hits $136 Million," iDownloadBlog, January 9, 2019, https://www.idownloadblog.com/2019/01/09/tim-cook-compensation-fiscal-2018/.

4   Rani Molla, "CEO's — Especially Those in Tech - Are Making More Money Than Ever: Worker Pay, However, Is Stagnating," Vox Media, May 2, 2019, https://www.vox.com/recode/2019/5/2/18522927/ceo-pay-ratio-tech-employee-salary-2018.

5   Stephen Nellis, "Apple to Build Iowa Data Center, Get $207.8 Million in Incentives," Reuters, August 24, 2017, https://www.reuters.com/article/us-apple-iowa/apple-to-build-iowa-data-center-get-207-8-million-in-incentives-idUSKCN1B422L.

6   "Subsidy Tracker Individual Entry," Good Jobs First, Subsidy Tracker: Apple, https://subsidytracker.goodjobsfirst.org/subsidy-tracker/nc-apple; Jeremy C. Owens, "Why Governments Are Giving Billions in Tax Breaks to Apple, Amazon, and Other Tech Giants," MarketWatch, October 14, 2016, https://www.marketwatch.com/story/why-governments-are-giving-billions-in-tax-breaks-to-apple-amazon-and-other-tech-giants-2016-10-13.

7   Michael S. Rosenwald, "Cloud Centers Bring High-Tech Flash But Not Many Jobs to Beaten-Down Towns," *The Washington Post*, November 24, 2011, Business, https://www.washingtonpost.com/business/economy/cloud-centers-bring-high-tech-flash-but-not-many-jobs-to-beaten-down-towns/2011/11/08/gIQAccTQtN_story.html.

8   Elizabeth Dwoskin, "Google Reaped Millions in Tax Breaks as It Secretly Expanded Its Real Estate Footprint Across the U.S.," *The Washington Post*, February 15, 2019, Business, https://www.washingtonpost.com/business/economy/google-reaped-millions-of-tax-breaks-as-it-secretly-expanded-its-real-estate-footprint-across-the-us/2019/02/15/7912e10e-3136-11e9-813a-0ab2f17e305b_story.html.

9   Dwoskin, "Google Reaped Millions in Tax Breaks as It Secretly Expanded Its Real Estate Footprint Across the U.S."

10 "Bloomberg Billionaires Index: #11 Sergey Brin $56.8B," Bloomberg, accessed August 8, 2019, https://www.bloomberg.com/billionaires/profiles/sergey-brin/; "#10 Larry Page Real Time Net Worth $55.1B," *Forbes*, accessed August 9, 2019, https://www.forbes.com/profile/larry-page/#7b3d445d7893.

11 Bill Bradley, "Nike Made $25 Billion Last Year, Still Got a Tax Break From Oregon," *Next City*, August 16, 2013, https://nextcity.org/daily/entry/nike-had-25-billion-last-year-still-got-a-tax-break-from-oregon.

12 Tim Omarzu, "Google Building $600 Million Data Center Near Chattanooga," *Times Free Press*, June 25, 2015, https://www.timesfreepress.com/news/local/story/2015/jun/25/goodbye-coal-plant-hello-google-google-plans/311380/.

13 "Quick Facts: Jackson County, Alabama," United States Census Bureau, https://www.census.gov/quickfacts/jacksoncountyalabama.

[14] Rachel Layne, "Microsoft Reaches $1 Trillion Market Value for the First Time," CBS News, April 25, 2019, https://www.cbsnews.com/news/microsoft-1-trillion-market-value-reached-today/.

[15] "Subsidy Tracker Individual Entry," Good Jobs First, Subsidy Tracker: Microsoft, https://subsidytracker.goodjobsfirst.org/subsidy-tracker/ia-microsoft.

[16] "Microsoft Seeks Delays in Finishing Third West Des Moines Data Center," *Business Record,* December 26, 2018, https://businessrecord.com/Content/Tech-Innovation/Technology/Article/Microsoft-seeks-delays-in-finishing-third-West-Des-Moines-data-center/172/834/85097.

[17] "Mark Zuckerberg: Real Time Net Worth $70.6B," *Forbes,* accessed July 15, 2019, https://www.forbes.com/profile/mark-zuckerberg/#6973235b3e06.

[18] "Facebook Market Cap: 541.20B for Aug. 8, 2019," https://ycharts.com/companies/FB/market_cap.

[19] "Subsidy Tracker Parent Company Summary," Good Jobs First, Subsidy Tracker: Facebook, https://subsidytracker.goodjobsfirst.org/prog.php?parent=facebook.

[20] CNN Wire Service, "Facebook to Build Massive Data Center in Utah," Fox 6 News Now, May 30, 2018, https://fox6now.com/2018/05/30/facebook-to-build-massive-data-center-in-utah/.

[21] Jay Evensen, "Why Give Tax Breaks to Super-Rich Companies Like Facebook?" *Deseret News,* June 6, 2018, https://www.deseretnews.com/article/900020686/why-give-tax-breaks-to-super-rich-companies-like-facebook.html.

[22] Mitchell Schnurman, "Tax Breaks 'R' Us: Texas Ponies Up the Big Bucks for Corporate Incentives, Again," *Dallas News,* June 2, 2019, https://www.dallasnews.com/opinion/commentary/2019/06/02/tax-breaks-r-us-texas-ponies-big-bucks-corporate-incentives-again.

[23] Dominic Rushe, "'It's a Huge Subsidy': The $4.8bn Gamble to Lure Foxconn to America," *The Guardian Weekly,* July 2, 2018, https://www.theguardian.com/cities/2018/jul/02/its-a-huge-subsidy-the-48bn-gamble-to-lure-foxconn-to-america.

[24] Rick Romell, "Foxconn Falls Short of First Job-Creation Hurdle but Reiterates Ultimate Employment Pledge," *Milwaukee Journal Sentinel,* January 18, 2019, https://www.jsonline.com/story/money/business/2019/01/18/foxconn-falls-short-first-jobs-hurdle-reiterates-13-000-job-pledge/2617038002/.

[25] Robert Channick, "As Foxconn Changes Wisconsin Plans, Job Promises Fall Short," *Chicago Tribune,* February 8, 2019, https://www.chicagotribune.com/business/ct-biz-foxconn-plant-hiring-target-20190205-story.html.

[26] Dan Kaufman, "Did Scott Walker and Donald Trump Deal Away the Wisconsin Governor's Race to Foxconn?" *The New Yorker,* November 3, 2018, https://www.newyorker.com/news/dispatch/did-scott-walker-and-donald-trump-deal-away-the-governors-race-to-foxconn.

[27] Kaufman, "Did Scott Walker and Donald Trump Deal Away the Wisconsin Governor's Race to Foxconn?"

[28] E. Tammy Kim, "Do Corporations Like Amazon and Foxconn Need Public Assistance?" *NYR Daily,* March 14, 2019, https://www.nybooks.com/daily/2019/03/14/do-corporations-like-amazon-and-foxconn-need-public-assistance/.

[29] Josh Dzieza, "Foxconn Is Confusing the Hell Out of Washington," *The Verge,* April 10, 2019, https://www.theverge.com/2019/4/10/18296793/foxconn-wisconsin-location-factory-innovation-centers-technology-hub-no-news.

[30] Jerry Hirsch, "Elon Musk's Growing Empire Is Fueled by $4.9 Billion in Government Subsidies," *Los Angeles Times*, May 30, 2015, Business, http://www.latimes.com/business/la-fi-hy-musk-subsidies-20150531-story.html.

[31] Hirsch, "Elon Musk's Growing Empire Is Fueled by $4.9 Billion in Government Subsidies."

[32] Hirsch, "Elon Musk's Growing Empire Is Fueled by $4.9 Billion in Government Subsidies."

[33] Josh Harkinson, "Taxpayer Subsidies Helped Tesla Motors, So Why Does Elon Musk Slam Them?" *Mother Jones*, September/October 2013, http://www.motherjones.com/politics/2013/10/tesla-motors-free-ride-elon-musk-government-subsidies/.

[34] Robert Frank, "Jeff Bezos Is Now the Richest Man in the World with $90 Billion," CBNC, October 27, 2017, https://www.cnbc.com/2017/10/27/jeff-bezos-is-now-the-richest-man-in-the-world-with-90-billion.html.

[35] Emily C. Bell, "5 Reasons You Definitely Don't Want Amazon's New Headquarters in Your City," *Salon*, October 21, 2017, https://www.salon.com/2017/10/21/5-reasons-you-definitely-do-not-want-amazons-new-headquarters-in-your-city_partner/.

[36] Bell, "5 Reasons You Definitely Don't Want Amazon's New Headquarters in Your City."

[37] Jeffery Dastin, "Billions in Tax Breaks Offered to Amazon for Second Headquarters," Reuters, October 19, 2017, https://www.reuters.com/article/us-amazon-com-headquarters/billions-in-tax-breaks-offered-to-amazon-for-second-headquarters-idUSKBN1CO1IP.

[38] CNN Wire, "New York Mayor Says Amazon Headquarters Debacle Was 'An Abuse of Corporate Power'," FOX 43, February 17, 2019, https://fox43.com/2019/02/17/new-york-mayor-says-amazon-headquarters-debacle-was-an-abuse-of-corporate-power/; "Amazon HQ2," Wikipedia, accessed on May 31, 2019, https://en.wikipedia.org/wiki/Amazon_HQ2.

[39] Richard Florida, "Support a Non-Aggression Pact for Amazon's HQ2," Change.org (petition), https://www.change.org/p/elected-officials-and-community-leaders-of-amazon-hq2-finalist-cities-support-a-non-aggression-pact-for-amazon-s-hq2.

[40] Joseph Lawler, "Koch Group Warns Cities Against 'Corporate Welfare' for Amazon," *Washington Examiner*, February 21, 2018, https://www.washingtonexaminer.com/koch-group-warns-cities-against-corporate-welfare-for-amazon.

[41] JoAnn Adams, "Teachers, School Districts Take Hit While Corporate Welfare Thrives," *Courier Journal*, May 19, 2018, Opinion, https://www.courier-journal.com/story/opinion/contributors/2018/05/19/kentucky-teachers-pensions-schools-hurt-corporate-welfare-thrives/625797002/.

[42] Dana Rubinstein, "Facebook and Google Say They Didn't Get State Subsidies. Why Should Amazon?" *Politico New York*, November 8, 2018, https://www.politico.com/states/new-york/albany/story/2018/11/08/facebook-and-google-say-they-didnt-get-state-subsidies-why-should-amazon-688859.

[43] Douglas MacMillan, Eliot Brown, and Peter Grant, "Google Plans Large New York City Expansion," *Wall Street Journal*, November 7, 2018, https://www.wsj.com/articles/google-plans-large-new-york-city-expansion-1541636579.

Taxes and Tax Breaks

The taxpayer is the new permanent underclass.

—Andrew Wilkow

There is no art which one government sooner learns of another than that of draining money from the pockets of the people.

—Adam Smith

Taxes are necessary. We need a military, a judicial system, a police force, and a number of other institutions that are essential to a complex modern society. Those things are generally paid for with tax revenue.

What we do not need is a system of taxation that distorts free markets, rewards economic activity in accordance with the preferences of politicians and special interests, or especially, a system that favors the wealthy and well-connected at the expense of ordinary taxpayers.

We have already examined many of the deleterious tax policies and preferences that make inequality worse, including taxpayer payments to rich farmers and sugar barons, the oil and gas depletion allowance and targeted tax breaks to a handful of industries and companies. These subsidies, provided to some of America's largest and richest corporations, distort the free market and shortchange ordinary Americans.

The problem of unfair tax policies has become especially acute during the current era when economic inequality is on the rise. During the January 2019, World Economic Forum at Davos, Dutch historian Rutger Bregman, an expert on global inequality, called out the rich for not paying their fair share of taxes. "I hear people talking the language of participation and justice and equality and transparency," he said. "But then almost no one raises the real issue of tax avoidance. And of the rich just not paying their fair share. It feels like I'm at a firefighters conference and no one is allowed to speak about water."[1]

Bregman's remarks were understandably controversial. Yet even some of America's wealthiest people believe the wealthy should pay more. Microsoft's Bill Gates has stated that he himself should probably pay more, and Warren Buffett (2019 net worth: $84 billion) is famous for pointing out that his tax rate is normally less than his secretary's. George Soros, in 2019, added his support for a "moderate wealth tax on the fortunes of the richest 1/10 of the richest 1% of Americans—on us."[2]

Stephen Prince, the New Jersey inventor of the now ubiquitous plastic gift card, is the founder of Patriotic Millionaires, an organization whose mission includes advocating for a fairer tax system. Said Prince, in a recent *New York Times* interview (conducted from his private yacht, anchored in the South Pacific), "The vast majority of my friends are wealthy, too, and they think I'm an idiot. I get called a traitor to my class all the time."[3]

But Prince has enlisted a number of allies, including Disney heiress Abigail Disney, who is a member of Patriotic Millionaires. Interviewed in 2019 on CNBC, the philanthropist and filmmaker noted that there is something fundamentally wrong with a tax system that allows her to pay at a lower tax rate than her office assistant because her income takes the form of capital gains. She also finds the $65 million paid to Disney's CEO Bob Iger an embarrassment.[4]

But despite the efforts of Prince and other like-minded individuals, the situation is getting worse. The Institute on Taxation and Economic Policy estimates that since 2001, "significant federal tax changes have reduced the government's revenue by $5.1 trillion." They note further that the lion's share of the tax reductions has accrued to the wealthy.[5]

Libertarians like the authors of this book are generally in favor of low taxes and limited government spending. So when the government grants a tax break that lowers people's taxes, that's a plus. But our system today provides tax breaks for biased and usually loaded reasons. When a single individual or company, or certain groups of individuals or companies, are granted tax favors that no one else gets, a fundamental injustice occurs that distorts free markets, weakens competition, and undermines the economy. All those who don't get targeted tax breaks are penalized; the loopholes and other subsidies are then appropriately called "tax expenditures," because the government is giving up identifiable revenue by allowing favored parties to pay less than others.

In the follow pages, we'll review a number of today's most dysfunctional tax policies, including some remarkable favors dished out to the wealthy by the states.

The 2017 Tax Cuts and the Tax Burden Borne by the Wealthy

In 2017, the Trump administration pushed through the Tax Cuts and Jobs Act (TCJA), the largest tax overhaul in recent history. The biggest changes in the TCJA were the lowering of the federal income tax rates (including lowering the top tax rate from 39.6 percent to 37 percent), cutting the corporate tax rate from 35 percent to 21 percent, and doubling the exemption on the estate tax exemption (also called the "inheritance tax" and the "death tax") from $5.45 million to $11.1 million for singles, and from $10.9 million to $22.4 million for couples.[6] The U.S. Congress's Joint Committee on Taxation estimates the loss of $1.5 trillion in federal tax revenue from 2018–2028 as a result of these changes.[7]

Virtually all taxpayers enjoyed a reduction in their taxes from these changes, with some of the biggest cuts going to the wealthy. As the president announced to a crowd of cheering fellow one-percenters after passage of the bill, "You all just got a lot richer!"[8] They certainly did. According to most analyses of the impact of these reforms, the rich gained the most, enjoying the largest reductions in tax burdens (Figure 8-1).

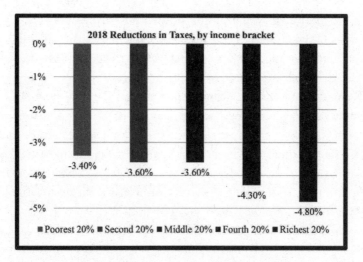

Figure 8-1: 2018 reductions in taxes, by income bracket.
Source: Institute of Taxation and Economic Policy

Consequently, the wealthy also enjoyed the biggest increases in after-tax income (Figure 8-2).

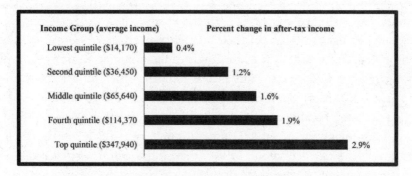

Figure 8-2: How the distribution of the Trump tax cuts favored the wealthy.
Source: Tax Policy Center estimates

These data, however, fail to fully reflect the higher taxes regularly paid by the top income quintiles. Chris Edwards, a tax expert at the Cato Institute, has analyzed the impact of the 2017 tax cuts, and found that "middle income groups…get by far the largest cuts as a percentage of current income taxes. For example, households earning between $50,000 and $75,000 [will] get a 24% cut in 2019, while those earning over $1 million...get just a 6 percent cut."[9] Thus, the widely publicized notion that the 2017 bill was loaded for the affluent deserves some qualification.

Relatedly and worth noting is the fact that the wealthy, both before and after the 2017 tax law changes, pay by far the highest income tax rates. In 2018 the government's Joint Committee on Taxation published an analysis showing that top earners ($1,000,000 or more) paid 26.3 percent of their income in federal income taxes. Those making $200,000–$500,000, paid 13.4 percent, with all lower income levels paying less.[10]

This issue is fraught with complexities and controversies. When we consider only federal income taxes, it is clear that the wealthy pay much higher rates than those who make less. However, when payroll taxes of 6.2 percent for Social Security, and 1.45 percent for Medicare are included, those with lower incomes end up paying rates that begin to rise closer to the rates paid by higher income earners. Further complicating the matter, most economists feel that workers end up paying the employer's share of the Social Security and Medicare taxes (the same 6.2 percent and 1.45 percent) because their wages would be higher if the employer wasn't paying the tax. To the extent this is true, all employees are paying 15 percent of their salaries in payroll taxes, which in the lower brackets, is usually the lion's share of their income-related taxation. Equally regressive are state and local sales taxes, which hit lower-income folks much harder than the wealthy because more of their earnings go to the purchase of daily needs, most of which incur a sales tax.

Economists disagree about the appropriate way to calculate the extent to which the rich pay more, or less, than those with lower incomes. It is fair to say, we believe, that considering federal and state income taxes alone, the wealthy pay the most—the highest rates and the most dollars. When all other taxes are accounted for, the differences in rates diminish.

That said, there are numerous tax policies and programs that are designed specifically to benefit the wealthy.

Special Tax Rates That Benefit the Lucky Few

An excellent example of a prejudicial tax break is the treatment of carried interest, a special tax calculation used to compensate private equity and hedge fund managers, theoretically in exchange for their success in providing investors a good return on their money. Current tax rules let such managers pay taxes on carried interest at the capital gains rate (maximum 20 percent) rather than the higher tax rate that normally applies to ordinary income (up to 37 percent).

The main argument offered in defense of the carried interest loophole is that there is risk involved in the investment and hedge fund business. But Victor Fleisher, a law professor at the University of San Diego, who studies tax issues, disagrees, explaining it this way:

> The real issue is that carried interest is compensation for services performed for the investment fund. The theory behind [carried interest] is that somehow, holding something for a longer period of time makes it more like a financial investment. But why would that be the case? If you write a book and it takes three or four years before you earn a royalty, that doesn't make the income a capital gain. If a movie takes three years to generate a return, that doesn't make it a capital gain. There is no reason why financial services should be any different.

Some lobbyists and industry representatives argue that closing the carried interest loophole would mean that fewer people would launch careers in finance. Fleisher scoffs at this argument. "We don't need to further subsidize people who go to work in this sector by giving them a lower tax rate," he says. "There's no shortage of people who want to go into private equity and earn millions or billions of dollars."[11]

Warren Buffett agrees. He testified on the matter to Congress, saying, "If you believe in taxing people who earn income on their occupation, I think you should tax people on carried interest."[12]

During his presidential campaign, candidate Trump vowed to do away with the carried interest deduction, telling CBS News, "…the hedge fund guys didn't build this country. These are guys that shift paper around, and they get lucky…They make a fortune; they pay no tax. It's ridiculous…They have to pay taxes."[13] It was an example of the kind of "populist" rhetoric that distinguished Trump from many traditional Republicans, and which some commentators believe helped him win the White House. But when Trump was in office and the time came for tax reform, the carried-interest loophole remained unchanged.

Treasury Secretary Steven Mnuchin, himself a former hedge fund manager, during negotiations regarding the tax cut package, implied that the carried interest loophole "wasn't that expensive."[14] But American taxpayers would likely disagree. According to the Treasury department, closing this loophole and making carried interest taxable at the same rate as ordinary income would generate $1.8 billion a year in tax revenue.[15] In the name of fairness to ordinary taxpayers, the carried interest loophole should be eliminated.

The capital gains tax, which taxes certain types of revenue at lower rates than ordinary earned income, has long been a target of those interested in tax reform, but this special tax rate remained entrenched under the 2017 Tax Reform Bill. The increase in the value of stocks, homes, and other assets is considered a long-term capital gain if held for a year or more. Such gains are taxed at a lower rate than ordinary income when the underlying assets are sold (Figure 8-3). Thus, the maximum capital gains rate for even the wealthiest taxpayers is 20 percent, as compared with a maximum rate of 37 percent on most other forms of income.

	Taxable Income	
Long Term Capital Gains Rate	Single Taxpayers	Married Filing Jointly
0%	Up to $38,600	Up to $77,200
15%	$38,600-$425,800	$77,200-$479,000
20%	Over $425,800	Over $479,000

Figure 8-3: Federal income tax rates on capital gains.
Source: United States Internal Revenue Service

Taxing capital gains at the same rate as ordinary income would almost certainly make the system fairer. After all, the poor and middle class receive most of their income from job earnings, and it is hard to justify taxing their income at a higher rate than the gains from property investment. As one observer put it, "there's no reason why income earned by money should be taxed at lower rate than income earned by sweat." According to a 2016 report from the Congressional Budget Office, raising the tax rates on capital gains by a mere two percentage points per tax bracket (i.e. taxing capital gains for high earners at 22 percent) would raise revenues by $6.7 billion annually.[16]

Those who defend the lower capital gains rates argue that they encourage vital investments. But as recently as the three years from 1988 to 1990, under President George H.W. Bush, capital gains were taxed the same as ordinary income, and there was no indication that investment levels suffered; indeed, according to the Federal Reserve, gross private domestic investment during 1988–1990 rose from $1.712 billion to $2.067 billion.[17]

The Cato Institute's Chris Edwards, however, offers three arguments for maintaining low tax rates for capital gains. The first argument is based on the impact of inflation. If Uncle Joe buys a stock for $100 and sells it ten years later for $120, that $20 gain may be mostly or entirely a result of inflation. Having to pay a tax on inflation is certainly wrong.

Edwards's second point is based on the phenomenon of "lock-in." Capital gains taxes are not levied until a property is sold. This means that the owners of properties that have gained value tend to hold on to them rather than sell and trigger an immediate capital gains tax bill—and, of course, this tendency will be greater the higher the tax rate is. Lock-in reduces market efficiency, as it chokes off the movement of funds from lower- to higher-yielding investments.

Finally, Edwards argues, capital gains taxes can be punishing for major one-time sales of, say, a family business. Such sales create a temporary income spike that results in a high tax rate that year, another arguably unfair impact of high taxes on capital gains.[18]

How the Mortgage Interest Deduction Is Tilted Toward the Wealthy

According to Bill Emmons, an economist with the St. Louis Federal Reserve, "It's rare to find a policy that's both popular among the public and almost universally disliked by economists. But the mortgage interest deduction is one such policy."[19] Under current tax policy, the interest a homeowner pays on a mortgage is deductible against income for tax purposes. And Emmons is right about this policy's popularity; a recent *Economist* survey found that 50 percent of homeowners are against eliminating the deduction. (So are 28 percent of renters, even though they don't benefit from it.)[20]

The 2017 TCJA reduced this deduction somewhat. Previously, the interest on mortgages for two homes up to $1 million each had been allowed (for joint filers). Now the deduction is limited to the interest on two mortgages of up to $750,000 each. The fact that the deduction is allowed for both primary and second homes is one feature that tilts the policy in favor of the wealthy, since only those in the top tax brackets are likely to have the means to own a second home. And the deduction reduces government revenues significantly. In 2016, the Pew Research Center reported that the mortgage interest deduction cost taxpayers $77 billion in foregone tax revenue just for that year.[21]

Emmons says there are several reasons why economists don't like the deduction. First, it encourages larger homes. Home buyers may be tempted to build or buy a bigger house because a portion of the mortgage costs will be shared with the taxpayers; in fact, they are often encouraged to do so both by lenders and real estate agents, who suggest that, with the deduction, a buyer can afford more house.[22] But bigger homes and bigger mortgages can drive up default rates and often waste valuable space. The mortgage interest deduction also tends to drive up housing prices, putting many homes beyond the reach of potential buyers.

Finally, the mortgage interest deduction is regressive—that is, it benefits the wealthy more than those of modest means. In 2018, taxpayers with incomes over $200,000 received 60 percent of the benefit.[23]

Matthew Desmond, author of the bestseller *Evicted: Poverty and Profit in the American City* observed in 2017:

> America's national housing policy gives affluent home-
> owners large benefits; middle-class homeowners, smaller
> benefits; and most renters, who are disproportionately
> poor, nothing. It is difficult to think of another social pol-
> icy that more successfully multiplies America's inequality
> in such a sweeping fashion…[in 2015], the federal gov-
> ernment dedicated nearly $134 billion to homeowner
> subsidies. The Mortgage Interest Deduction accounted
> for the biggest chunk of the total, $71 billion.[24]

"[T]his national wealth-creation policy has several negative side effects," notes Derek Thompson, writing in the *Atlantic Monthly* in 2017: One is a distorted perception of the role of government in the housing market. As Thompson observes, "high-income households don't consider their tax benefits to be a form of government policy at all. For example, 60 percent of people who claim the mortgage interest deduction say they have never used any government program, ever. As a result, rich households can be skeptical of public housing policies while benefiting from a $71 billion annual tax benefit which is, functionally, a public-housing policy for the rich."[25] Ironically, in 2015, the mortgage interest deduction cost more in foregone taxes than the government spent on subsidizing housing for the poor.[26]

After the 2017 tax reforms, the mortgage interest deduction is less important overall, but even more tilted toward the wealthy. The TCJA increased the standard (non-itemized) deduction from $6,300 to $12,000 for single taxpayers and to $24,000 for couples. This means that many homeowners will choose that option and not itemize on their returns at all. [27] As a result, the Tax Policy Center estimates that the number of taxpayers making use of the mortgage interest deduction will fall from 34 million to 14 million.[28] While this is good news, those who continue to use the deduction will be, on average, very rich. Because of its regressive nature, and the fact that its benefits go largely to people who really don't need any help from the taxpayers, the mortgage interest deduction should be eliminated.

The Debate Over the Estate Tax

Supporters and critics argue endlessly over the estate tax, which applies only to the estates of relatively wealthy Americans. Estates of single persons up to an assessed value of $5.5 million were exempt from 2010 until 2017, when under the TCJA, the exemption amount was doubled to $11.1 million. This means that the number of people affected is quite small; on average, only about eighteen hundred U.S. taxpayers leave estates in excess of this amount each year. However, thirteen states charge their own estate taxes. Oregon and Massachusetts tax all estates over $1 million; Vermont and Washington tax any estate over $2.8 million (VT) or $2.2 million (WA). Other states have more generous exemptions— New York's, for example, is $5.25 million. Tax rates run from 8 percent to 16 percent, and in one case, up to 20 percent (in Washington State).

Opponents of the estate tax point out that, while the number of estates affected is small, any substantial excesses over the exclusion amount are taxed heavily. An estate assessed at $20 million, for example, will be subject to a federal tax of more than $3 million. Critics of the tax point out that this may make it necessary to break up and sell parts of a successful farm or corporation just to pay the tax. They also note that taxes (especially property taxes) have often been paid on large estates during the benefactor's lifetime, and that no credit is allowed for such payments.

Finally, critics such as Cato's Edwards argue that the tax penalizes savings. Why save money if you know that once you die your heirs will have to pay a big chunk of what you leave behind to the IRS? Edwards says that the tax "rewards a selfish 'die-broke ethic,'" and that many other countries get along fine with no estate tax at all.[29] For these reasons, Edwards and others believe the estate tax should be eliminated altogether. Polls suggest that around thirty percent of Americans agree.[30]

On the other side of the argument are those who feel that only estates of, perhaps, one or two million dollars should be exempt. This level would exempt most average Americans' inheritance, while the tax on large inheritances would help reduce the wealth gap between the wealthy and the middle class. At the current exemption level of $11.1 million, critics assert, many undeserving beneficiaries will continue to be rich, thus exacerbating income and wealth inequality. "[B]ecause most recipients of large bequests are themselves wealthy," says Isabel Sawhill of the Brookings Institution, "and did nothing to earn their inheritance, these [untaxed] bequests are, in essence, welfare for the rich." [31]

Our view is that the previous exemption level of $5.5 million was about right. While this level would result in unjust consequences for certain large properties, inherited wealth is not *per se* virtuous. What's more, the charitable option is available for those who wish to keep their money in the private sector, since there is no estate tax on any amount of funds or property bequeathed to qualifying nonprofits.

The Tax Deduction for Charitable Contributions—Merely a Tax Dodge?

Another tax policy around which controversy swirls is the provision that permits a taxpayer who itemizes deductions to deduct from adjusted gross income the amount given to qualified charities in any tax year. Using this provision, a wealthy individual in the 37 percent tax bracket can make a charitable contribution of $1,000 for a net personal cost of just $630, since, after the deduction, the taxpayer's federal tax will be reduced by $370. By contrast, a person with more modest income, in, say, the 25 percent bracket, will pay a net cost of $750 for her $1,000 contribution.

When explained this way, it sounds as if the law favors the rich. But in order to get the tax break, the donor at any income level must give away $1,000. That money is gone; it no longer belongs to him or her. It belongs to the charity—and no one gets richer by giving money away. Indeed, the purpose of the charitable contribution deduction is precisely to encourage the wealthy (and the not-so-wealthy) to give their money to charity. The higher one's income, and thus the higher one's marginal tax rate, the greater the incentive to make charitable contributions.

Up to this point, we see no problem with this policy. It has helped encourage Americans to increase their charitable giving to a remarkable $410 billion (2017), lending support for thousands of programs that help the poor, support education and the arts, provide health care, and much more.[32] (Full disclosure: Phil makes extensive use of the charitable deduction in his own personal finances.)

On the other hand, the system can be abused. Deductions are allowed for private as well as public charities, though private charities face more restrictions, and a donor may make contributions to his or her own private foundation and still retain control over that foundation and its funding, as long as the money is spent on charitable purposes.

Fortunately, abuses of this system are rare—but they do occur, as illustrated by some of the questionable activities associated with Presidents Trump's private foundations. In a 2018 exposé, *The Washington Examiner* reported:

> In the run-up to the 2016 Iowa Caucuses, Trump skipped a debate and instead hosted a Trump Foundation fundraiser for veterans and troops. The Trump Foundation [then] cut six-figure checks to three Iowa-based veterans' charities…You'd have to play dumb to deny what was going on here; the Trump Foundation was acting as an arm of the Trump campaign.[33]

This was a clear abuse of power and a violation of the rules. After New York State brought a lawsuit against Trump, he accepted a settlement in November 2019, that required him to pay $2 million in damages to a number of nonprofit groups (though Trump posted a defiant statement on Twitter that called the misdeeds to which he confessed "some small technical violations).[34]

Other investigations suggest that, in 2007, the Trump Foundation even paid $20,000 for a portrait of Donald Trump that ended up hanging in one of his hotels.[35] And the foundation's largest-recorded gift helped restore a fountain outside of the Trump Plaza in New York. These and a number of other expenditures were questioned by the IRS, and as a result of all the bad publicity, Trump closed the foundation in 2018.

Does the charitable deduction advantage the rich? Insofar as the deduction reduces taxes the most for high-level taxpayers, it benefits them. But shouldn't the wealthy be encouraged to give to charity? The resulting shift of charitable dollars from the public to the private sector is in our opinion, very healthy. Like all acts of fraud and lawbreaking, the occasional abuses of the charitable deduction should be exposed and appropriately penalized. But overall, this tax break almost certainly has a positive impact on American society.

A Word About Social Security Taxes

While the Social Security program does not directly move funds from lower to upper income persons, the entire Social Security system is designed in such a way as to have that very same effect. While every wage earner must pay the same 6.2 percent (plus 1.45 percent for Medicare) Social Security tax, the system is loaded against low-income wage earners.

First, the tax must be paid on the very first dollar of earned income. If a high school student earns as little as $200 or $300 on a summer job, he/she will nonetheless pay the tax on those small amounts. Unlike income taxes, the Social Security tax must be paid by even the low-est-income workers.

Second, high school graduates (and dropouts) who do not go to college begin paying the tax much earlier in their lives than their more educated peers. Those who go on to college receive training that directly enhances their earning power a few years later, but until that time, they pay no Social Security tax. By the time upper-income earners begin pay-ing the tax, they are several years older than the lower-rung workers who have already been paying the tax for several years.

Third, the tax is paid only on income up to $132,900. All income above that amount is untaxed for Social Security.

Finally, low-income earners generally die at a younger age than those in the higher economic echelons, and thus collect fewer Social Security benefits in old age. Workers in the top income groups have a life expec-tancy of more than eighty years, while those in the lowest quintile die, on average, in their 70s. This means that low-income earners realize significantly fewer Social Security benefits after retirement than their bet-ter-paid counterparts.

They start paying the tax sooner, yet receive fewer benefits later.

All in all, Social Security is loaded for the rich and against low-income workers and the poor. No wonder economist Milton Friedman once remarked that the system is so regressive it could never be enacted today.

Tax Breaks That Are Prone to Abuse

Some kinds of tax deductions, cuts, and credits are more prone to abuse than others—some to such an extent that we think the country would be better off without them.

One example is the Research and Development (R&D) Tax Credit, which allows companies that are engaged in R&D to write off some of those costs. Created in 1981, under the Economic Recovery Tax Act, this credit's original purpose was to provide an economic stimulus to help lift the country out of the then-current recession.[36] It was made permanent in 2015, and since then, it has been regularly abused.

A recent study found that 82 percent of the benefits from this tax credit are claimed by the largest 1 percent of American businesses—big and wealthy companies that presumably need the help the least.[37] In 2019, when the Internal Revenue Service released its "Dirty Dozen" list of the worst tax evasion tactics for the year, the R&D tax credit was featured. Its report noted:

> The IRS continues to see significant misuse of the research credit. Improper claims for this credit generally involve a failure to participate in or substantiate qualified research activities, and/or a failure to satisfy the requirements related to qualified research expenses…
>
> The IRS often sees expenses from non-qualified activities included in claims for the research credit.[38]

This tax credit costs American taxpayers over $9 billion in lost reve-nue per year ($10.3 billion in 2018).[39]

Giant Amazon, for example, makes full use of the R&D credit. According to the Institute on Taxation and Economic Policy, Amazon paid no federal corporate income taxes in 2018 on their $11.2 billion in revenue—none.[40] One reason is that Amazon received $419 million in tax credits that year, most in the form of R&D credits.[41]

Lower taxes are generally desirable, but this particular provision of the tax code seems to invite abuse and to benefit only the largest companies. It should be eliminated.

Then there are so-called tax extenders—in reality, tax *cut* extenders—which are provisions slipped into larger tax bills that extend temporary tax cuts year after year without subjecting them to the scrutiny required to become regular line items in the federal budget. Every time Congress passes a budget, a plethora of special interests fight to defend their narrow tax breaks, and year after year, Congress extends them with minimal oversight. Notable examples include tax cut extenders for:

- *Owners of racehorses.* This tax break allows owners to accelerate the depreciation on their racehorses. In 2018, it cost taxpayers an estimated $37 million in lost revenue.[42] Perhaps not coincidentally, Mitch McConnell, Senate Majority Leader, represents the state of Kentucky, home of the Kentucky Derby.
- *Owners of NASCAR racetracks.* This break allows NASCAR racetrack owners to deduct taxable expenses on an accelerated basis. This tax break is worth $13 million a year.[43]
- *A tuna packing plant in American Samoa.* This tax break, called The American Samoa Economic Development Credit, benefits a Starkist Tuna packing plant in American Samoa. In 2018, the credit cost $11 million in lost federal revenue.[44]

There are hundreds, perhaps thousands, of these narrowly targeted tax breaks littering the federal budget. According to the Joint Committee on Taxation, these specialized breaks will cost the taxpayer $16 billion in lost revenue in the next decade.[45] As custom-designed gifts from government to specific beneficiaries—most often, individuals and companies that are already doing well financially—they undermine the ideal of equal treatment under the law, and they should be eliminated from the tax code.

Opportunity Zones

The 2017 tax reforms included the creation of Opportunity Zones, which have been touted as a way to create incentives for investors to support economic activity in underserved parts of the country. Opportunity Zones offer temporary deferral of inclusion in taxable income for gains realized on funds invested in an Opportunity Fund (which is the mechanism for investing in an Opportunity Zone). The law also includes a step-up in basis for investments that are held in the Opportunity Fund for five years or more. For example, an investor who puts $50,000 in an Opportunity Fund and sees his investment grow to $60,000 could sell after seven years, owing capital gains tax on only $2,500, the difference between his selling price and the stepped-up basis ($57,500). Furthermore, if the investment is held for ten years or more, investors receive a permanent exclusion of capital gains tax.

Economic development zones are not new. British Prime Minister Margaret Thatcher created some of the earliest opportunity zones in England in the 1980s (under the name "enterprise zones"), with the goal of encouraging development in blighted areas of London. President Ronald Reagan embraced the concept, using the term Urban Enterprise Zones. Similar programs followed under succeeding U.S. presidents— Empowerment Zones under President Clinton, and Promise Zones under President Obama.

The strategy has occasionally worked well, when accompanied by major liberalization of the economic rules governing business. For example, the designation of Shenzhen City as a special economic zone in China in the late 1970s was accompanied by major reductions in the tax and regulatory burdens there. The result was an astonishing record of economic growth for decades afterwards, transforming Shenzhen into a modern metropolis.

Some U.S.-based programs similar to opportunity zones have also done well. Larry Kosmont, chairman and CEO of Kosmont Companies in Manhattan Beach, California, has won several awards in for his work in the real estate and economic development sectors. We met Larry, a handsome, friendly, and confident Latino man, on a sunny afternoon in April 2019. He serves on the boards of and routinely gives speeches to real estate development associations, and counsels investors and municipalities all over California on the promise of Opportunity Zones. Kosmont points to highly successful developments he has already completed under related economic development models.

One of Kosmont's recently completed projects is the 370,000-square-foot South Gate Azalea Shopping Center in the city of South Gate, California, which is 95 percent Hispanic or Latino, and with 95,000 residents, the densest community in Los Angeles County. The shopping center sits on the site of an old manufacturing plant site and was built during the 2008–2012 recession, when the city had a 16 percent unemployment rate. Today, the shopping center is 98 percent leased. It has created fourteen hundred jobs, 50 percent of them filled by local residents, and boasts a public event space, recycled water features, electric car chargers, and free Wi-Fi throughout.

It is this kind of economic development in underserved areas that Kosmont is promoting for Opportunity Zones across the country. "If we do it right, we *can* help underserved areas. We can provide jobs. We can improve communities, while making good returns for our investors."[46]

Unfortunately, few developers are as committed to serving underserved areas as Kosmont. The same month we talked with him, Bloomberg News ran a story about a low-income community in Florida that was likely to be bulldozed to make way for a gentrification project that would fall under the Opportunity Zone designation. The article describes an August 2018 "salon discussion" hosted by Florida billionaire Richard LeFrak, which featured Treasury Secretary Steve Mnuchin explaining to a collection of millionaire developers the benefits of the new Opportunity Zones.

These developers had convinced Florida Governor Rick Scott to designate a census tract in North Miami an Opportunity Zone, making them eligible for numerous tax breaks. One of the neighborhoods that helped the census zone qualify is the Highland Village trailer park, a collection of aging mobile and manufactured homes where the rents are cheap and the average household income is under $30,000 a year. Under the plan, the area is supposed to be converted into Solé Mia, a $4 billion, 184-acre community. [47]

An interview with local residents revealed decidedly negative assessments of the Solé Mia development. Brenda Evans, a forty-nine-year-old Home Depot cashier who's lived in the Highland Village neighborhood for more than a decade, pays $600 a month for three bedrooms for her mom, two daughters, and grandson. She worries the development will soon drive up rents. "I'm sure one day we'll be pushed out," she said."[48] Other residents share the belief that the Opportunity Zone program is just a way to further enrich wealthy real estate developers, rather than a plan to help the needy.

In general, academic analysis has not been kind to enterprise zones in the U.S., regardless of their name or political provenance. In 2002, Alan H. Peters and Peter S. Fisher at the University of Iowa did an exhaustive study of the impact of enterprise zones in thirteen states, and concluded, "the direct revenue effects of enterprise zone incentives are very likely to be negative, and rather strongly so…the evidence shows that enterprise zones have little or no impact…on employment growth."[49] Echoing the University of Iowa study, in 2019, the Tax Foundation warned that place-based incentive programs (i.e. Opportunity Zone programs) do not generate new economic activity, but merely subsidize activity that would have happened anyway, and end up displacing low-income residents by increasing property values and encouraging higher skilled workers to move into the newly improved areas.[50] While this process has many pluses, it does little for those who lived there when the Opportunity Zone process began.

Further complicating the picture, in 2019 the *Wall Street Journal* reported problems with the zone designation process. For example, university areas often qualify as "poor" because students generally are low-income. "California's initial cut of potential zones included parts of Stanford University, San Diego State University, and University of California, Berkeley, as well as rapidly gentrifying sections of San Francisco."[51] Surely these are not the kinds of needy communities lawmakers intended when they created the Opportunity Zone program. And of course, like all special tax breaks, Opportunity Zones create revenue gaps that other taxpayers must fill. The *Wall Street Journal* reports that the current Opportunity Zone program will cost about $10 billion in foregone capital gains tax revenue during the next decade.[52]

To get a close look at some start-up Opportunity Zone activities, we visited High Point, North Carolina in early 2019. In the middle of this small southern city sit showrooms for the hundreds of furniture and housing decoration companies that flock here twice a year for the Furniture International trade show. We met with High Point's Economic Development Corporation Executive Vice President, Sandy Dunbeck, and Ray Gibbs, Executive Director of Forward High Point, an organization created in 2015 to bring the city a sports stadium (presently under construction).[53]

Forward High Point is now turning its focus to Opportunity Zone development. In a small windowless room on the top floor of the City Hall building, Sandy Dunbeck pulled up a city map showing the proposed Opportunity Zones. They are primarily downtown, close to the future stadium as well as the Furniture International hub. Gibbs seemed especially hopeful that this would help jumpstart downtown redevelopment. "North Carolina prohibits property tax abatement; we can't give businesses that break," he said. "So this is a way for us to offer investors something—that capital gains tax break—to get them to build here."

We asked, what about the mission of serving the underserved in distressed economic areas? Both Sandy and Ray looked uncomfortable. Clearly, they viewed Opportunity Zones as a tool to lure investors to expand and improve the commercial areas of downtown, to promote tourism and gentrify the city. "We are looking at properties we can buy up and hold for future development," Ray said, pointing to lots on the property map. There was no mention of affordable housing, public services, or new jobs.

As with so many taxpayer giveaways, the ostensible purpose of the Opportunity Zones program and the way it plays out in reality are two different things.

Special Breaks for Real Estate Moguls

As a real estate developer, and as probably the wealthiest president to ever hold the office, Donald Trump's tax avoidance history is quite remarkable. It's not surprising. Real estate developments nearly always get special tax treatment.

"One reason there are so many real estate billionaires," noted the *New York Times* in 2019, "is the law allows the industry to perpetually defer capital gains in properties by trading one for another…In addition, real estate industry executives can depreciate the value of their investment for tax purposes, even when the actual value of the property appreciates."[54]

Another real estate break is the conservation easement deduction. It allows a tax break for those who take their land out of use and leave it to the extent possible, in its natural state. The goals are noble: to protect water quality, improve wildlife habitat, and foster healthy plant and tree growth. Many land trusts manage these donated lands in pursuit of these environmental goals. But the system has become rife with abuse.

Adam Looney, with the Urban-Brookings Tax Policy Center, reports that "…donors are abusing the [easement] provision by applying grossly inflated appraisals to the value of the easement to increase their charitable deduction, or by taking donations for easements that do not fulfill bona fide conservation purposes."[55] The IRS even published a report on such abuses, noting:

> The IRS has seen abuses of this tax provision that compromise the policy Congress intended to promote. We have seen taxpayers, often encouraged by promoters and armed with questionable appraisals, take inappropriately large deductions for easements. In some cases, taxpayers claim deductions when they are not entitled to any deduction at all.[56]

In 2014, taxpayers claimed $1.2 billion in deductions for conservation easements, including agricultural easements. By 2016, that number had ballooned to $6.6 billion.[57]

The 2017 TCJA includes a tax break specifically offering conservation easement credits to owners of golf courses. This is convenient for the president, as *Forbes* reports: "Last August [2016] Donald Trump's campaign gave the Associated Press a 94-page list of $102 million worth of donations he and his companies had made since 2010. The first entry: $63.825 million for various conservation easements."

These "donations," of course, reduced Trump's taxable income. He has used this break on golf courses in California, at his Mar-a-Lago Club in Palm Beach, Florida, and on his Bedminster, New Jersey golf course.[58] The deductions may be perfectly legal; one tax advisor describes them as a savvy investment for his clients. But conservation easements for golf courses are simply unjustified.

Consider Millstone golf course outside Greenville, South Carolina, which closed in 2006 and sat vacant for years. Littered with abandoned irrigation pipes and rusted food and beverage carts, the property abutted a trailer park, all conditions that lowered the property's value. In 2015, a group of investors purchased the property for $5.4 million. Then, with the help of an appraiser, they declared it to be worth $41 million for purposes of an easement deduction. They were able to deduct the full $41 million as a charitable contribution against their other income. Thus, these investors got $4 in deductions for every $1 they put into the deal. [59] Not a bad return on investment, but bad land policy and bad tax law.

Real estate tax breaks are also one of the ways states and municipalities compete for business. In his years as a developer, Trump benefitted from preferential tax treatment in New York, New Jersey, Florida, and Nevada.[60] In New York, for the Grand Hyatt Hotel Trump built on 42nd Street, he got a "40-year tax break that has cost New York City $360 million to date in forgiven, or uncollected, taxes, with four years still to run, on a property that cost only $120 million to build in 1980." Including other such deals, the *New York Times* has calculated that Trump has received at least $885 million in tax breaks from New York City over the years.[61]

In 2017, the Trump organization sued the town of Ossining, New York, in an effort to reduce the property tax bill on the Trump golf course there. On the campaign trail in 2016, Trump bragged that the property was worth $50 million. At tax time, the town assessed its value at $15.1

million—to which Trump responded by suing to have the valuation lowered to $7.5 million.[62] Gloria Fried, the receiver of taxes for Ossining, noted at the time, "It is very difficult when you see someone who has all these assets at his disposal, who would rather pay lawyers to avoid his civic duty of paying taxes."[63]

In Clinton, Mississippi, a Trump-managed hotel (under his Scion brand) will cost $20 million to build, and will receive $6 million in taxpayer-funded tax incentives and rebates.[64] Trump's partners in the hotel project, developers Dinesh and Suresh Chawla, are long-time Mississippi developers who own dozens of hotels across the South. Shortly after their first meetings with the Trump organization in 2016, they made donations of $50,000 to the Trump campaign and the Republican National Committee. Soon, they were signing the deal on the Trump hotel.[65]

Some Notable State Tax Boondoggles

As we've already suggested, government is not alone in lavishing tax breaks on those who need them least. The states have also gotten into the act, some of them in a very big way.

In Texas, there is an especially convoluted system for delivering special taxpayer favors to corporations building their own facilities. The system utilizes—of all things—local school districts to disseminate corporate welfare.

Schools in Texas are funded by property taxes that developers go to considerable means to avoid. The Texas Economic Development Act, called Chapter 313 after its placement in the Texas tax code, allows school districts to grant state tax abatements and tax refunds. Under a system devised in 2001, if a developer decides to build within a certain school district's border, the developer applies to the school district for a tax abatement. The school district board members review the applications, then vote whether to grant the abatement. If it is granted, the school district then sends a bill for the lost property tax revenue to the state, which reimburses the school district in full. In the last ten years, the state of Texas has given away $7 billion in taxpayer dollars via such schemes, and tax abatement costs through the end of the decade are projected at $10 billion.[66]

Given that there is no loss of revenue to the school district if they *do* grant the abatement, they generally accede to all requests. And putting the nominal onus for these subsidies onto school district board members tends to disguise the taxpayer burden.

Touted by supporters as a way to lure businesses and jobs to Texas, the program has become a serious drain on the Texas economy. A report by the State Comptroller's office found that Texas taxpayers have paid roughly $314,000 for each job "created" through the Chapter 313 program. And in most cases, when companies are turned down, they end up building the developments anyway, showing that the tax break was not necessary.[67] University of Texas Professor Nathan Jensen, an expert on tax incentives, recently released a study on the effectiveness of Chapter 313's economic development strategy. He concluded: "An analysis of the program finds that 85–90% of projects would have located in Texas without the 313 program, and [thus], 80% of the program's dollars are lost revenue for the state's school finance system."[68]

Giant corporations have been among the big winners from Chapter 313. Writing in the *Texas Observer*, Patrick Michels concludes, "At a time when the Legislature can spend months scrapping over $100 million for pre-K, when $55 million to air condition Texas prisons is a nonstarter, corporations such as Exxon and Dow Chemical need only ask and Texas hands them billions."[69] He's right. According to a 2017 analysis by the *Houston Chronicle*, the Dow Chemical Company raked in $442 million in tax breaks under Chapter 313 agreements, between 2014 and 2018. Their plants are all located in the Brazosport School District, which has a student population of 12,300 students served by eight hundred teachers. At the time of Dow Chemical's applications for tax abatement, they promised to bring 410 jobs to the area, but in those four years, there have been just seventy-four jobs created—a cost of almost $6 million per job. Meanwhile, the chairman of Dow Chemical, Andrew Liveris, received a compensation package of over $23 million in 2016, landing him on the *Forbes* 200 list of highest paid CEOs.[70]

Exxon's latest taxpayer funded project through Chapter 313 will cost the taxpayers $531 million. It received approval from the Gregory-

Portland and San Patricio School Districts near Corpus Christi, in 2018.[71] The project in question is part of a joint $20 billion Growing the Gulf joint venture with the Saudi Arabia Basic Industries Corporation, a Saudi company, and will include the world's largest ethylene plant.

In early 2018, Texas State Senator Konni Burton (R) introduced S.B. 600, which sought to eliminate Chapter 313, arguing that it is "corporate welfare at its worst."[72] However, she faced fierce assaults from industry lobbyists, and the measure never made it to a vote.

You might agree with Senator Burton that the Texas tax boondoggle sounds like "corporate welfare at its worst." But Broderick Bagert wouldn't agree with you. Leader of Together Louisiana, an organization fighting for property tax reform in Louisiana, Bagert says, "I'd be happy if Louisiana had [the Texas] system. That would be a big step up from where we are at right now."

We spoke with Bagert in his small family home in downtown New Orleans, surrounded by floor-to-ceiling bookshelves and a few children's toys scattered on the floor.[73] Broderick's engaging grin belies a fierce intellect and passion for the good fight. A descendant of local politicians and civic leaders, he is proud of the battle he and his organization recently won against the entrenched property tax dodgers in his state, including the likes of Dow, Exxon Mobil, and others who he says have long been feeding at the public trough.

A few years ago, Bagert and others began looking into why Louisiana, rich in natural resources, and with unprecedented access to the Gulf of Mexico and its refinery and shipping capacity, ranked dead last on the *U.S. News and World Report*'s ranking of "State Well-Being." Part of the answer, Bagert discovered, was the dismal level of tax revenue, and the main culprit was multinational chemical and energy corporations that had enjoyed a property-tax-free life in Louisiana for decades, paying no property taxes on their oil refineries and other processing facilities.

The story goes back to 1936, when the legislature established the Louisiana State Board of Commerce and Industry to approve property tax exemption requests through its Industrial Tax Exemption Program. Until recently, this entity routinely approved almost every application that came its way. According to the findings of Together Louisiana, in the previous decade, the state gave up $16.7 billion in revenue to these corporations. "I knew we were on to something when I saw that those numbers were starting with a 'B' for billion, not 'M' for million," Bagert said.[74]

In 2016, Together Louisiana took the fight to the legislature, arguing that struggling school districts, police departments, and other public service entities should have a say in whether these companies get property tax exemptions. They also insisted that such tax giveaways be tied to some kind of job creation metric, noting:

> ...31,150 permanent jobs...were created by the companies receiving the subsidies, which calculates to $535,343 per job. Lost local revenue over the past 10 years cut into law enforcement and corrections by $316.6 million, parish governments by $281 million, libraries by $75 million, roads by $60.5 million, and levees by another $27.8 million. The $587 million in tax revenue lost to local school districts is more than three times the $185 million needed to pay for universal pre-kindergarten statewide.[75]

The job creation issue has been an ongoing one. According to investigative reporting by *The Advocate*, a local newspaper, Exxon Mobil profited from over a half-billion dollars in tax exemptions, while cutting almost 1,900 jobs.[76]

Thanks to the efforts of Together Louisiana, the situation has changed. Governor John Bel Edwards issued an executive order in June 2016, making changes to the Board's practices. "Beginning today," the announcement read, "Louisiana Economic Development (LED) will create Cooperative Endeavor Agreements for each ITEP [tax exemption] application, with local governments (parish governing bodies, municipal governing bodies, school boards, and sheriffs) providing input on the percentage of tax exemption to be granted, based upon the...economic impact of each project. Each manufacturer applying for the exemption also must agree to create new jobs beyond existing employment, retain existing jobs, or both."[77]

Much to the shock and dismay of the corporations involved, school districts and other public entities now help determine whether tax breaks are given out. But actual outcomes may change slowly. In November 2018, in the first test of the new rules, the Calcasieu Parish School Board in Western Louisiana granted $2 billion in tax exemptions requested by a liquefied natural gas facility. One of the school board members said, sheepishly, "Should we have negotiated with them? Maybe. But the benefits of them coming far outweigh the risk of haggling with them and having them go to Corpus Christi or Houston, or even Lafayette."[78]

On the other hand, in January 2019, the East Baton Rouge Parish school board turned down a $3 million tax exemption request from Exxon Mobil. Now more school districts around the state are recognizing the benefits of denying the exemptions so that everyone pays their fair share. In response, the corporations in 2019 were gathering support for a 2020 run for governor by Eddie Rispone, who vowed to overturn the new rules.

The High Cost of Corporate Welfare

If you're a believer in low taxes—as we are—you may wonder how much damage is really done by the various tax breaks we've described in this chapter. But the cause of overall lower taxes is actually *harmed* when governments provide selective breaks to favored businesses.

Scholars at the Mercatus Center at George Mason University have calculated how much corporate and personal tax rates could be reduced in various states if corporate tax incentives were eliminated. In their 2018 report The Opportunity Cost of Corporate Welfare, the authors found that in almost every state, eliminating corporate incentives could lead to the reduction of major tax burdens on state taxpayers:

> Several states, including Missouri and New York, could reduce their corporate tax rates by more than 90 percent if policymakers eliminated corporate incentives. Michigan, Nebraska, and Oklahoma could completely

eliminate corporate taxation and still have room for cuts in other taxes if they eliminated all corporate incentives.

Lawmakers in Louisiana, Michigan, and Nebraska could reduce their states' personal income tax rates by 14.2, 10.8, and 16.2 percent, respectively, if they eliminated corporate incentives. Tennessee lawmakers could reduce their state's personal income tax rate by nearly 98 percent if they eliminated all corporate incentives...

Taxpayers in Nebraska could enjoy a 23.2 percent reduction in their sales tax rate if state lawmakers eliminated corporate incentives. Similarly, if lawmakers in New York eliminated corporate incentives, they could reduce the state sales tax rate by 34.1 percent. More dramatically, Michigan state lawmakers could reduce their state sales tax rate by 49.3 percent in the absence of corporate incentives. [79]

Why should ordinary citizens, small to mid-sized businesses, and start-up companies be stuck with higher tax rates to compensate for corporate welfare lavished on giant firms with political and lobbying clout? The answer is plain as day—they shouldn't.

1   Eli Rosenberg, "An Angry Historian Ripped the Ultrarich Over Tax Avoidance at Davos. Then One Was Given the Mic.," *The Washington Post*, January 31, 2019, Business, https://www.washingtonpost.com/business/2019/01/31/an-angry-historian-ripped-ultra-rich-over-tax-avoidance-davos-then-one-was-given-mic/?utm_term=.ed376f5dd3d9.

2   Tom Metcalf and Suzanne Woolley, "'We Are Part of the Problem': Billionaires and Heirs Demand Wealth Tax," Bloomberg, June 24, 2019, https://www.bloomberg.com/news/articles/2019-06-24/billionaires-from-soros-to-pritzker-heirs-call-for-wealth-tax.

3   David Gelles, "They're Rich and They're Mad About Taxes (Too Low!)," *The New York Times,* February 12, 2019, https://www.nytimes.com/2019/02/12/business/rich-people-against-tax-cut.html.

4   Isaac Stanley-Becker, "Disney's CEO Made 1,424 Times as Much as His Employees. An Heir to the Disney Fortune Thinks That's 'Insane.'," *The Washington Post*, April 22, 2019, Morning Mix, https://www.washingtonpost.com/nation/2019/04/22/disneys-ceo-made-times-much-his-employees-an-heir-disney-fortune-thinks-thats-insane/?utm_term=.cbfff2140e36.

5   Teresa Ghilarducci, "Why Some of the Rich Want to Pay More Taxes," *Forbes*, February 11, 2019, https://www.forbes.com/sites/teresaghilarducci/2019/02/11/why-some-of-the-rich-want-to-pay-more-taxes/#38f6194b6cf9.

6   Kimberly Amadeo, "Trump's Tax Plan and How It Affects You," *The Balance*, June 25, 2019, https://www.thebalance.com/trump-s-tax-plan-how-it-affects-you-4113968.

7   Jugal K. Patel and Alicia Parlapiano, "The Senate's Official Scorekeeper Says the Republican Tax Plan Would Add $1 Trillion to the Deficit," *The New York Times*, December 1, 2017, https://www.nytimes.com/interactive/2017/11/28/us/politics/tax-bill-deficits.html.

8   Kathryn Watson, "'You All Just Got A Lot Richer,' Trump Tells Friends, Referencing Tax Overhaul," CBS News, December 24, 2017, https://www.cbsnews.com/news/trump-mar-a-lago-christmas-trip/.

9   Chris Edwards, "The Senate Tax Bill Favors the Middle Class, Not the Rich," Cato Institute, December 5, 2017, Commentary, https://www.cato.org/publications/commentary/senate-tax-bill-favors-middle-class-not-rich.

10   Chris Edwards, "Taxing Wealth and Capital Income," Tax and Budget Bulletin, no. 85 (August 1, 2019), https://www.cato.org/publications/tax-budget-bulletin/taxing-wealth-capital-income.

11   James B. Stewart, "A Tax Loophole for the Rich That Just Won't Die," *The New York Times*, November 9, 2017, https://www.nytimes.com/2017/11/09/business/carried-interest-tax-loophole.html.

12   James Surowiecki, "Special Interest," *The New Yorker*, March 7, 2010, https://www.newyorker.com/magazine/2010/03/15/special-interest-2.

13   Donald Trump, Chris Christie, Ted Cruz, Julianna Goldman, Michael Scherer, Anne Gearan, Manu Raju, Ruth Marcus, and Ken Burns, interview by John Dickerson, *Face the Nation*, August 23, 2015, https://www.cbsnews.com/news/face-the-nation-transcripts-august-23-2015-trump-christie-cruz/.

14   Alan Rappeport, "Trump Promised to Kill Carried Interest. Lobbyists Kept It Alive," *The New York Times*, December 22, 2017, https://www.nytimes.com/2017/12/22/business/trump-carried-interest-lobbyists.html.

15 Victor Fleischer, "How A Carried Interest Tax Could Raise $180 Billion," *The New York Times*, June 5, 2015, https://www.nytimes.com/2015/06/06/business/dealbook/how-a-carried-interest-tax-could-raise-180-billion.html.

16 "Raise the Tax Rates on Long-Term Capital Gains and Qualified Dividends by 2 Percentage Points," Congressional Budget Office, December 8, 2016, https://www.cbo.gov/budget-options/2016/52249.

17 "Gross Private Domestic Investment," FRED, 2019, https://fred.stlouisfed.org/series/GPDI.

18 Chris Edwards, Advantages of Low Capital Gains Tax Rates," Tax & Budget Bulletin, no. 66 (December 2012), https://www.cato.org/sites/cato.org/files/pubs/pdf/tbb-066.pdf.

19 Christine Smith, "Why Economists Don't Like the Mortgage Interest Deduction," *Open Vault Blog*, May 9, 2018, https://www.stlouisfed.org/open-vault/2018/may/why-economists-dont-like-mortgage-interest-deduction.

20 Kathy Frankovic, "People Are Unwilling to See Tax Deductions Go Even If They Don't Benefit from Them," YouGov, October 30, 2017, https://today.yougov.com/topics/politics/articles-reports/2017/10/30/tax-deductions-are-hard-part.

21 Drew DeSilver, "The Biggest U.S. Tax Breaks," Pew Research Center, April 6, 2016, https://www.pewresearch.org/fact-tank/2016/04/06/the-biggest-u-s-tax-breaks/.

22 Gina Pogol, "How the Mortgage Interest Tax Deduction Lowers Your Payment," The Mortgage Reports, July 20, 2017, https://themortgagereports.com/30247/how-the-mortgage-interest-tax-deduction-lowers-your-payment; Ric Edelman, *The Truth About Money* (Harper Collins, 2003).

23 Scott Eastman, "The Home Mortgage Interest Deduction," Tax Foundation, October 15, 2019, https://taxfoundation.org/home-mortgage-interest-deduction/.

24 Matthew Desmond, "How Homeownership Became the Engine of American Equality," *The New York Times*, May 9, 2017, https://www.nytimes.com/2017/05/09/magazine/how-homeownership-became-the-engine-of-american-inequality.html?action=click&pgtype=Homepage&region=CColumn&module=MostViewed&version=Full&src=mv&WT.nav=MostViewed&_r=0.

25 Derek Thompson, "The Shame of the Mortgage-Interest Deduction," *The Atlantic*, May 14, 2017, Business, https://www.theatlantic.com/business/archive/2017/05/shame-mortgage-interest-deduction/526635/.

26 Kathy Orton, "Federal Government Spends More Subsidizing Homeowners Than It Does Helping People Avoid Homelessness," *The Washington Post*, October 11, 2017, Where We Live, https://www.washingtonpost.com/news/where-we-live/wp/2017/10/11/the-federal-government-spends-more-than-twice-as-much-subsidizing-homeowners-as-it-does-helping-people-avoid-homelessness/?utm_term=.735942f18218.

27 Erica York, "Nearly 90 Percent of Taxpayers Are Projected to take the TCJA's Expanded Standard Deduction," Tax Foundation, September 26, 2018, https://taxfoundation.org/90-percent-taxpayers-projected-tcja-expanded-standard-deduction/.

28 William G. Gale, "Chipping Away at the Mortgage Deduction," *Wall Street Journal*, April 9, 2019, https://www.wsj.com/articles/chipping-away-at-the-mortgage-deduction-11554851420.

29 Chris Edwards, "Repealing the Federal Estate Tax," Tax and Budget Bulletin, no 36 (June 2006), https://www.cato.org/sites/cato.org/files/pubs/pdf/tbb-0606-36.pdf.

30 Karlyn Bowman, "Eliminating the Estate Tax: Where is the Public?" *Forbes*, October 31, 2017, https://www.forbes.com/sites/bowmanmarsico/2017/10/31/eliminating-the-estate-tax-where-is-the-public/#6bbb52db4607.

31 Isabel V. Sawhill and Eleanor Krause, "American Workers Need a Pay Raise - the Estate Tax Could Help," The Brookings Institute, November 2, 2017, Social Mobility Memos, https://www.brookings.edu/blog/social-mobility-memos/2017/11/02/american-workers-need-a-pay-raise-the-estate-tax-could-help/.

32 "Giving Statistics," Charity Navigator, 2019, https://www.charitynavigator.org/index.cfm?bay=content.view&cpid=42.

33 Timothy P. Carney, "The Trump Foundation and Abuse of Both Power and Privilege," *Washington Examiner*, December 19, 2018, Opinion, https://www.washingtonexaminer.com/opinion/columnists/the-trump-foundation-and-abuse-of-both-power-and-privilege.

34 Alan Feuer, "Trump Ordered to Pay $2 Million to Charities for Misuse of Foundation," *The New York Times*, November 7, 2019, https://www.nytimes.com/2019/11/07/nyregion/trump-charities-new-york.html.

35 David A. Fahrenthold, "This is the Portrait of Donald Trump That His Charity Bought for $20,000," *The Washington Post*, November 1, 2016, Politics, https://www.washingtonpost.com/news/post-politics/wp/2016/11/01/this-is-the-portrait-of-himself-that-donald-trump-bought-with-20000-from-his-charity/?utm_term=.d1bbc9d959de.

36 Regina Mullen, "There's Never Been a Better Time to Claim R&D Tax Credits in the US: Here's Why," *Replicon*, August 4, 2017, https://www.replicon.com/blog/theres-never-better-time-claim-rd-tax-credits-us-heres/.

37 Jason J. Fichtner and Adam N. Michel, "Can a Research and Development Tax Credit Be Properly Designed for Economic Efficiency?" Mercatus Center, July 2015, https://www.mercatus.org/system/files/Fichtner-R-D-Tax-Credit.pdf.

38 "IRS 'Dirty Dozen' List of Tax Scams for 2018 Contains Warning to Avoid Improper Claims for Business Credits," IRS, March 13, 2018, https://www.irs.gov/newsroom/irs-dirty-dozen-list-of-tax-scams-for-2018-contains-warning-to-avoid-improper-claims-for-business-credits.

39 Jason J. Fichtner and Adam N. Michel, "The Research and Development Tax Credit Suffers from Design and Implementation Problems," Mercatus Center, August 5, 2015, https://www.mercatus.org/publication/research-and-development-tax-credit-suffers-design-and-implementation-problems; Gene Marks and Ben Gran, "7 Myths About the Research and Development Tax Credit for Small Business Owners," *The Hartford*, March 7, 2017, updated August 26, 2019, https://sba.thehartford.com/finance/7-myths-about-the-research-and-development-tax-credit/.

40 Matthew Gardner, "Amazon in Its Prime: Doubles Profits, Pays $0 in Federal Income Taxes," Institute on Taxation and Economic Policy, February 13, 2019, https://itep.org/amazon-in-its-prime-doubles-profits-pays-0-in-federal-income-taxes/?ftag=MSFd61514f.

41 Megan Cerullo, "Big Companies Paying Little to No Federal Income Tax," CBS News, March 4, 2019, https://www.msn.com/en-us/news/other/big-companies-paying-little-to-no-federal-income-tax/ar-BBUlrI1.

42 Sarah Kleiner, "A Controversial Tax Incentive for Racehorse Owners Is Back on Track," The Center for Public Integrity, https://apps.publicintegrity.org/tax-breaks-the-favored-few/#racehorse-owners.

43 John Dunbar, "Congress Gives NASCAR A Boost with A Tax Break for Improving Speedways," The Center for Public Integrity, https://apps.publicintegrity.org/tax-breaks-the-favored-few/#racetracks.

44 Lateshia Beachum, "Starkist Stands to Gain from American Samoa Tax Credit," The Center for Public Integrity, https://apps.publicintegrity.org/tax-breaks-the-favored-few/#starkist-company.

45 Dave Levinthal, "Congress Packed Budget Bill with Special Breaks for Washington Insiders," The Center for Public Integrity, March 13, 2018, https://apps.publicintegrity.org/tax-breaks-the-favored-few/.

46 Larry Kosmont (Chairman and CEO, Kosmont Companies), interview by Lisa Conyers, April 2019, Manhattan Beach, California.

47 Noah Buhayar, "Florida Paradise Offers Wealthy Developers a Big Trump Tax Break," Bloomberg, April 12, 2019, https://www.bloomberg.com/news/features/2019-04-12/lefrak-s-florida-sol-mia-is-headed-for-a-big-trump-tax-break.

48 Buhayar, "Florida Paradise Offers Wealthy Developers a Big Trump Tax Break."

49 Alan H. Peters and Peter S. Fisher, "State Enterprise Zone Programs: Have They Worked?" Upjohn Institute for Employment Research, 2002, https://doi.org/10.17848/9781417524433.

50 Scott Eastman and Nicole Kaeding, "Opportunity Zones: What We Know and What We Don't," Tax Foundation, January 8, 2019, https://taxfoundation.org/opportunity-zones-what-we-know-and-what-we-dont/.

51 Ruth Simon and Richard Rubin, "As States Pick 'Opportunity Zones' for Tax Breaks, A Debate Over Who Benefits," Wall Street Journal, March 20, 2018, https://www.wsj.com/articles/will-new-tax-incentives-for-poor-communities-work-some-are-skeptical-1521547201.

52 Scott Eastman, "Measuring Opportunity Zone Success," Tax Foundation, May 29, 2019, https://taxfoundation.org/measuring-opportunity-zone-success/.

53 Ray Gibbs (Executive Director, Forward High Point) and Sandy Dunbek (Executive Vice President, High Point Economic Development Corporation), interview by Lisa Conyers, North Carolina, February 2019.

54 Andrew Ross Sorkin, "Tax the Rich? Here's How to Do It (Sensibly)," The New York Times, February 25, 2019, DealBook, https://www.nytimes.com/2019/02/25/business/dealbook/taxes-wealthy.html?searchResultPosition=1.

55 Adam Looney, "Abuse of Tax Deductions for Charitable Donations of Conservation Lands Are on the Rise," Brookings Institute, June 1, 2017, https://www.brookings.edu/research/abuse-of-tax-deductions-for-charitable-donations-of-conservation-lands-are-on-the-rise/.

56 "Conservation Easements: More in Charities and Nonprofits," Internal Revenue Service, updated March 26, 2019, https://www.irs.gov/charities-non-profits/conservation-easements.

57 Adam Looney, "Estimating the Rising Cost of a Surprising Tax Shelter: The Syndicated Conservation Easement," Brookings Institute, December 20, 2017, Up Front, https://www.brookings.edu/blog/up-front/2017/12/20/estimating-the-rising-cost-of-a-surprising-tax-shelter-the-syndicated-conservation-easement/.

58 Richard Rubin, "Donald Trump's Donations Put Him in Line for Conservation Tax Breaks," Wall Street Journal, March 10, 2016, https://www.wsj.com/articles/donald-trumps-land-donations-put-him-in-line-for-conservation-tax-breaks-1457656717#livefyre-comment.

59 Peter Elkind, "The Billion-Dollar Loophole," *Fortune*, December 20, 2017, https://fortune.com/2017/12/20/conservation-easement-tax-deduction-loophole/.

60 Jim Zarroli, "As Trump Built His Real Estate Empire, Tax Breaks Played a Pivotal Role," NPR, May 18, 2017, https://www.npr.org/2017/05/18/528998663/as-trump-built-his-real-estate-empire-tax-breaks-played-a-pivotal-role.

61 Charles V. Bagil, "A Trump Empire Built on Inside Connections and $885 Million in Tax Breaks," *The New York Times*, September 17, 2016, https://www.nytimes.com/2016/09/18/nyregion/donald-trump-tax-breaks-real-estate.html?_r=1.

62 Allan Dodds Frank, "Trump Organization Seeks Hefty Tax Break for Westchester Golf Club," ABCNews, June 21, 2017, https://abcnews.go.com/Politics/trump-organization-seeks-hefty-tax-break-westchester-golf/story?id=48179222.

63 Frank, "Trump Organization Seeks Hefty Tax Break for Westchester Golf Club."

64 Steve Eder and Ben Protess, "Developers Seek $6 Million Tax Break for Trump-Managed Hotel," *The New York Times*, February 9, 2018, https://www.nytimes.com/2018/02/09/business/trump-hotel-mississippi-tax-break.html?hp&action=click&pgtype=Homepage&clickSource=story-heading&module=first-column-region&region=top-news&WT.nav=top-news.

65 Matt Drangle, "How Business Connections and Political Ties Helped Launch Trump's Newest Line of Hotels," *Forbes*, July 18, 2017, https://www.forbes.com/sites/mattdrange/2017/07/18/how-business-connections-and-political-ties-helped-launch-trumps-newest-line-of-hotels/#3c3d685b6260.

66 Patrick Michels, "Free Lunch," *The Texas Observer*, https://www.texasobserver.org/chapter-313-texas-tax-incentive/.

67 Olga Garza and Annet Nalukwago, "Chapter 313: Attracting Jobs and Investment, State Law Aims at Local Development," Fiscal Notes, April 2016, https://comptroller.texas.gov/economy/fiscal-notes/2016/april/chap313.php.

68 Nathan Jensen, "Texas Chapter 313 Program: Evaluating Economic Development Strategies," University of Texas at Austin, http://www.natemjensen.com/wp-content/uploads/2017/02/Jensen_TEXAS-CHAPTER-313-PROGRAM-2-Pager.pdf.

69 Michels, "Free Lunch."

70 Heather Jordan, "How Much Money Did Dow CEO Andrew N. Liveris Make in 2016?" *Mlive*, May 10, 2017, https://www.mlive.com/news/saginaw/2017/05/ceo_pay_report_shows_dows_live.html.

71 Rye Druzin, "South Texas School Board Approves $531 Million in Tax Breaks for Exxon Plant," *San Antonio Express-News*, March 22, 2017, updated January 9, 2018, https://www.expressnews.com/business/eagle-ford-energy/article/South-Texas-school-board-approves-1-2-billion-in-11021080.php.

72 Bob Sechler, "Senate Panel Weighs Future of State's Tax Abatement Law," *Statesman*, April 18, 2017, updated September 25, 2018, Business, https://www.statesman.com/business/20170418/senate-panel-weighs-future-of-states-tax-abatement-law.

73 Broderick Bagert (leader, Together Louisiana, Downtown New Orleans), interview by Lisa Conyers, January 2019.

74 Bagert, interview.

75 "Costly and Unusual: An Analysis of the Industrial Tax Exemption Program (ITEP), With Amounts of Foregone Revenue by Locality/Public Service and Public Cost Per Job Created.," Together Louisiana, Appendix B, http://togetherla.com/wp-content/uploads/2016/06/3_Appendix-B_Cost-to-every-parish-and-jurisdiction.pdf.

76 Rebekah Allen, "Louisiana's Costliest Incentive Program Allowed Manufacturing Companies to Cut Jobs While Saving Billions in Taxes," *The Advocate*, December 16, 2017, https://www.theadvocate.com/baton_rouge/news/politics/article_41faa140-d861-11e7-9ec8-83e329aeda19.html.

77 "Gov. Edwards Ties Industrial Tax Breaks to Job Creation and Local Approval (press release)," Office of the Governor, June 24, 2016, http://gov.louisiana.gov/news/gov-edwards-ties-industrial-tax-breaks-to-job-creation-and-local-approval.

78 Richard Fausset, "A School Board Says No to Big Oil, and Alarms Sound in Business-Friendly Louisiana," *The New York Times*, February 5, 2019, https://www.nytimes.com/2019/02/05/us/louisiana-itep-exxon-mobil.html.

79 Matthew D. Mitchell and Tamera Winter, "The Opportunity Cost of Corporate Welfare," Mercatus Center, May 22, 2018, https://www.mercatus.org/publications/corporate-welfare/opportunity-cost-corporate-welfare.

Do Banks Need Uncle Sam as Their Sugar Daddy?

It is well enough that people of the nation do not understand our banking and monetary system, for if they did, I believe there would be a revolution before tomorrow morning.

—Henry Ford

anking is so ingrained in our daily lives that it often escapes notice that the industry represents the third largest sector of our economy. Only real estate (which involves a lot of banking) and state and local government rank higher.[1] What's more, over time, this huge industry has become both bigger and more concentrated. In 1985, over 16,000 banks managed just over $2 trillion in assets. By 2000, the number of banks had been reduced by half, while the volume of deposits had doubled.[2] Today fewer than five thousand banks manage $10 trillion in deposits.

That means a lot of wealth and power in relatively few hands—which, as we've already seen in this book, creates plenty of potential for abuse. That potential came to fruition in a big way in the midst of the 2008 recession.

TARP and Too Big to Fail

In October 2008, with a major financial crisis in full swing, the U.S. government acted. The Democrat-controlled Congress passed and Republican President Bush signed into law the Troubled Asset Relief Program (TARP), which bailed out the big banks and their CEOs and rescued many from bankruptcy. TARP became the biggest corporate bailout in history—courtesy of American taxpayers, of course.

The lawmakers were motivated by fears that the financial crisis might trigger an economic collapse as devastating as the Great Depression of the 1930s. The recession that actually ensued wasn't that bad—but it was bad enough. A decade later, the Federal Reserve reported that the recession had reduced United States GDP by 7 percent and reduced the average lifetime earnings of Americans by over $70,000 each.[3] The crisis cost 8.7 million Americans their jobs and ten million Americans their homes.[4]

Whether the recession would have been worse (or perhaps less bad) without TARP and the other government-sponsored bailouts will remain a hotly debated topic for years to come. But there's no doubt that the bailouts raise huge questions about the relationship between government and the financial industry—especially the nation's biggest, richest, and most powerful banks.

In 2019, the research organization ProPublica stated, "Altogether, accounting for both the TARP and the Fannie and Freddie Mae bailout, $632B has gone out the door—invested, loaned, or paid out—while $390B has been returned."[5] They went on to note that the Treasury continues to earn interest on outstanding debt, and those earnings have offset the remaining deficits. That news has led many to believe that the bailout has been fully repaid, at no cost to the taxpayer. But that accounting understates the enormous risks involved in extending $700 billion in loans and bailout money, especially the unsecured loans to some of the weaker banks.

The story of the BB&T Bank provides excellent insights into the nature of the 2007 financial crisis and the often-haphazard ways the government dealt with it.

Headquartered in Winston-Salem, North Carolina, BB&T was headed by Chairman and CEO John Allison. In 2007, the bank held assets of $132 billion, making it one of the largest in the country. It was also one of the banks that was forced to receive bailout money under the TARP program. A 30-year veteran of BB&T leadership, Allison weathered the crisis at the helm of that company. Since his retirement in 2009, he has thought and written a lot about the bailouts. His 2013 *New York Times* bestseller, *The Financial Crisis and the Free Market Cure,* provides an insider's account of what led up to the crisis, why the bailouts were a terrible idea, and what needs to happen to avoid another collapse. Hailed as one of the five best books written on the crisis, it was also the only book to focus on the central role played by the government.

We met with Allison on a sunny winter day in 2019, on the campus of Wake Forest University in Winston-Salem, North Carolina, in the carriage house that is home to the University's Eudaimonia Institute. Noted Allison, "Eudaimonia—Greek for happiness or human flourishing—is a reference to Aristotle, of whom I'm very fond."[6]

Having shed his CEO mantle at BB&T in 2009, and then guided Washington D.C.'s preeminent libertarian think tank, the Cato Institute, through a successful leadership transition from 2012 through 2015, Allison has now retired to a life of writing and teaching. He seems to have shed a few years in the process. He appeared youthful, cheerful, and upbeat as he shared stories from the 2007–2008 crisis.

"The primary cause of the Great Recession was a massive mis-investment in residential real estate," Allison said, in his soft-spoken gentleman's drawl. "We built too many houses, too large houses, and houses in the wrong places. The over-investment in residential real estate was more than three trillion dollars." This was caused by the government's insistence that mortgage loans be made available to a riskier and riskier pool of buyers—buyers with no or bad credit, and buyers with no savings. Noted Allison:

> Much of this was driven through the rules forced on lenders by the 1977 Community Reinvestment Act, legislation that was intended to increase homeownership among those of lower income, and to combat inequality

in the housing market. The consequence of this act was a weakening of lending rules, including those that normally call for verification of income level, credit history and savings history—the very financial facts that alert banks to risky borrowers. The federally guaranteed Fannie Mae and Freddie Mac corporations became the de-facto enforcers of these relaxed lending rules, with predictable results.

It used to be that buyers had to come to the table with twenty percent down to buy a house. And then the government got involved. They decided that every American should be able to live the American dream of homeownership, and expanded lending by allowing for riskier and riskier buyers to get loans.[7]

Allison went on to observe, "Look, twenty percent is not a magic number, but what that twenty percent savings process did was instill in buyers a habit of saving, and it also insured that they had some equity in their home."[8] In his book, Allison details how Americans' access to easy mortgage terms, and the fallacious arguments from lenders that a house was equivalent to a savings account, explain the rapid over-investment in housing leading up to the crunch. Banks began bundling bad loans and good loans together and selling them to investors. The crisis was slowly developing—driven in large part, as Allison and others have pointed out, by misguided government policies.[9]

What annoys Allison most is the way the bailout played out. During the course of 2007 and early 2008, it had become increasingly clear that there were headwinds in the economy. Having helped to blanket the country in mortgage debt, abetted by federal government mortgage lending rules that encouraged lending to Americans who had no business taking on mortgage loans and other credit, banks found themselves at their day of reckoning. At 11:00 a.m. on Wednesday, September 18, 2008, Henry Paulson, the treasury secretary, and Ben Bernanke, the chair of the Federal Reserve, appeared before Congress and told them that $5.5 trillion in wealth would disappear by 2:00 p.m. that day unless Congress intervened and rescued the banks. Bernanke shocked the room when he stated that there was a possibility that there wouldn't be an economy at all by Monday. "That meeting was one of the most astounding experiences I've had in my 34 years in politics," Senator Charles Schumer of New York later recalled.[10]

It took a couple of weeks of political horse-trading, but on October 3, 2008, the bailout was approved. The Troubled Asset Relief Program (TARP) bailed out several banks whose failure was deemed likely to cause unacceptable distress to the banking system and the economy. Taxpayers provided the $700 billion that guaranteed the solvency of America's "too big to fail" banks.

What happened to BB&T during the crisis was remarkable. "The day the legislation passed," Allison told us, "I got a call from the bank regulators, who told me that they wanted BB&T to participate in the TARP program. I was vehemently opposed. BB&T was a strong, healthy bank that did not need, nor did we want, to take government money." Allison paused, a look of annoyance crossing his face. "Well, they said, there would be new rules coming out in the next few days, and they were concerned that under these new, arbitrary, secret rules that they couldn't share with us, our finances wouldn't look good and they would then be forced to intervene, so we should probably just join the TARP program right then and there. The message was clear. We were being threatened with a fabricated failure if we didn't participate. So we said okay, sign us up."

That decision went on to cost BB&T $100 million in interest. Furthermore, the much stricter rules imposed on all the banks after the crisis forced BB&T to withdraw its support from a number of otherwise viable business clients who subsequently—and unnecessarily—went out of business.

"An interesting question is why the Federal Reserve wanted the healthy banks to participate in TARP," says Allison. "[Bernanke] believed…if the healthy banks participated, the market would not see the program as a bailout…it would be seen as an industry rescue… Therefore, the Fed effectively forced all banks with a hundred billion dollars and over to participate."

The bailouts maintained the lifestyles of well-off bankers even while risking billions of taxpayer assets. One former trader at Citibank, one of the major bailed-out banks, featured in an *Atlantic Monthly* article in 2016, assumed that the crisis would cost him his job at Citibank, but the bailout changed that. Instead of catastrophe, normal business resumed. "When our stock fell below three dollars per share," he said, "I texted my wife, 'ready to become farmers?' [But] I didn't have to become a farmer, and neither did anybody around me. Thanks to a government bailout, not only didn't we lose our jobs, but we also got paid well over the next few years. Really well."[11]

Should the government have intervened in the market? John Allison doesn't think so:

> Sure, some of those banks would have failed. And good riddance. The bad actors would have been gone, and the rest of us could have moved on. Instead, the bailouts of badly managed banks kept those banks afloat, ignoring the problem. This is what happens when the government intervenes in the market. It just makes things worse. In the case of the banks, those who had the ear of Paulsen and Bernanke were able to convince them to help their banks out, and they made all the rest of us victims of this crony behavior. It was stupid…
>
> Was saving Goldman and AIG about systems risk or about crony capitalism? The government just picked the winners and losers. Save Bear Stearns, let Lehman go. Save Citigroup, let Wachovia and Washington Mutual go. And they protected Goldman Sachs.

(We might note that Hank Paulson, the Secretary of the Treasury, who drove these decisions, also had close ties to Goldman-Sachs, where he had earned over $16 million as Goldman's CEO in 2006.)

"One reason Wall Street has such a bad reputation," Allison continued, "is because of the connection between Wall Street and the U.S. government. Unfortunately, Goldman is the ultimate crony capitalist… Goldman makes huge contributions to political parties and politicians. Many Goldman alumni are in various high-level policy positions in Washington…Crony capitalism is caused by politicians."

In 2018, ten years after the TARP bailouts, Americans were asked what they thought of the program. When asked if they thought "too big to fail" was still a problem, 72 percent said yes. Sixty-eight percent believe that rescuing of any industry increases the likelihood of future bailouts, and 75 percent believe that earlier bailouts in the decades before the TARP bailouts led to an expectation that the government would always bail out industries in trouble. Fifty-nine percent believe that the bailouts served primarily shareholders and management, while only 11 percent believe they helped consumers.

Clearly, American taxpayers do not have faith that government has fixed the problem, or that it should be in the bailout business.[12]

The Export–Import Bank—Government Lending With No Meaningful Purpose

The 2008 bailout illustrated the privileged position enjoyed by the biggest private banks in America. But they're not the only financial institutions with a hand in the taxpayers' pockets. There are government-sponsored banks that represent equally egregious examples of welfare for the well-to-do.

Founded in 1934, the Export-Import Bank (Ex-Im) is a taxpayer-funded bank tasked with promoting the export of U.S.-made goods and services. The bank gives subsidized financial support to U.S. firms that export to foreign markets, and to foreign buyers who use the loans to purchase American exports. It is a very small player in the import/export world, involved in only 0.3 percent of American foreign trade, but it nonetheless deploys many billions of dollars and has historically enjoyed the support of Congress—despite the fact that an examination of who benefits from the Ex-Im Bank reveals that the bank often works *against* taxpayer interests and the interests of America overall.

First, notice that Ex-Im funding has often gone to countries most Americans view as, at best, potential adversaries of the U.S. For instance:

> *Russia.* In 2012, Vnesheconombank (VEB), a Russian state-owned bank, secured $1.2 billion in Ex-Im

loan guarantees. This is the same Russian bank that President Obama sanctioned after Russian interference in Ukraine. Pete Hegseth, CEO of Concerned Veterans of America, wrote in a 2019 piece for *USA Today*, "VEB has an operating agreement with Russian arms dealer Rosoboronexport—which is responsible for more than 80% of Russian weapons exports—to 'promote exports of Russian military products and boost their competitive edge in the world market'...The company is the primary source of arms to Syria's Bashar al-Assad, and has also sent advanced weapons systems to Iran."[13]

Saudi Arabia. In 2012, a $5 billion loan—the largest ever granted through the Ex-Im Bank—was awarded to Sadara Chemical Company, a joint venture between Dow Chemical and the Saudi Arabian Oil Company, a state-owned oil company. Former Florida Senator Bob Graham, in 2019, asserted that "terrorism financing originating in Saudi Arabia has been a significant source of funds for international terrorist organizations, including al-Qaeda."[14] The same year, the CIA concluded that the crown prince of Saudi Arabia ordered the killing of American journalist Jamal Kashoggi.[15] American taxpayers are thus on the hook for $5 billion in loans to a major financier of terrorism and a regime comfortable suppressing free speech by murdering journalists.

On the corporate side, the Ex-Im bank has shown a special fondness for channeling funds to giant companies that logically would seem to be far too wealthy to need help from the taxpayers. A couple of examples:

Boeing. The giant aircraft manufacturer is the Ex-Im bank's biggest client and cheerleader.[16] Over the 2007–2017 decade, 34 percent of all the aid provided by Ex-Im went to foreign airlines with contracts to buy planes from Boeing. But Boeing hardly needs the help; in 2018, with no help from the Ex-Im bank, Boeing enjoyed its best year ever, with worldwide sales of $101.1 billion. No wonder the Ex-Im bank has been nicknamed "Boeing's Bank."

The largesse to Boeing is especially egregious, considering that many U.S. airlines view the support provided to foreign carriers as damaging to their interests. Former Delta Air CEO Richard Anderson long fought the special relationship between Boeing and the Ex-Im bank, and opposes using taxpayer dollars to help subsidize Delta's competition.[17] And in 2015, Mark Dunkerley, CEO of Hawaiian Airlines' holding company, called loans to the likes of Emirates, Korean Air, and Turkish Airlines "a complete unwarranted subsidy to the injury of U.S. airlines."[18]

> *Caterpillar.* Caterpillar is another major recipient of Ex-Im aid. In 2013, the bank authorized almost $700 million in loan guarantees to Australian mining company Roy Hill to purchase equipment from Caterpillar.[19] Caterpillar has a net worth of $22.7 billion and is on the *Forbes* Global 2000 list of world's largest companies, while the Roy Hill Corporation earned $558 million in 2018. Clearly, neither company should need taxpayer help.

"The Export-Import Bank is naked corporate welfare," asserted former Senator Ron Paul in 2002. "It never ceases to amaze me how members of Congress who criticize welfare for the poor see no problem with the even more objectionable programs that provide welfare for the rich."[20]

Efforts have been made over the years to shut down the Ex-Im Bank. For three years, beginning in 2015, the bank did not have its quorum of five board members, the minimum required to authorize loans over $10 million. This hiatus ended in 2019 when President Trump and Congress re-energized the bank, filling the empty seats. But the hiatus itself offered some fascinating evidence regarding the value of Ex-Im's work. As noted by Veronique de Rugy, a scholar with the Mercatus Institute at George Mason University, writing in *The New York Times*:

For the fiscal years from 2014 to 2018, approvals by the bank fell to $3.6 billion from $21 billion…a good proxy for an Ex-Im-less world…If Ex-Im's supporters are correct, this extreme drop in corporate financial aid should have caused exports to fall. But in fact, exports rose to a record $2.5 trillion in the 2018 fiscal year, from $2.3 trillion in the 2014 fiscal year.

In other words, America's international export market performed just fine without the bank's help. Further, de Rugy continued:

This evidence strongly suggests that Ex-Im has no effect on total exports—a finding consistent with an extensive body of economic literature showing that export subsidies have a negligible effect on the overall level of exports in such a large economy. …[even] in its heyday, Ex-Im backed less than 2 percent of United States exports (that figure has since dropped to 0.3 percent).[21]

So why does the Ex-Im Bank continue to exist if its effectiveness is negligible, at best? Lobbying clearly plays a major role.

When President Trump was a candidate, he promised to get rid of the Ex-Im Bank, and in 2017, he even nominated former Representative Scott Garrett, a staunch opponent of the bank, to serve as its president, hoping Garrett would use the role to dismantle the bank. However, Congress shot that nomination down. Then, in an abrupt about-face, in May 2019, President Trump nominated Kimberly Reed as bank president and former Rep. Spencer Bachus and Judith DelZoppo Pryor as board members. Congress approved them all, giving the bank back its quorum.[22] This allows the bank to go back to authorizing expenditures over $10 million, letting the big boys back in the game.

What happened to change the attitude of the Trump administration? It's impossible to prove a cause-and-effect relationship. But according to the *Washington Post*, when the bank was being threatened with closure, "Both the National Association of Manufacturers and Boeing, two of the most vocal forces pressuring lawmakers to renew the bank, spent more

on lobbying in 2015 than any other year going back at least 17 years…
General Electric, another staunch Ex-Im supporter, spent $21 million
on lobbying that year."[23]

We agree with the critics of the Ex-Im Bank. It's an example of crony
capitalism at its worst, and it should be abolished.

OPIC and Associates—Scandal-Plagued Government Lenders

Ex-Im isn't the only case of government-backed banking that channels taxpayer funds to the already-prosperous. The U.S. International
Development Finance Corporation (USIDFC) was created in 2018
by merging the former Overseas Private Investment Corporation
(OPIC) with the Development Credit Authority of the U.S. Agency
for International Development (USAIDCA). By the end of 2019,
USIDFC will be tasked with managing $60 billion in taxpayer dollars
for loans, grants, and guarantees to countries and private corporations
around the world.

Both OPIC and USAIDCA are notorious for perpetrating boondoggles on the taxpayer dime. These include a $58 million loan to a Jordanian
businessman who said he planned to build a hotel and apartments across
the street from the American Embassy in Kabul, Afghanistan—only to
abandon the projects after most of the funds were wasted. The unfinished
hotel in Kabul, initially funded in 2009, was the subject of an Inspector
General (IG) investigation into "troubling management practices and
lax oversight" on the part of OPIC.[24] The final IG report noted, "OPIC
did not regularly visit the site or provide consistent on-site monitoring
during the construction of either the hotel or apartment building…and
instead relied on information provided by the loan recipients regarding
the status of the projects…"[25] As a result, the $85 million in loans is
gone, the buildings were never completed and are uninhabitable, and the
U.S. Embassy is now forced to provide security for the site at additional
cost to U.S. taxpayers.

Another OPIC fiasco involved a $1 billion loan to five solar farms
(2013) and a hydroelectric dam (2014) in Chile that were unable to
attract funding by other investors, and ultimately failed. This project was

the subject of another blistering IG report, which not only questioned OPIC's ability to manage these specific projects, but concluded that OPIC did not have the management skills or capacity to manage *any* of their projects, stating, "OPIC lacks the business practices necessary to ensure it upholds its statutory requirements…"[26] In other words, OPIC is not up to the task of responsibly managing taxpayers' funds.

USAIDCA, meanwhile, is responsible for a $5.5 billion lending budget that provides foreign assistance to support development objectives through the Development Credit Authority (DCA) which guarantees loans designed to generate additional lending to underserved markets.[27] It has been plagued with scandals, corruption, and investigations for decades.[28]

Those who pay for these costly failures, of course, are American taxpayers. Pending the merger with the USAIDCA, OPIC continues to grant funds to questionable projects, including a $200 million toll road outside Santiago, Chile; a $270 million commitment to the development and construction of a Central Spent Nuclear Fuel Storage Facility located in the Chornobyl Exclusion Zone in the Ukraine; and $450 million in commitments to CitiBank for banking insurance coverage in Pakistan, Jordan, and Egypt.[29] None of these countries or projects would likely impress American taxpayers looking for an investment return on their dollars.

Congress has repeatedly pushed Ex-Im and OPIC to provide more support for small business enterprises, activities that have much wider public support than financing America's giant corporations. Have these government banks responded by moving in that direction?

To answer that question, in June 2019, we attended the two-day U.S. Commercial Service U.S.-Caribbean Business Conference jointly hosted by the District Export Council of South Florida and the Department of Commerce's U.S. Commercial Service, which is touted as the premier international business conference for U.S. businesses that desire to do business in the region.[30] Representatives from Ex-Im bank and OPIC attended. There, we learned that there is little to no support for small businesses in this network.

Here's an illustrative story. Thory Coquillo, CEO of Krysko International, LLC, a small business start-up out of New Jersey, came to the conference seeking funds to start an agricultural enterprise on the island of Haiti. "We need $1.5 million to get started, for equipment, seeds and fertilizers, and improvements to the buildings," he told the authorities.

On the morning of the second day, Coquillo met Elio Muller, an experienced hand at Ex-Im and OPIC financing. Muller pulled no punches. "You have a $1.5 million budget?" he told Coquillo. "You aren't going to get any help from OPIC or Ex-Im, or really anyone here. They aren't cut out for projects like yours."

Coquillo was crestfallen. "But I was told by the State Department that I should come here and line up assistance."

Muller scoffed. "I can't speak to that, but I can tell you that unless you have a project worth $10 million at the very least, they aren't in a position to help you. I can tell you, I worked at OPIC for a long time, and Ex-Im and OPIC and the other development banks don't do small projects, and yours is a small project."[31]

This story played out several times during the course of the conference. Over and over again, we saw energetic younger entrepreneurs shot down, while representatives from big companies, including LNG Allies and Solar Axiom, got support.

These government lending institutions are not needed. The great majority of U.S. exports are managed without them; they do little or nothing for small enterprises; they often foster corruption and incompetence; and on more than one occasion, they have worked against U.S. interests. They should be abolished.

1   Benjamin Elisha Sawe, "The Biggest Industries in the United States," *WorldAtlas*, https://www.worldatlas.com/articles/which-are-the-biggest-industries-in-the-united-states.html.
2   ILSR, "Number of Banks in the U.S., 1966-2017," Institute for Local Self-Reliance (graph), May 14, 2019, https://ilsr.org/number-banks-u-s-1966-2014/.
3   Stephen Grenville, "What Did the 2008 Crisis Cost America?" *The Interpreter*, August 23, 2018, https://www.lowyinstitute.org/the-interpreter/what-did-2008-crisis-cost-america; Regis Barnichon, Christian Matthes, and Alexander Ziegenbein, "The Financial Crisis at 10: Will We Ever Recover?" Federal Reserve Bank of San Francisco, August 13, 2018, Economic Research, https://www.frbsf.org/economic-research/publications/economic-letter/2018/august/financial-crisis-at-10-years-will-we-ever-recover/.
4   Jim Puzzanghera, "A Decade After the Financial Crisis, Many Americans Are Still Struggling to Recover," *The Seattle Times*, September 10, 2018, updated September 11, 2018, Nation & World, https://www.seattletimes.com/nation-world/a-decade-after-the-financial-crisis-many-americans-are-still-struggling-to-recover/.
5   Paul Kiel and Dan Nguyen, "Bailout Tracker: Tracking Every Dollar and Every Recipient," ProPublica, February 25, 2019, https://projects.propublica.org/bailout/.
6   John A. Allison (former Chairman and CEO, BB&T), interview by Lisa Conyers, Winter 2019, Wake Forest University; Raleigh, North Carolina.
7   John A. Allison, *The Financial Crisis and the Free Market Cure: Why Pure Capitalism is the World Economy's Only Hope*, (New York: The McGraw-Hill Companies, 2013), 9.
8   John A. Allison (former Chairman and CEO, BB&T), interview by Lisa Conyers, Winter 2019, Wake Forest University; Raleigh, North Carolina.
9   Yaron Brook, "The Government Did It," *Forbes*, July 18, 2008, https://www.forbes.com/2008/07/18/fannie-freddie-regulation-oped-cx_yb_0718brook.html#da4c1e6364b4.
10 Andrew Ross Sorkin et al., "As Credit Crisis Spiraled, Alarm Led to Action," *The New York Times*, October 1, 2008, https://www.nytimes.com/2008/10/02/business/02crisis.html.
11 Chris Arnade, "What Breaking Up the Banks Wouldn't Fix," *The Atlantic*, February 19, 2016, Business, https://www.theatlantic.com/business/archive/2016/02/too-big-too-fail-kashkari/464184/.
12 "New Survey: Americans Believe Washington Has Not Learned the Hard Lessons from Bailouts-A Decade Later," Charles Koch Institute, September 19, 2018, https://www.charleskochinstitute.org/news/tarp-bailouts-anniversary/.
13 Pete Hegseth, "Ex-Im Bank's Phony 'National Security' Cred: Column," *USA Today*, May 14, 2015, Opinion, https://www.usatoday.com/story/opinion/2015/05/14/export-import-bank-economy-security-column/27188991/.
14 Bob Graham and Pionnula Ni Aolain, "Saudi Arabia Still Isn't Doing Enough to Fight the Financing of Terrorism," *The Washington Post*, February 19, 2019, Opinions, https://www.washingtonpost.com/opinions/global-opinions/saudi-arabia-still-isnt-doing-enough-to-fight-the-financing-of-terrorism/2019/02/19/bdb300d4-3454-11e9-a400-e481bf264fdc_story.html.
15 Shane Harris, Greg Miller, and Josh Dawsey, "CIA Concludes Saudi Crown Prince Ordered Jamal Khashoggi's Assassination," *The Washington Post*, November 16, 2018, National Security, https://www.washingtonpost.com/world/national-security/cia-concludes-saudi-crown-prince-ordered-jamal-khashoggis-assassination/2018/11/16/98c89fe6-e9b2-11e8-a939-9469f1166f9d_story.html.

16 Allen Benjamin Johnson III, "America's Corporate Welfare Bank Is Forced to Tighten Its Belt," *Morning Consult*, April 4, 2018, Opinion, https://morningconsult.com/opinions/americas-corporate-welfare-bank-is-forced-to-tighten-its-belt/.

17 Gillian Rich, "Boeing, GE, Caterpillar Overseas Sales Hopes Just Got A Big Lift," *Investor's Business Daily*, May 8, 2019, News, https://www.investors.com/news/export-import-bank-quorum-bank-of-boeing-ge-caterpillar/.

18 Jon Ostrower, "Delta CEO Reiterates Objections to Ex-Im Bank Widebody-Jet Financing: Richard Anderson Also Warns of 'Huge Bubble' in Single-Aisle Jets," *Wall Street Journal*, June 24, 2014, https://www.wsj.com/articles/delta-head-warns-of-single-aisle-jet-bubble-1403651272.

19 Lawton King, "Ex-Im Bank Approves $694 Million to Finance Export of U.S. Mining and Rail Equipment to Australia," Export-Import Bank of the United States (press release), December 19, 2013, https://www.exim.gov/news/ex-im-bank-approves-694-million-finance-export-us-mining-and-rail-equipment-australia.

20 James T. Bennet, *Corporate Welfare: Crony Capitalism That Enriches the Rich,* (New York: Routledge, 2017).

21 Veronique de Rugy, "Corporate Welfare Wins Again in Trump's Washington," *The New York Times*, May 7, 2019, Opinion, https://www.nytimes.com/2019/05/07/opinion/export-import-bank-trump-corporate-welfare.html.

22 Alex Gangitano, "Biz Group Takes Victory Lap on Ex-Im Bank," *The Hill*, May 10, 2019, https://thehill.com/business-a-lobbying/business-a-lobbying/443000-biz-groups-take-victory-lap-on-ex-im-bank.

23 Catherine Ho, "Ex-Im Backers Spent Record Amounts Lobbying Government in 2015," *The Washington Post*, January 28, 2016, PowerPost, https://www.washingtonpost.com/news/powerpost/wp/2016/01/28/ex-im-backers-spent-record-amounts-lobbying-government-in-2015/.

24 Rebecca Hersher, "How $85 Million Failed to Build a Swanky Hotel in Kabul," NPR, November 17, 2016, https://www.npr.org/sections/thetwo-way/2016/11/17/502428985/how-85-million-failed-to-build-a-swanky-hotel-in-kabul.

25 John F. Sopko, "SIGAR-17-13-SP Review Letter: Abandonment of OPIC Projects in Kabul," Office of the Special Inspector General for Afghanistan Reconstruction, November 14, 2016, https://www.sigar.mil/pdf/special%20projects/SIGAR-17-13-SP.pdf.

26 "OPIC Investments Increased Chile's Energy Capacity, but Weak Processes and Internal Controls Diminish OPIC's Ability to Gauge Project Effects and Risks (audit report 9-OPC-19-002-P)," Office of Inspector General; U.S. Agency for International Development, February 1, 2019, https://www.oversight.gov/sites/default/files/oig-reports/9-OPC-19-002-P.pdf.

27 "DCA One-Pager for Financial Partners," Development Credit Authority, https://www.usaid.gov/sites/default/files/documents/1865/DCA_One-Pager_2018.pdf.

28 Jake Johnston, "USAID Failing to Ensure Sustainability of Programs in Haiti, Says GAO Report," Center for Economic and Policy Research, June 4, 2015, http://cepr.net/blogs/haiti-relief-and-reconstruction-watch/usaid-failing-to-ensure-sustainability-of-programs-in-haiti-says-gao-report.

29 "Active OPIC Projects," OPIC, https://www.opic.gov/opic-action/active-opic-projects.

30 "U.S. Commercial Service U.S.-Caribbean Business Conference," District Export Council of South Florida and the Department of Commerce's U.S. Commercial Service (paper brochure), June 2019.

31 Thory Coquillo (CEO, Krysko International, LLC) and Elio Muller (former employee, PIC), interview by Lisa Conyers, June 2019.

10.

Lobbying—The Right of Which People?

We have the best government money can buy.

—Mark Twain

We are a nation of factions—groups of citizens with divergent interests, beliefs, values, and policy preferences. Making government work while balancing and addressing the often-conflicting demands of factions is an inherent challenge to democracy. George Washington warned of the dangers of political factions, and James Madison, recognizing that factions are inevitable ("The latent causes of faction are...sown in the nature of man"), also wrote of their dangers.[1]

Today's factions—often referred to as special interests—are different in their particulars from the ones the founders anticipated. But the existence of intensive lobbying by factions ranging from Boeing and Exxon to the AARP and the American Medical Association would probably not surprise them. What *would* surprise the founders is the size of the federal government that the lobbyists importune. Washington takes in and spends over 20 percent of all the wealth produced by Americans each year. That reality, more than any other factor, drives the scope of special interest lobbying.

After all, the $3.4 billion spent on lobbyists jostling for favors from the federal government constitutes less than one tenth of one percent of the money spent annually by the federal government, and an even smaller fraction of America's annual corporate profits.

In a $4 trillion federal budget, the number of opportunities to profit from minor changes, additions, or tweaks is staggering. Re-designation of one one-hundredth of one percent of the Social Security budget, for example would move more than $90 million to an enterprising lobbyist's client yet would be practically invisible in the budget. When the opportunities for making so much money are so great and so numerous, intensive lobbying is inevitable. Indeed, for some companies, lobbying may be essential for defense against government actions.

Thus, we shouldn't blame professional lobbyists for doing what they are paid to do. There is nothing insidious or inherently unethical about openly representing a special interest. The problem is that the federal government's tentacles reach into nearly every corner of the economy (as well as other facets of our lives). Given the fact that there are 27 million businesses in the U.S., 1.5 million nonprofits, and thousands of associations, all with interests that inevitably collide, it's no wonder that the lobbying landscape has become so complex, so costly, and so pervasive.

Lobbying has grown and proliferated to the point where it is strangling the legislative process (Figure 10-1). Jonathan Rauch likens this environment to the busy activity on a forest floor: "Congressmen are at the mercy of the intricate ecology that surrounds them. It is the aphids and earthworms and dung beetles and termites and algae, the busy little creatures all in their niches—the farm lobbies and veterans lobbies and real-estate lobbies and education lobbies and a million other species—that shape the jungle's topography."[2]

Some additional perspective: The $3.4 billion annual lobbying cost represents over $6 million for each member of Congress, and the presence of more than 11,000 registered lobbyists means that there are twenty or more lobbyists per representative.[3] And lobbying efforts are not confined to Congress. Lobbyists also deal with such federal agencies as the Environmental Protection Agency (EPA), the U.S. Department of Agriculture (USDA), The Federal Trade Commission (FTC), the Federal Communications Commission (FCC), the Occupational Safety and

Health Administration, (OSHA), the Consumer Financial Protection Bureau (CFPB), the Securities and Exchange Commission (SEC), and several hundred others. In fact, no one is quite sure how many federal agencies there are. USA.gov lists thirty-seven independent executive agencies and 268 units in the cabinet, while other estimates vary.[4]

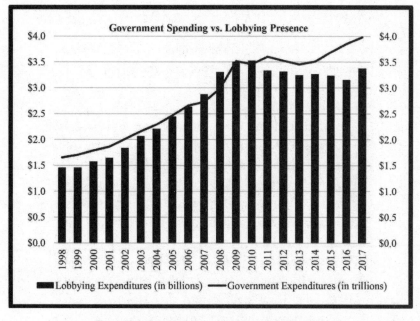

Figure 10-1: Comparative growth of government spending
and lobbying expenditures, 1998-2017.
Source: The White House, and Statista, 2019

What's more, registered lobbyists do not work alone. There are many more unregistered players—consultants, attorneys, and advisers who do much of the same work while trying to avoid violating the rules that would require them to register. So there's plenty of fuel to feed all that activity on the forest floor.

A major contributing factor to this teeming landscape is that laws and regulations have been accumulating for decades—even centuries— and new laws and regulations are added every year. But old programs almost never die. As economist Milton Friedman once observed, there is nothing so permanent as a temporary program in Washington. "Like

barnacles attaching to a rock, government programs and subsidies…
almost never go away," notes Lee Drutman, in his book *The Business of
America is Lobbying.*[5] A graphic example comes from Rauch's description
of what has happened to the federal government's wool and mohair subsidies. They were introduced during World War II to assure sufficient
wool and mohair for military uniforms, but over the years they have
morphed into widely derided boondoggles. Then:

> In 1993, a remarkable thing happened. Congress…
> managed to eliminate the wool and mohair subsidy…
> [E]ffective on December 31, 1995, the National Wool
> Act was repealed.
>
> Well, that didn't seem entirely fair, now did it?
> So in April 1996, Congress passed a new farm bill,
> whose Section 759 was titled "National Sheep Industry
> Improvement Center." This, it turned out, was an entity
> empowered with up to $50 million of federal funds to
> "enhance production and marketing of sheep or goat
> products in the United States" and to "design unique
> responses to the special needs of the sheep or goat indus-
> tries on both a regional and national basis." [Further],
> in 1998, the Texas people and the Mohair Council
> of America slipped into a giant appropriations bill, a
> provision letting mohair growers take out interest-free
> federal loans.[6]

And since that time? As of 2018, the National Sheep Industry
Improvement Center, headquartered in Rockland, Maryland, was alive
and well, benefitting from a $50 million revolving fund, and the Mohair
Council of America has set up shop in San Angelo, Texas, near the herds
of angora goats that benefit from the Council's largesse.

Are these programs necessary? Of course not. But they will almost
certainly last for decades to come, like thousands of other government
programs that benefit one or another of our nation's countless factions.
Most of those programs have spawned lobbying efforts designed largely

to keep them functioning, whether or not the original need or rationale for the program still exists, and regardless of the cost to taxpayers.

For this reason, there is actually more lobbying effort expended to prevent changes in government policies or programs than to create innovations. "[T]he most important reason for lobbying," Drutman found, "is preserving the status quo."[7] "Most people hire lobbyists because they want to stop the government from doing something that will harm their business," adds former lobbyist Jack Abramoff.[8]

Who Plays the Lobbying Game?

The tendency of lobbying to protect the status quo is exacerbated by the size of most corporations that lobby. Most are big companies that have adapted successfully to the existing set of rules and carved out their own pieces of the government pie. No wonder they don't want change—and will lobby hard to prevent it.

Lobbying is a competitive sport. A given rule or law may favor one company, industry, or other group, while harming others. Thus, there is a defensive element to lobbying. "If you're not at the table, you're probably on the menu" has become a cliché in the lobbying world.

Trade associations (such as the U.S. Chamber of Commerce and the National Association of Retailers) and private corporations dominate the lobbying industry, along with a few nonprofits (for example, the Open Society Policy Center and Citizens United).

Major corporations, especially those with high profiles, sometimes have little choice.

Microsoft learned this the hard way. Hoping to stay out of politics, back in 1990s, Microsoft had only a one-person lobbying shop located in a shopping mall in suburban DC. But then, goaded by lobbyists from Microsoft's competitors, the Justice Department filed an anti-trust suit against the firm in 1998, forever disabusing company executives of the idea that they could stay out of the political game.[9] "Today," notes F.H. Buckley, author of *The Republic of Virtue*, "Microsoft has one of the biggest government-relations offices in Washington, having discovered that every business in a crony nation is in partnership with the federal government, and woe to those who forget it."[10]

But surprisingly, only a very small percentage of businesses have lobbyists in Washington. Even among publicly traded corporations—generally America's biggest firms—90 percent do not employ federal lobbyists.[11] When you add in privately-held companies, sole proprietorships, S-Corps, and LLCs, there are about 33 million American businesses, only a minuscule fraction of whom engage in lobbying.[12]

The fact is that most businesses don't need to lobby. Unless a federal law is passed or a rule is promulgated that directly impacts their business, most managers simply won't be bothered with tracking activity in Washington—nor need they. And some larger businesses avoid lobbying on principle. Lee Drutman reports his discussions with several corporate CEOs, who have a "true disdain for government…The last thing that they would do is to get involved in D.C."[13] Ryan Young at the Competitive Enterprise Institute believes that part of the reason is that most businessmen have a sense of fairness. "[M]ost (but not all) businessmen and entrepreneurs have a sense of virtue and honor that prevents them from seeking special favors. It is much more satisfying to make an honest living than a dishonest one."[14]

The distance separating the overwhelming majority of American businesses from the political game may be an important characteristic of the U.S. economy. While a few hundred of our biggest firms are jostling at the trough in Washington (or, in many cases, merely trying to keep the government out of their hair), most of the activity driving economic progress is outside the lobbying world. That seems like a very good thing.

The Case Against Lobbying

Lobbying has had its defenders. In 1956, then-U.S. Senator John F. Kennedy pointed out some positives of lobbying. "[L]obbyists are, in many cases, expert technicians and capable of explaining complex and difficult subjects in a clear, understandable fashion," Kennedy observed. "…the lobbyists who speak for the various economic, commercial, and other functional interests of this country serve a very useful purpose and have assumed an important role in the legislative process."[15]Lobbyist Robert Raben defends lobbying, noting that, in recent decades, lobbying has become more democratized. With increasing instances of "grassroots and grasstops leaders" working in communities, Raben contends that lobbying "is core to our nation's democracy."[16]

We agree that the increase in grassroots lobbying is healthy and that lobbying offers some important pluses. If lawmakers are going to enact rules that will impact industry, it's important for them to hear from business experts who can explain the likely real-world impact of those rules. But the lobbying process as it has evolved in contemporary America is still rife with trouble.

One big problem is that lobbying substantially abets a great many bad programs and policies. We have already seen a number of examples. There's a sugar program pumping undeserved profits to sugar growers— so there's a sugar lobby to defend the program. As power plants switch from coal to cleaner natural gas, the coal lobby springs into action. When Sen. John McCain and many others tried to end the expensive and dysfunctional Jones Act, lobbyists thwarted the effort. In the majority of cases, lobbyists can keep almost any program or policy functioning no matter how bad the program or policy may be.

A related problem is that lobbying's complexity and below-the-radar strategies make much of lawmaking invisible to the public, seldom serving the public good. Thanks in part to the unseen efforts of lobbyists, many legislative changes are carried out by way of patches and grafts on existing laws—seemingly minor revisions that their proponents often try to enact with little fanfare. Author Steven Teles calls this approach "kludgeocracy," a kludge being "an ill-assorted collection of parts." Teles adds that corporations and lobbyists "are most likely to get their way when political issues are out of the public gaze...Policy complexity is valuable for those seeking to extract rents from government because it makes it hard to see just who is benefitting and how."[17]

When Jack Abramoff was looking for a change in federal law that would permit the Tigua Indian tribe, an important client of his, to open a casino in Texas, Abramoff looked for a low-profile fix. "I need legislative language we can slip into a bill," he told an associate. "Something so cryptic, so enigmatic, so opalescent, that it would take a computer to discern what we were trying to do." His colleague handed him a piece of paper that read: "Public Law 100-89 is amended by striking section 207 (101 Stat. 668,672)."

"It was a thing of beauty," says Abramoff. "No one would know that these abstruse words would magically open the doors to the Tigua casino."[18]

Finally, although advocating for the interests of a particular group of citizens is not in itself unethical, lobbying is subject to and sometimes invites ethical, moral, and legal violations.

The very nature of lobbying makes this true. The "special interests"—Madison's factions—want something from government, and they hire lobbyists to get it. If I want something from you, I'll have an incentive to provide you with favors. If what I want is worth a great deal of money, I will be tempted to shower you with very generous favors. Sure enough, for many years, lobbyists provided members of Congress with expensive travel packages, meals, VIP-box seating at sporting events, vacation retreats, and other largesse.

In 2007, Congress enacted the Honest Leadership and Open Government Act (HLOGA), which restricts these practices. But the pressure on lobbyists to capture Congresspersons' votes, and therefore the temptation to resort to underhanded tactics, is always there. Factor in campaign contributions and fundraising events hosted by special interest lobbyists and their clients—which are generally legal—and it is easy to see why so many Americans think of the lobbying game as sleazy.

In defense of these practices, it's often asserted that generous campaign contributions may "buy access" to lawmakers, but rarely buy changes in votes or policies.[19] That may be so, but the distinction is permeable. When wealthy Farm Bill beneficiaries get involved in political campaigns, for example, it's hard to tell access from policy. The subsidized farmers who ended up on Jeb Bush's "Iowa Farm Team" during the 2015 primary election cycle were high-powered, high-income donors assembled to bring Iowa voters into Jeb Bush's camp. Their success in fulfilling that goal was undoubtedly helped by the $9.2 million in farm subsidies this group of fourteen raked in at the expense of American taxpayers from 2010–2014.

Wisconsin Governor Scott Walker's "Leadership Team" during the same election cycle had the same mission and included many farmers from the Environmental Working Group list of wealthy farmers. The largest subsidy recipient on Walker's election teams pulled in $1,367,891 in agricultural subsidies during 1995–2012; another got over $800,000. Such cozy relationships between legislators and Farm Bill beneficiaries are unquestionably also a way of influencing policy.

Similarly, the sugar industry gave over $5 million to members of Congress the 2014–15 election cycle. As David Guest, an attorney with Earthjustice who has fought the major sugar companies for over twenty years, noted in a 2011 interview, "Big Sugar trades cash in the form of campaign donations for political favors in the form of subsidies...They are unlike any other industry in Florida in that they aren't in the agricultural business, they are in the corporate welfare business."[20] While this conclusion may be oversimplified, it is not far-fetched.

Considering all the ways lobbying impacts the legislative process, author Lee Drutman believes that lobbying is undermining American democracy. If current lobbying trends continue, he writes, "American democracy will continue to decline."[21]

From Legislators to Lobbyists: The Revolving Door Problem

Perhaps the most denigrated practice in the world of lobbying is the process by which Congressional representatives and staff members are themselves attracted to the profession of lobbying after they leave the government—the so-called revolving door phenomenon. Lobbying companies' boasts about the previous government experience of their partners reveals how important this is. For example, the lobbying firm Ogilvy Government Relations asserts that "All of our partners have served in senior-level positions throughout the legislative and executive branches of the federal government. In addition, many have played key roles in presidential and congressional campaigns."[22]

Numbers reveal the extent of the problem. As Lee Drutman reports, "[B]etween 2001 and 2011, almost 5,400 former congressional staffers had registered as lobbyists"[23] The lure is enticing. Experienced and well-connected lobbyists earn on the order of $300,000 a year, with the possibility of much more.

One might argue that it's only reasonable, and perhaps even laudable, for lobbying firms to want to hire people with government experience. Bertram Levine, a former lobbyist for Johnson & Johnson, and more recently a Fellow at Colgate University, notes that the majority of the lobbyists who had formerly served in government "really respected the institution. They were truthful and had a solid understanding of the system, and they came with an institutional memory. That was especially valuable."[24]

But it's easy to see that a representative or a congressional staff member who knows they could one day be trading in their government paycheck for a much larger salary from a lobbying firm might well be inclined to pay particularly respectful attention to the arguments made by lobbyists for or against a controversial bill. The revolving door encourages legislative officials and lobbyists to think of themselves as members of "the same team," with personal financial interests that are ultimately aligned. No wonder author F. H. Buckley argues that the hope or expectation of a highly paid lobbying job is inherently corrupting for congresspersons and their staffs.[25] Former lobbyist Jack Abramoff agrees, calling the revolving door "the greatest source of corruption in government."[26]

Efforts have been made to limit the revolving door phenomenon. The 2007 HLOGA Act, which restricts lobbyists' gift-giving, requires that senators wait two years after leaving office before lobbying Congress. It also mandates that top-level House and Senate staffers must wait a full year after leaving the Hill before they can lobby their former colleagues. But despite these restrictions, the problem persists. In 2017, *The LA Times* noted that ex-congressmen were becoming "stealth lobbyists," citing a study that showed that twenty-nine of 104 former legislators and staffers were already involved in influencing legislation, most without actually registering as lobbyists. One way around the HLOGA restrictions is simply not to register. As the *LA Times* explained, "To be formally considered a lobbyist, for example, an ex-legislator must be engaged in lobbying activities for 20% or more of his or her time for an individual client. So by spreading their services among many clients, or by providing 'strategic advice' rather than 'lobbying services,' any ex-lawmaker can evade the ban."[27]

F. H. Buckley has also noted the inadequacy of the legal restrictions. "[T]he cooling off periods of a year or two are entirely too short," he says. "When the most recent period expired in 2015, about 30 percent of the former congressmen and staffers had already begun work in corporate government-relations departments or as registered lobbyists."[28]

What To Do?

Dozens of other fixes have been suggested to clean up or otherwise improve the lobbying game. The proposals include stricter rules against the revolving door (for example, prohibiting congresspersons from ever becoming lobbyists); making campaign contributions anonymous, so members of Congress can't know who funded their campaigns; and improving the salaries of congressional staff, thereby reducing the allure of a post-government lobbying career.

But at the end of the day, the only sure way to reduce the scope and intensity of the lobbying enterprise is to reduce the amount of government spending. That could begin with killing off bad programs; eliminate subsidies for rich farmers, and kill the Jones Act and the Sugar program. Cancelling programs that a majority of unbiased economists agree are dysfunctional would save several hundred billion dollars yearly and reduce the power of the lobbying game considerably.

A variation on this would devolve control over many of the federal governments' programs to the states. Some years ago, Alice Rivlin, who served as vice chairman of the Federal Reserve Board during the Clinton administration, proposed a plan under which "the federal government would cede to the states control of most or all programs in education, job training, economic development, housing, transportation, social services, and some other fields."[29]

Such a plan would have substantial advantages. However, it would require Congress to give up some of its power, and would make it more difficult for it to meddle in the lives of American citizens. Perhaps that could happen in the same year that the wool and mohair subsidies are permanently eliminated.

1 "Federalist No. 10 (1787)," Bill of Rights Institute, https://billofrightsinstitute.org/founding-documents/primary-source-documents/the-federalist-papers/federalist-papers-no-10.

2 Jonathan Rauch, *Government's End: Why Washington Stopped Working* (New York: Perseus Books Group, 1999); 226.

3 "Lobbying Database," OpenSecrets.org, https://www.opensecrets.org/lobby/.

4 Wayne Crews, interview with Phil Harvey, August 20, 2015.

5 Lee Drutman, *The Business of America Is Lobbying: How Corporations Became Politicized and Politics Became More Corporate* (New York: Oxford University Press, 2015), 26.

6 Rauch, *Government's End*, 140.

7 Drutman, *The Business of America Is Lobbying*, 73.

8 Jack Abramoff, *Capitol Punishment: The Hard Truth About Washington Corruption from America's Most Notorious Lobbyist* (Washington, D.C.: WND Books, 2011), 63.

9 F.H. Buckley, *The Republic of Virtue: How We Tried to Ban Corruption, Failed, and What We Can Do About It* (New York: Encounter Books, 2017), 179.

10 Buckley, *The Republic of Virtue*, 179.

11 Drutman, *The Business of America Is Lobbying*, 224.

12 Adam Grundy, "Nonemployer Statistics and County Business Patterns Data Tell the Full Story," United States Census Bureau, September 18, 2018, https://www.census.gov/library/stories/2018/09/three-fourths-nations-businesses-do-not-have-paid-employees.html.

13 Drutman, *The Business of America Is Lobbying*, 225.

14 Ryan Young, "Virtuous Capitalism, or, Why So Little Rent-Seeking?" Competitive Enterprise Institute, October 20, 2015, https://cei.org/blog/virtuous-capitalism-or-why-so-little-rent-seeking.

15 Mark Fagan, *Lobbying: Business, Law and Public Policy: Why and How 12,000 People Spend $3+ Billion Impacting Our Government* (Vandeplas Publishing, 2015), 10.

16 "Robert Raben's Approach to Lobbying Highlighted by CQ Magazine," The Raben Group, February 13, 2018, https://rabengroup.com/2018/02/robert-rabens-approach-lobbying-highlighted-cq-magazine/; Kate Ackley and Sean McMinn, "K Street Reinvents Itself in the Era of Trump," *Roll Call*, February 15, 2018, https://www.rollcall.com/news/politics/k-street-reinvents-itself-in-the-era-of-trump.

17 Steven M. Teles, "Kludgeocracy in America," *National Affairs*, Fall 2013, https://www.nationalaffairs.com/publications/detail/kludgeocracy-in-america.

18 Abramoff, *Capitol Punishment*, 198.

19 Jonathan Rauch, interview with Phil Harvey, March 30, 2018; Drutman, *The Business of America Is Lobbying*, 16.

20 Virginia Chamlee, "How Big Sugar Get What It Wants from Congress," *The Colorado Independent*, September 20, 2011, https://www.coloradoindependent.com/2011/09/20/how-big-sugar-gets-what-it-wants-from-congress/.

21 Drutman, *The Business of America Is Lobbying*, 238.

22 "Expertise," Ogilvy Government Relations, https://www.ogilvygr.com/expertise/.

23 Drutman, *The Business of America Is Lobbying*, 161.

24 Bertram J. Levine, *The Art of Lobbying: Building Trust and Selling Policy* (Washington, D.C.: CQ Press, 2009), 67.

25 F.H. Buckley, *The Republic of Virtue: How We Tried to Ban Corruption, Failed, and What We Can Do About It* (New York: Encounter Books, 2017), 188.

26 Abramoff, *Capitol Punishment,* 223.
27 Michael Hiltzik, "The Revolving Door Spins Faster: Ex-Congressmen Become 'Stealth Lobbyists'," *Los Angeles Times,* January 6, 2015, Business, https://www.latimes.com/business/hiltzik/la-fi-mh-the-revolving-door-20150106-column.html.
28 Buckley, *The Republic of Virtue,* 188.
29 Rauch, *Government's End,* 244.

11.

Joining Forces and Fighting Back

We pay the taxes that make the country run, but history shows that if we aren't watching, politicians will give our money to their friends.

—Somchai Kaisorn, Las Vegas
Taxi Driver, Thai immigrant

As we have shown in several chapters in this book—for example, our account of the recent success of Together Louisiana in chapter 6—when citizens get together and cry foul, their representatives can be persuaded to change, and sometimes to change quickly. In this chapter, we'll offer some specific advice about what you can do to help remedy the serious problems we've described throughout this book.

One step you can take is to run for public office yourself. The opportunities to serve are surprisingly numerous. There are fifty states in this country, presided over by fifty governors. But there are 3,142 counties and county-equivalents (including parishes and boroughs), 285 cities with over 100,000 people, and thousands of smaller towns and villages, each with its mayor, board of supervisors, or other elected officials. While the average citizen may not aspire to be elected to Congress, they can easily run for their county, city, or town legislature. And as we have seen, many of the corporate welfare dollars that flow to the wealthy via state and local governments were the result of targeted local lobbying and horse-trading. If self-interested people can influence policy this way, it stands to reason that a committed citizen working as a force for good can have similar success.

A reform-minded citizen serving in government can play a meaningful role in jump-starting change. But a group of citizens who band together to advocate for reform can be even more powerful. The first task is to get organized. There is no better way to reap the many benefits of community action than to rally around a common cause. We encourage you to engage with your fellow citizens on causes you care about. When such efforts help family, friends, and neighbors keep more of their hard-earned money, all the better.

There are many other ways Americans can engage as activists in the battle against welfare for the rich. They include the following:

- *Attend town meetings.* Study the advance agendas that are often posted online or in the local media, and when a new regulation or budget line is being considered that promises to feather someone's nest, show up to ask a few hard questions rather than allowing it to pass uncontested.

- *Contact your representatives and senators.* Contrary to popular belief, elected officials do care about what the voters think. Smart members of Congress know that every constituent who calls or emails with a strong opinion likely represents ten more who share the same view. When an outrageous proposal is being considered on Capitol Hill, make your feelings known. Even if you receive only a formulaic response, your opinion is almost certainly being tallied by a staff member, and if enough people weigh in, it may impact your representative's final vote.

- *Support companies that don't accept subsidies.* A bit of research can help you discover which businesses are most reliant on government largesse, and which are most self-sufficient. Try to give your business to the latter, and consider writing a letter to the CEO explaining your reason. Companies need to know that

Americans *do* care about the problem of unjustifiable government subsidies, and that many consumers are willing to vote against such subsidies with their pocketbooks.

- *Look at the benefits you personally receive from government; if you're a businessperson, look at those your company may be receiving.* Are there steps you can take to wean yourself off reliance on taxpayer support?
- *During election season, make the issue of welfare for the rich one of your priorities as a voter.* Attend campaign gatherings and ask the candidates hard, specific questions about wasteful government spending and subsidies for business. Let them know that your support will go to those with a real commitment to tackling the problem.

Get the Facts

Citizen activism is only effective when it's based on solid factual information. Thankfully, there are a number of organizations that are doing a great job of researching the complicated issues surrounding crony capitalism and other wasteful practices, and sharing their findings with the general public.

To get current data on local, state and federal spending, access these research organizations, which publish all their work online in easily accessible formats:

- Good Jobs First (www.goodjobsfirst.org) is a giant in the field of corporate welfare reform. The organization touts itself as a "national policy resource center for grassroots groups and public officials, promoting corporate and government accountability in economic development, [that provides] timely, accurate information on best practices in state and local job subsidies, [and] works with a broad spectrum of organizations, providing research, training, communications and consulting assistance."[1] Their biggest success came in 2015, when they led and won the fight for the issuance of Governmental Accounting Standards

Board Statement 77 on Tax Abatement Disclosures, a tax law that requires states and most local governments to report how much revenue they lose to economic development tax breaks (subsidies to developers). [2] Thanks to this transparency, ordinary citizens can easily access information on corporate welfare expenditures in their area, and use that information to inform the public, expose fraud, waste and abuse, and fight for change.

- Open The Books (openthebooks.com) focuses on budgetary transparency. They provide information on government spending at all levels. Open The Books prides themselves on the accessibility of their data, noting "Perhaps our most important microscope for long-term impact, we have worked to make our data easy to use, accurate, and accessible. OpenTheBooks.com is the world's largest private database of government spending. Our goal is to put every government expense—local, state, and federal—online in real time. The data is accessible via cell phone, iPad, and computer to everyone including public citizens, investigative reporters, academics, think tanks, politicians, and more."[3] If information is power, then this website can help make citizens powerful.

- The Sunlight Foundation (sunlightfoundation.com) is a national nonpartisan, nonprofit organization that uses civic technologies, including open data, to make government and politics accountable and transparent. Their goal is technology solutions that enable more complete, equitable and effective democratic participation by making changes to the law to require real-time, online transparency for all government information.[4] That means anything that any public official does will be accessible by his/her constituents, allowing for a fairer playing field.

- The Center for Responsive Politics and its website OpenSecrets.org, touts itself as "the nation's premier research group tracking money in U.S. politics and its effect on elections and public policy."[5] Their vision is for Americans to be empowered by access to clear and unbiased information about money's role in politics and policy, and to use that knowledge to strengthen our democracy. They produce and disseminate data and analysis on money in politics to inform and engage Americans, champion transparency, and expose disproportionate undue or improper influences on public policy.

All four of these organizations work with journalists, activists, and others interested in exposing government spending and actions to public scrutiny. Any citizen can use their datasets to amass information and use it pressure public officials for change. This is democracy in action, and we urge you to make use of their great stores of information.

Think Tanks—Expertise for the Public Good

America's think tanks are valuable sources of information, and they are consistent advocates for government change. We list four of them here. All are influential in Washington, and all, from Heritage on the political right to Brookings on the left, adamantly oppose the kind of crony capitalism and other forms of subsidy we describe in this book. Their scholars have expertise in a wide variety of areas; they are accessible and happy to help put their work to good use on causes they believe in.

- The Cato Institute is a libertarian public policy research organization dedicated to the principles of individual liberty, limited government, free markets, and peace. Its scholars and analysts conduct independent, nonpartisan research on a wide range of policy issues, including the constitution, law and the courts, civil liberties, government, politics and economics.[6] They have published widely on the harms caused by corporate welfare.
- The Brookings Institution, considered left of center politically, has over three hundred experts in government and academia from all over the world who provide research, policy recommendations, and analysis on a full range of public policy issues.[7] The research agenda and recommendations of Brookings's experts are rooted in open-minded inquiry; topics they cover include foreign policy, economics, development, governance and metropolitan policy.

- The Heritage Foundation is a conservative institution, promoting "an America where freedom, opportunity, prosperity, and civil society flourish."[8] The stated mission of The Heritage Foundation is to formulate and promote conservative public policies based on the principles of free enterprise, limited government, individual freedom, traditional American values, and a strong national defense.
- The American Enterprise Institute (AEI) leans right politically and is dedicated to defending human dignity, expanding human potential, and building a freer and safer world. They state, "The work of our scholars and staff advances ideas rooted in our belief in democracy, free enterprise, American strength and global leadership, solidarity with those at the periphery of our society, and a pluralistic, entrepreneurial culture."[9]

Clearly, the information you need to become an effective community activist and force for change is out there, as are people who are eager to help you along the way. If you believe that it is time for change, time to rein in government largesse to the rich, time to level the playing field and restore fairness to taxpayers who foot the bill, we urge you to tap into these resources and get started fighting back.

Recommendations on Specific Issues

In addition to the policy recommendations we've offered throughout the book, there are reforms related to specific issues that we believe deserve your support and advocacy. Here are some of the positions we recommend, together with the names of organizations that are working on behalf of those positions and deserve your support.

Licensing Reform. As discussed in Chapter 5, licensing requirements for jobs that don't need them are preventing hundreds of thousands of Americans from working at the jobs they seek. Nearly 25 percent of all jobs, from tree trimmers to decorators, require a costly license. There is simply no need to put these roadblocks in the paths of people who want to earn a living. Licensing requirements should be substantially cut back.

The Institute for Justice (IJ), which calls itself the National Law Firm for Liberty. They are leaders in the fight for reduced licensing requirements. They also work to eliminate "policing for profit"—the use of civil asset forfeiture to seize money and property from citizens, especially low-income citizens, most of whom have committed no offense. They litigate to limit the size and scope of government power and to ensure that all Americans have the right to control their own destinies as free and responsible members of society.[10]

Tax Policy. A sweeping tax reform bill proposed by several congressmen in the 1990s. It called for a flat rate of about 20 percent, with a generous standard deduction of $20,000, above which the flat 20 percent rate would apply. It also greatly simplified the tax code by eliminating virtually all deductions, thereby making it far more difficult for lawmakers or regulators to tilt the playing field for or against particular people, groups, or businesses. We favor a tax policy along these lines.

If tax policy is of specific interest to you, there are several organizations that focus on tax policies and their effects. The organizations below are good resources for those who want to learn about and change tax policy.

The Tax Policy Center (taxpolicycenter.org) is a joint venture between the Urban Institute and the Brookings Foundation, both long-established Washington D.C. think tanks which focus on public policy research and analysis. Their website offers tax data, analyses, and estimates of the effects of current and proposed legislation. It also includes in-depth data on federal, state, and local taxes. They note, "The United State faces a dismal fiscal future in part because projected revenues fall far short of anticipated spending needs…We examine the implications of current policies and proposed tax changes on the well-being of future generations."[11]

The Institution on Taxation and Economic Policy (itep.org) does research on tax issues, with a focus on the consequences of both current law and proposed changes in order to educate policymakers, advocates, the media and the general public about the fairness, adequacy and sustainability of proposed changes to federal, state, and local tax systems. They are perhaps best known for their microsimulation tax model, "a tool for calculating tax revenue yield and incidence, by income group, of federal, state, and local taxes. The ITEP model is frequently used to analyze federal and state tax proposals and to look at the impact of current tax policies on issues of public concern."[12] This allows users to see the effects of different tax scenarios—a useful tool when trying to explain how a tax law change would affect people's lives.

Term Limits for Politicians. Term limits have long been promoted as a way to reduce the kinds of cronyism that lead to government favors to the rich. U.S. Term Limits (USTL) is an organization that has focused on this issue for many years. USTL advocates for term limits at all levels of government, and has assisted in enacting term limits on state legislators in fifteen states. USTL continues to be highly active in the term limits movement. They state: "To this day, voters in states and municipalities across the country are enacting and reaffirming term limit laws one election cycle after another."

Defense Spending. The Project on Government Oversight (pogo.org) focuses on the Pentagon budget. According to POGO, "Our investigations into waste, fraud, corruption, and abuse of power allow us to find deficiencies in federal government policies, programs, and projects. Much of our focus is where government and powerful private interests intersect, a nexus where corruption and abuse of power can thrive if oversight isn't strong..." This is also the area where crony capitalism can be most damaging, with the Pentagon lavishing favors on its multi-billion-dollar contractors. POGO adds: "[Our] investigators are experts in working with whistleblowers and other sources inside the government who come forward with information that we then verify using the Freedom of Information Act, interviews, and other fact-finding strategies. We publish these findings and release them to the media, Members of Congress and their constituents, executive branch agencies and offices, public interest groups, and our supporters."

Open the Government (openthegovernment.org) provides useful tips in its Citizen's Guide, including "How to write a Letter to the Editor" and filing a FOIA (Freedom of Information Act) request. Their focus is on prying open the secrecy around America's bombing raids overseas and the civilian deaths that routinely result.

Agriculture. We favor the complete elimination of subsidy payments to farmers, except those who qualify for welfare. Failing that, at the very least, the Farm Bill should be separated from the food stamp program. Combining the two is nothing more than a cynical political ploy to keep taxpayer money flowing to megafarms and agribusiness.

Zoning Regulations should be loosened dramatically, especially in our coastal cities, so that the needed millions of additional houses and apartment units can be built, especially in areas close to public transportation.

Restraining Government Growth. Here we side with Cato's Chris Edwards, who proposed a 3 percent annual limit on the growth of the federal budget; that is, no federal budget may exceed by more than 3 percent the budget of the previous year. This simple step would do wonders for curtailing government growth and hence the growth of deficits.

Fixing the problem of welfare for the rich is a giant task. The vast apparatus that channels taxpayer funds to those who need them least has grown up over generations, and it won't be eliminated overnight. Even trimming its size is difficult because, as we've seen, each piece of the machine provides concrete benefits to powerful people, groups, or businesses who will fight hard to protect the status quo.

The good news is that the cause of combatting wasteful government spending is a popular one. According to a 2017 survey, a majority of Americans agree that the free market is the best system to generate wealth, yet they also believe that big business distorts the functioning of markets to its own advantage, and that a few rich people and corporations have too much power in this country. [13] Eliminating corporate welfare would lead to meaningful progress towards balancing the scales and placing prosperity within reach of all Americans, not just the rich. All that's needed to make it happen is to energize the majority sen-timent of American voters and demand that our elected officials pay attention. It won't be easy—but it can happen if enough of us make this cause our own.

1   "About Us," Good Jobs First, 2019, https://www.goodjobsfirst.org/about-us.
2   "About Us." Good Jobs First.
3   "About Us," Open The Books, 2019, https://www.openthebooks.com/about_us/.
4   "Our Mission," Sunlight Foundation, https://sunlightfoundation.com/about/.
5   "Our Vision and Mission: Inform, Empower & Advocate," Center for Responsive Politics, http://www.opensecrets.org/about/.
6   "About CATO," Cato Institute, 2019, https://www.cato.org/about.
7   "About Us," Brookings Institution, 2019, https://www.brookings.edu/about-us/.
8   "About Heritage," The Heritage Foundation, 2019, https://www.heritage.org/about-heritage/mission.
9   "About," American Enterprise Institute, 2019, https://www.aei.org/about/.
10 "About Us," Institute for Justice, 2019, https://ij.org/about-us/.
11 "TPC," Tax Policy Center, https://www.taxpolicycenter.org/sites/default/files/20190516_tpc_1_pager.pdf.
12 "ITEP Microsimulation Tax Model — Frequently Asked Questions," Institute on Taxation and Economic Policy, https://itep.org/modelfaq/.
13 Luigi Zingales, *A Capitalism for the People* (New York: Basic Books, 2012), 29-30.

Bibliography

"#10 Larry Page Real Time Net Worth $55.1B." *Forbes*. accessed August 9, 2019. https://www.forbes.com/profile/larry-page/#7b3d445d7893

"#40: Elon R Musk: $23.5B." *Bloomberg*. October 22, 2019. https://www.bloomberg.com/billionaires/profiles/elon-r-musk/

"#67 Richard Kinder." *Forbes*. October 22, 2019. https://www.forbes.com/profile/richard-kinder/#49cc0beb2f62

Abel, Jaison, Jason Bram, Richard Deitz, Thomas Klitgaard, James Orr, Katherine Bradley, Tricia Kissinger, Rae Rosen, and Javier Silva. "Report on the Competitiveness of Puerto Rico's Economy." Federal Reserve Bank of New York. June 29, 2012. https://www.newyorkfed.org/medialibrary/media/regional/PuertoRico/report.pdf

Abramoff, Jack. *Capitol Punishment: The Hard Truth About Washington Corruption from America's Most Notorious Lobbyist* (Washington, D.C.: WND Books, 2011).

"About CATO." Cato Institute. 2019. https://www.cato.org/about

"About Heritage." The Heritage Foundation. 2019. https://www.heritage.org/about-heritage/mission

"About Us." Brookings Institution. 2019. https://www.brookings.edu/about-us/

"About Us." Good Jobs First. 2019. https://www.goodjobsfirst.org/about-us

"About Us." Institute for Justice. 2019. https://ij.org/about-us/

"About Us." Open The Books. 2019. https://www.openthebooks.com/about_us/

"About Us." Pinnacle West Capital Corporation. http://www.pinnaclewest.com/about-us/default.aspx

"About." American Enterprise Institute. 2019. https://www.aei.org/about/

"Accountable USA — Hawaii." Good Jobs First. Major Subsidy Deals. https://www.goodjobsfirst.org/states/hawaii

Ackley, Kate, and Sean McMinn. "K Street Reinvents Itself in the Era of Trump." *Roll Call.* February 15, 2018. https://www.rollcall.com/news/politics/k-street-reinvents-itself-in-the-era-of-trump

"Active OPIC Projects." *OPIC.* https://www.opic.gov/opic-action/active-opic-projects

Adams, JoAnn. "Teachers, School Districts Take Hit While Corporate Welfare Thrives." *Courier Journal.* May 19, 2018. Opinion. https://www.courier-journal.com/story/opinion/contributors/2018/05/19/kentucky-teachers-pensions-schools-hurt-corporate-welfare-thrives/625797002/

"Advanced Energy Now 2019 Market Report." Advanced Energy Economy. https://www.advancedenergynow.org/aen-2019-market-report?utm_campaign=Press%2FMedia%20Outreach&utm_source=hs_email&utm_medium=email&utm_content=72063212&_hsenc=p2ANqtz-9Q4tlOGFZp4GYx-oXwCse1EVqBnx2dnVp3pXFH1VYzP3tuHIxe27GBHC9VhBNreTAGQ5sJ-FT64e7zt3HPUpu9LPXXD5JooDBnt9HB_G8o6-0m95k&_hsmi=72063212

"Advanced Technology Vehicles Manufacturing Loan Program." Wikipedia. https://en.wikipedia.org/wiki/Advanced_Technology_Vehicles_Manufacturing_Loan_Program

Aeppel, Timothy. "Whirlpool's Washer War Is Balancing Act for Trump." *Reuters.* October 4, 2017. https://www.reuters.com/article/us-trump-effect-trade-washers/whirlpools-washer-war-is-balancing-act-for-trump-idUSKCN1C91EL

"Agency Fees." State of Vermont Agency of Agriculture, Food and Market. https://agriculture.vermont.gov/license-and-registrations/agency-fees#33

Allen, Rebekah. "Louisiana's Costliest Incentive Program Allowed Manufacturing Companies to Cut Jobs While Saving Billions in Taxes." *The Advocate.* December 16, 2017. https://www.theadvocate.com/baton_rouge/news/politics/article_41faa140-d861-11e7-9ec8-83e329aeda19.html

Allison, Bill and Sarah Harkins. "Fixed Fortunes: Biggest Corporate Political Interests Spend Billions, Get Trillions." Sunlight Foundation.

November 17, 2014. https://sunlightfoundation.com/2014/11/17/fixed-fortunes-biggest-corporate-political-interests-spend-billions-get-trillions/

Allison, John A. *The Financial Crisis and the Free Market Cure: Why Pure Capitalism is the World Economy's Only Hope*. (New York: The McGraw-Hill Companies, 2013).

Allison, John. "Red Tape Is Strangling the Recovery." *U.S News & World Report*. October 19, 2012. https://www.usnews.com/opinion/blogs/economic-intelligence/2012/10/19/lift-the-regulatory-burden-on-small-businesses

Amadeo, Kimberly. "Trump's Tax Plan and How It Affects You." The Balance. June 25, 2019. https://www.thebalance.com/trump-s-tax-plan-how-it-affects-you-4113968

"Amazon HQ2." Wikipedia. accessed on May 31, 2019. https://en.wikipedia.org/wiki/Amazon_HQ2

"America's Most Affordable Cities." *Forbes*. accessed October 22, 2019. https://www.forbes.com/pictures/mhj45hkhe/4-houston-tx/#6b3eadb2ba01

"Americans Paid $7 Billion More For Shoes at Retail Than Needed in 2018." Footwear Distributors and Retailers of America. Tariff Reduction Initiatives. https://fdra.org/key-issues-and-advocacy/legislative-initiatives/

Amiti, Mary, Stephen J. Redding, and David Weinstein. "The Impact of the 2018 Trade War on U.S. Prices and Welfare." NBER Working Paper no. 25672. National Bureau of Economic Research. Cambridge, Massachusetts. March 2019. https://www.nber.org/papers/w25672

Anderson, Patrick. "What Trump's Budget Would Mean For South Dakota." *Argus Leader*. May 23, 2017. updated May 24, 2017. https://www.argusleader.com/story/news/2017/05/23/what-trumps-budget-would-mean-south-dakota/339573001/

Anonymous. "How the Other Half Lives." R.U. Seriousing Me? (blog), April 5th, 2012. http://www.ruseriousingme.com/2012/04/how-other-half-lives.html

Anonymous. "Is the Levi's Stadium Going to Pay Off for Santa Clara? They Seem to Have Started on a Good Path with Sponsorship Revenues, But What Does the ROI Look Like?" Quora. September 18, 2016. https://www.quora.com/Is-the-Levis-stadium-going-to-pay-off-for-Santa-Clara-They-seem-to-have-started-on-a-good-path-with-sponsorship-revenues-but-what-does-the-ROI-look-like

Arnade, Chris. "What Breaking Up the Banks Wouldn't Fix." *The Atlantic*. February 19, 2016. Business. https://www.theatlantic.com/business/archive/2016/02/too-big-too-fail-kashkari/464184/

Arp, Jason. "Anatomy of a Regional Cities Project, a Bad One." *Indianapolis Review*. July 26, 2017. http://inpolicy.org/2017/07/anatomy-of-an-eco-deco-project-a-bad-one/

Avent, Ryan. *The Gated City*. (Amazon Digital Services LLC, Kindle Single, August 31, 2001)

Bagil, Charles V. "A Trump Empire Built on Inside Connections and $885 Million in Tax Breaks." *The New York Times*. September 17, 2016. https://www.nytimes.com/2016/09/18/nyregion/donald-trump-tax-breaks-real-estate.html?_r=1

Bain, Marc. "Your Sneakers Are A Case Study in Why Trump's America-First Trade Policy Is Nonsense." *Quartz*. December 20, 2016. https://qz.com/859628/your-nike-sneakers-are-a-case-study-in-why-trumps-protectionist-america-first-trade-policy-is-nonsense/

Baker, David R. "Feds Probe Solyndra's Upbeat July Report." *SF Gate*. September 13, 2011. https://www.sfgate.com/business/article/Feds-probe-Solyndra-s-upbeat-July-report-2309983.php

Baker, John. "Revisiting the Explosive Growth of Federal Crimes." The Heritage Foundation. June 16, 2008. https://www.heritage.org/report/revisiting-the-explosive-growth-federal-crimes

Baker, Russ. "What They Don't Tell You About Oil Industry Tax Breaks." *Business Insider*. May 23, 2011. https://www.businessinsider.com/what-they-dont-tell-you-about-oil-industry-tax-breaks-2011-5

Ballard, Mark, and Gordan Russell. "Giving Away Louisiana- Fracking Tax Incentives." *The Advocate* (blog). http://www.cleanwaterlandcoast.com/giving-away-louisiana-fracking-tax-incentives/

Ballard, Mark, and Gordon Russell. "Giving Away Louisiana- Fracking Tax Incentives." *The Advocate* (blog). December 4, 2014. https://www.theadvocate.com/baton_rouge/news/article_3958382c-1062-5702-81af-d793f62c9918.html

Barnett, Ted. "ConocoPhillips Angers Senator by Declaring Tax Proposal 'Un-American'." *Political Ticker…CNN Politics* (blog). May 11, 2011.

http://politicalticker.blogs.cnn.com/2011/05/11/conocophillips-angers-senator-by-declaring-tax-proposal-un-american/

Barnichon, Regis, Christian Matthes, and Alexander Ziegenbein. "The Financial Crisis at 10: Will We Ever Recover?" Federal Reserve Bank of San Francisco. August 13, 2018. Economic Research. https://www.frbsf.org/economic-research/publications/economic-letter/2018/august/financial-crisis-at-10-years-will-we-ever-recover/

Baskt, Daren, editor. Farms and Free Enterprise: A Blueprint for Agricultural Policy (Washington, D.C.: The Heritage Foundation, 2016). http://thf-reports.s3.amazonaws.com/2016/Farms_and_Free_Enterprise.pdf

Beachum, Lateshia. "Starkist Stands to Gain from American Samoa Tax Credit." The Center for Public Integrity. https://apps.publicintegrity.org/tax-breaks-the-favored-few/#starkist-company

"Becoming a Certified & Licensed Fertilizer Applicator." Office of Indiana State Chemist. https://www.oisc.purdue.edu/pesticide/how_do_i_fert.html

Bell, Emily C. "5 Reasons You Definitely Don't Want Amazon's New Headquarters in Your City." Salon. October 21, 2017. https://www.salon.com/2017/10/21/5-reasons-you-definitely-do-not-want-amazons-new-headquarters-in-your-city_partner/

Bennet, James T. Corporate Welfare: Crony Capitalism That Enriches the Rich. (New York: Routledge, 2017).

Benson, Tim. "Steyer's Renewable Mandate Would Punish Arizona's Poor." The Heartland Institute. October 3, 2018. https://www.heartland.org/news-opinion/news/steyers-renewable-mandate-would-punish-arizonas-poor

Berezow, Alex. "Panel Power: Solar Advocates Openly Celebrate Crony Capitalism." American Council on Science and Health. May 9, 2018. https://www.acsh.org/news/2018/05/09/panel-power-solar-advocates-openly-celebrate-crony-capitalism-12941

Berman, Nat. "10 Things You Didn't Know About Chevron CEO Michael Wirth." Money Inc. https://moneyinc.com/chevron-ceo-michael-wirth/

Bernard, Zach. "'Boutique Hotel' Plans for Downtown Fort Wayne Revealed." 89.1 WBOI NPR News and Diverse Music. November

7, 2017. https://www.wboi.org/post/boutique-hotel-plans-downtown-fort-wayne-revealed#stream/0

Blackmon, David. "Oil and Gas Tax Provisions Are Not Subsidies for 'Big Oil'." *Forbes*. January 2, 2013. https://www.forbes.com/sites/davidblackmon/2013/01/02/oil-gas-tax-provisions-are-not-subsidies-for-big-oil/#4952b88252e8

"Bloomberg Billionaires Index: #11 Sergey Brin $56.8B." *Bloomberg*. accessed August 8, 2019. https://www.bloomberg.com/billionaires/profiles/sergey-brin/

Boaz, David. "The Hidden Costs of Tariffs." Cato Institute. July 9, 2018. https://www.cato.org/blog/hidden-costs-tariffs

Borrell, Brendan. "Are Proposition 65 Warnings Healthful or Hurtful?" *Los Angeles Times*. November 2, 2009. https://www.latimes.com/health/la-he-pro-con2-2009nov02-story.html

Bowman, Karlyn. "Eliminating the Estate Tax: Where is the Public?" *Forbes*. October 31, 2017. https://www.forbes.com/sites/bowmanmarsico/2017/10/31/eliminating-the-estate-tax-where-is-the-public/#6bbb52db4607

Boyd, Dan. "New Mexico Film Impact Estimated at $1.5 Billion." *Albuquerque Journal*. July 23, 2014. https://www.abqjournal.com/433752/new-mexico-film-impact-estimated-at-15-billion.html

Bracken, Amy. "A Sweet Deal: The Royal Family of Cane Benefits from Political Giving." *Aljazeera America*. July 23, 2015. http://america.aljazeera.com/multimedia/2015/7/fanjul-family-benefits-political-donations.html

Bradley, Bill. "Nike Made $25 Billion Last Year, Still Got a Tax Break from Oregon." Next City. August 16, 2013. https://nextcity.org/daily/entry/nike-had-25-billion-last-year-still-got-a-tax-break-from-oregon

Breiner, Andrew, and Alan Pyke. "How Republicans Who Took Millions in Farm Subsidies Justify Cutting Food Stamps." ThinkProgress. June 18, 2013. Climate Progress. https://thinkprogress.org/how-republicans-who-took-millions-in-farm-subsidies-justify-cutting-food-stamps-6dc850ed748a/

Brenner, Marie. "In the Kingdom of Big Sugar." *Vanity Fair*. January 5, 2011. Business. https://www.vanityfair.com/news/2001/02/floridas-fanjuls-200102

Brinson, Will. "Here's How Many NFL Owners Are Worth More Than a Billion Dollars." *CBSSports.com*. March 2, 2016. https://www.cbssports.com/nfl/news/heres-how-many-nfl-owners-are-worth-more-than-a-billion-dollars/

Bromley, Ben. "Is Erick Thohir a Billionaire? A Look at What We Know About His Finances and His Ownership of D.C. United." *SB Nation*. May 19, 2014. https://www.blackandredunited.com/opinion/2014/5/19/5731378/erick-thohir-billionaire-dc-united-stadium-inter-milan

Brook, Yaron. "The Government Did It." *Forbes*. July 18, 2008. https://www.forbes.com/2008/07/18/fannie-freddie-regulation-oped-cx_yb_0718brook.html#da4c1e6364b4

Brooks, David. "How We Are Ruining America." *The New York Times*. July 11, 2017. https://www.nytimes.com/2017/07/11/opinion/how-we-are-ruining-america.html

Bryant, Dave. "Trump's China Tariffs - The List of Products Affected and What You Can Do." ECOMCREW. updated August 23, 2019. https://www.ecomcrew.com/trumps-china-tariffs/

Bryce, Robert. "Wind-Energy Sector Gets $176 Billion Worth of Crony Capitalism." *National Review*. July 18, 2019. https://www.nationalreview.com/2016/06/wind-energy-subsidies-billions/

Buckley, F.H. *The Republic of Virtue: How We Tried to Ban Corruption, Failed, and What We Can Do About It* (New York: Encounter Books, 2017).

"Budget Issues That Shaped the 2014 Farm Bill." Every CRS Report. April 10, 2014. https://www.everycrsreport.com/reports/R42484.html

Buhayar, Noah. "Florida Paradise Offers Wealthy Developers a Big Trump Tax Break." *Bloomberg*. April 12, 2019. https://www.bloomberg.com/news/features/2019-04-12/lefrak-s-florida-sol-mia-is-headed-for-a-big-trump-tax-break

C.R. "Protectionism Doesn't Pay: America's Department of Commerce Imposes a Tariff of 292% on Bombardier's C-Series Jets." *The Economist*. December 20, 2017. Gulliver. https://www.economist.com/gulliver/2017/12/20/americas-department-of-commerce-imposes-a-tariff-of-292-on-bombardiers-c-series-jets

Candee, Adam. "Raiders Stadium By The Numbers: What to Expect At The New Jewel Just Off The Strip." *Las Vegas Sun*. November 27,

2017. https://lasvegassun.com/news/2017/nov/27/raiders-stadium-by-the-numbers/

Carney, Timothy P. "The Trump Foundation and Abuse of Both Power and Privilege." *Washington Examiner*. December 19, 2018. Opinion. https://www.washingtonexaminer.com/opinion/columnists/the-trump-foundation-and-abuse-of-both-power-and-privilege

Carpenter II, Dick M., Ph.D., Lisa Knepper, Kyle Sweetland, and Jennifer McDonald. "License to Work; A National Study of Burdens from Occupational Licensing, 2nd ed." Institute for Justice. 2019. https://ij.org/report/license-work-2/

Carrington, Damian and Harry Davies. "US Taxpayers Subsidising World's Biggest Fossil Fuel Companies." *The Guardian*. May 12, 2015. https://www.theguardian.com/environment/2015/may/12/us-taxpayers-subsidising-worlds-biggest-fossil-fuel-companies

Carroll, Rory. "The US Shipping Industry is Putting a Multimillion Dollar Squeeze on Puerto Rico." *Business Insider*. July 9, 2015. https://www.businessinsider.com/r-us-shippers-push-back-in-battle-over-puerto-rico-import-costs-2015-7

Casselman, Ben. "Promising Billions to Amazon: Is It a Good Deal for Cities?" *The New York Times*. January 26, 2018. https://www.nytimes.com/2018/01/26/business/economy/amazon-finalists-incentives.html

Cato Institute. (October 18, 2017). https://www.cato.org/publications/policy-analysis/zoning-land-use-planning-housing-affordability

Cerullo, Megan. "Big Companies Paying Little to No Federal Income Tax." *CBS News*. March 4, 2019. https://www.msn.com/en-us/news/other/big-companies-paying-little-to-no-federal-income-tax/ar-BBUlrI1

Chamlee, Virginia. "How Big Sugar Get What It Wants from Congress." *The Colorado Independent*. September 20, 2011. https://www.coloradoindependent.com/2011/09/20/how-big-sugar-gets-what-it-wants-from-congress/

Chan, Szu Ping. "When's a Van a Van and When's it a Car?" *BBC News*. October 18, 2018. Business. https://www.bbc.com/news/business-45875405

Channick, Robert. "As Foxconn Changes Wisconsin Plans, Job Promises Fall Short." *Chicago Tribune*. February 8, 2019. https://www.chicagotribune.com/business/ct-biz-foxconn-plant-hiring-target-20190205-story.html

Chapin, Adele. "7 Cool Design Facts to Know About DC United's Audi Field." Curbed. July 20, 2018. https://dc.curbed.com/2018/7/20/17595234/dc-united-audi-field-design

Chase, Chris. "Changes to California's Labeling Law Prop 65 to Take Effect by Month-End." Seafood Source. August 22, 2018. https://www.seafoodsource.com/news/foodservice-retail/changes-to-california-labeling-law-prop-65-taking-effect-by-month-end

"Chevron." OpenSecrets.org Center for Responsive Politics. https://www.opensecrets.org/orgs/summary.php?id=D000000015&cycle=2016

Chokshi, Niraj. "Trump Waves Jones Act for Puerto Rico, Easing Hurricane Aid Supplies." *The New York Times*. September 28, 2017. https://www.nytimes.com/2017/09/28/us/jones-act-waived.html

"Chuck Grassley." Open Secrets. 2015. https://www.opensecrets.org/personal-finances/net-worth?cid=N00001758

"City Fixes Limit on Tall Buildings." *The New York Times,* July 26, 1916. https://timesmachine.nytimes.com/timesmachine/1916/07/26/issue.html

Clark, Krissy. "The Uncertain Hour." *NPR* (podcast). https://www.npr.org/templates/story/story.php?storyId=476015630

Clarke, Liz. "The Rams' $5 Billion Stadium Complex Is Bigger Than Disneyland. It Might Be Perfect for L.A." *The Washington Post*. January 26, 2019. Sports. https://www.washingtonpost.com/sports/the-rams-5-billion-stadium-is-bigger-than-disneyland-it-might-be-perfect-for-la/2019/01/26/7c393898-20c3-11e9-8e21-59a09ff1e2a1_story.html?utm_term=.20122e7d9664

Clendinen, Dudley. "Court Ban on Work at Home Brings Gloom to Knitters in Rural Vermont." *The New York Times*. December 3, 1983. https://timesmachine.nytimes.com/timesmachine/1983/12/03/issue.html

CNN Wire Service. "Facebook to Build Massive Data Center in Utah." *Fox 6 News Now*. May 30, 2018. https://fox6now.com/2018/05/30/facebook-to-build-massive-data-center-in-utah/

CNN Wire. "New York Mayor Says Amazon Headquarters Debacle Was 'An Abuse of Corporate Power'." *FOX 43*. February 17, 2019. https://fox43.com/2019/02/17/new-york-mayor-says-amazon-headquarters-debacle-was-an-abuse-of-corporate-power/

"Coal and Air Pollution." Union of Concerned Scientists. December 19, 2017. https://www.ucsusa.org/resources/coal-and-air-pollution

Colburn, Tom A., M.D. "Subsidies of the Rich and Famous." November 2011. http://big.assets.huffingtonpost.com/SubsidiesoftheRichandFamous.pdf

Coleman, Robert. "The Rich Get Richer: 50 Billionaires Got Federal Farm Subsidies." Environmental Working Group. April 18, 2016. AgMag. https://www.ewg.org/agmag/2016/04/rich-get-richer-50-billionaires-got-federal-farm-subsidies

Collins, Paul. "The Beautiful Possibility." *Cabinet Magazine*. Spring 2002. Issue 6. http://www.cabinetmagazine.org/issues/6/beautiful possibility.php

ConocoPhillips. "ConocoPhillips Highlights Solid Results and Raises Concerns Over Un-American Tax Proposals at Annual Meeting of Shareholders." ConocoPhillips (news release), May 11, 2011. http://www.conocophillips.com/news-media/story/conocophillips-highlights-solid-results-and-raises-concerns-over-un-american-tax-proposals-at-annual-meeting-of-shareholders/

"Conservation Easements: More in Charities and Nonprofits." Internal Revenue Service. updated March 26, 2019. https://www.irs.gov/charities-non-profits/conservation-easements

"Costly and Unusual: An Analysis of the Industrial Tax Exemption Program (ITEP), With Amounts of Foregone Revenue by Locality/Public Service and Public Cost Per Job Created." Together Louisiana. Appendix B. http://togetherla.com/wp-content/uploads/2016/06/3_Appendix-B_Cost-to-every-parish-and-jurisdiction.pdf

Crain, W. Mark, and Nicole V. Crain. "The Cost of Federal Regulation to the U.S. Economy, Manufacturing and Small Business." National Association of Manufacturers. September 10, 2014. https://www.nam.org/wp-content/uploads/2019/05/Federal-Regulation-Full-Study.pdf

Crane, Edward H., and Carl Pope. "Fueled by Pork." *Cato Institute*. July 30, 2002. https://www.cato.org/publications/commentary/fueled-pork

Craven, Steven @OldPaddler replying to @David_Boaz @cpgrabow. "I once did a talk show for Hawai'i Public Radio. We wanted to look at the Jones Act and it was easy to find opponents to come on the air, but we couldn't get a single pro-Jones Act guest." Twitter. July 1, 2018. https://twitter.com/David_Boaz/status/1012459559804375040

"Crop Insurance Acreage Sets New Mark in 2017." National Crop Insurance Services. February 6, 2018. https://cropinsuranceinamerica. org/crop-insurance-acreage-sets-new-mark-2017/

"Crop Insurance in the United States." EWG's Farm Subsidy Database. https://farm.ewg.org/cropinsurance.php?fips=00000&regionname= theUnitedStates&_ga=2.130354696.682960410.1505326591- 842112084.1489101636

"Custom Manure Applicators." State of Vermont Agency of Agriculture, Food and Markets. https://agriculture.vermont.gov/custom-applicator

"Customs Rulings Online Search System: Elizabeth Orzol." U.S. Customs and Border Protection Securing America's Borders. https:// rulings.cbp.gov/search?term=Elizabeth%20Orzol&collection= ALL&sortBy=RELEVANCE&pageSize=30&page=1

Daher, Natalie. "Here Are the Top Cities Where U-Haul Says People Are Packing up and Moving." *CNBC Make It.* May 27, 2017. https://www.cnbc.com/2017/05/27/houston-chicago-among-top- destination-cities-for-movers-u-haul-says.html

Daniels, Jeff. "California Regulators Approve Plan to Mandate Solar Panels on New Home Construction." *CNBC.* May 9, 2018. https:// www.cnbc.com/2018/05/09/california-approves-plan-to-mandate- solar-panels-on-new-homes.html

Daniels, Steve. "Charges for Green Power, Nuke Subsidies Hike Electric Bills." Crain's Chicago Business. June 14, 2017. https://www. chicagobusiness.com/article/20170614/NEWS11/170619959/ comed-customers-paying-extra-starting-this-month-to-support- nuclear-renewable-power

Darby, Chris. "Plan in Works to Expand Industrial Park, Widen Hillegas Road." *Wane.com.* November 8, 2017. https://www.wane. com/news/local-news/plan-in-works-to-expand-industrial-park- widen-hillegas-road/

Dastin, Jeffery. "Billions in Tax Breaks Offered to Amazon for Second Headquarters." *Reuters.* October 19, 2017. https://www.reuters. com/article/us-amazon-com-headquarters/billions-in-tax-breaks- offered-to-amazon-for-second-headquarters-idUSKBN1CO1IP

"Data Files: U.S. and State-Level Farm Income and Wealth Statistics." United States Department of Agriculture Economic Research Service. https://www.ers.usda.gov/data-products/farm-income-and-wealth-statistics/data-files-us-and-state-level-farm-income-and-wealth-statistics/

Davis, Bruce. "Tire Makers Invest $10 Billion In Expansions, Improvements." *Rubber & Plastic News*. September 13, 2016. https://www.rubbernews.com/article/20160913/NEWS/309059996/tire-makers-invest-10-billion-in-expansions-improvements

Daysong, Rick. "Special Report: CEO Pay Soars, HEI Receives 'F' for Executive Pay." *HawaiiNewsNow*. updated July 11, 2013. https://www.hawaiinewsnow.com/story/22084152/ceo-pay-soars-hei-receives-f-for-executive-pay/

"DCA One-Pager for Financial Partners." Development Credit Authority. https://www.usaid.gov/sites/default/files/documents/1865/DCA_One-Pager_2018.pdf

De Avila, Joseph. "New Ballpark Adds to Hartford's Financial Strain." *Wall Street Journal*. April 11, 2017. https://www.wsj.com/articles/new-ballpark-adds-to-hartfords-financial-strain-1491912002

de la Merced, Michael J., and Andrew Ross Sorkin. "Owners of D.C. United Soccer Team Are Said to Consider Selling." *The New York Times*. July 30, 2017. https://www.nytimes.com/2017/07/30/business/dealbook/dc-united-soccer-owners-potential-sale.html

de Rugy, Veronique. "Corporate Welfare Wins Again in Trump's Washington." *The New York Times*. May 7, 2019. Opinion. https://www.nytimes.com/2019/05/07/opinion/export-import-bank-trump-corporate-welfare.html

deMause, Neil. "DC United Asks for More Money and Public Parkland for Second Stadium Before First One Has Even Opened." Field of Schemes. December 27, 2017. http://www.fieldofschemes.com/2017/12/27/13282/dc-united-asks-for-more-money-and-public-parkland-for-second-stadium-before-first-one-has-even-opened/

DeSilver, Drew. "The Biggest U.S. Tax Breaks." Pew Research Center. April 6, 2016. https://www.pewresearch.org/fact-tank/2016/04/06/the-biggest-u-s-tax-breaks/

Desmond, Matthew. "How Homeownership Became the Engine of American Equality." *The New York Times*. May 9, 2017. https://www.nytimes.com/2017/05/09/magazine/how-homeownership-became-the-engine-of-american-inequality.html?action=click&pgtype=Homepage&region=CColumn&module=MostViewed&version=Full&src=mv&WT.nav=MostViewed&_r=0

DiChristopher, Tom. "Trump Administration Moves to Keep Failing Coal and Nuclear Plants Open, Citing National Security." *CNBC*. June 1, 2018. https://www.cnbc.com/2018/06/01/trump-plan-bails-out-coal-and-nuclear-plants-for-national-security.html

"Dietary Studies." *JAMA Internal Medicine*(commentary). July 5, 2016. https://media.jamanetwork.com/news-item/dietary-studies-commentary-in-jama-internal-medicine/

"Direct Federal Financial Interventions and Subsidies in Energy in Fiscal Year 2016." U.S. Energy Information Administration. April 24, 2018. https://www.eia.gov/analysis/requests/subsidy/

DiSavino, Scott, Chris Reese, ed., and Diane Craft, ed., "New Jersey Governor Signs Nuclear Power Subsidy Bill into Law." *Reuters*. May 23, 2018. https://www.reuters.com/article/us-new-jersey-pseg-exelon-nuclear/new-jersey-governor-signs-nuclear-power-subsidy-bill-into-law-idUSKCN1IO2RL

Divounguy, Orphe. "Building Fairness and Opportunity: The Effects of Repealing Illinois' Prevailing Wage Law." Illinois Policy. https://www.illinoispolicy.org/reports/building-fairness-and-opportunity-the-effects-of-repealing-illinois-prevailing-wage-law/

Dlouhy, Jennifer A. "Trump Prepares Lifeline for Money-Losing Coal Plants." *Bloomberg*. May 31, 2018. https://www.bloomberg.com/news/articles/2018-06-01/trump-said-to-grant-lifeline-to-money-losing-coal-power-plants-jhv94ghl

Dolan, Kerry A. "World's Richest Green Billionaires 2011." *Forbes*. April 19, 2011. https://www.forbes.com/sites/kerryadolan/2011/04/19/worlds-greenest-billionaires-2011/#2fbe05d749a5

Dorfman, Jeffrey. "Publicly Financed Sports Stadiums Are A Game That Taxpayers Lose." *Forbes*. January 31, 2015. https://www.forbes.com/sites/jeffreydorfman/2015/01/31/publicly-financed-sports-stadiums-are-a-game-that-taxpayers-lose/#7e0da5c64f07

Doyle, Kathryn. "Foods from Subsidized Commodities Tied to Obesity." *Reuters*. July 5, 2016. Health News. https://www.reuters.com/article/us-health-diet-farm-subsidies/foods-from-subsidized-commodities-tied-to-obesity-idUSKCN0ZL2ER

Drangle, Matt. "How Business Connections and Political Ties Helped Launch Trump's Newest Line of Hotels." *Forbes*. July 18, 2017. https://www.forbes.com/sites/mattdrange/2017/07/18/how-business-connections-and-political-ties-helped-launch-trumps-newest-line-of-hotels/#3c3d685b6260

Drutman, Lee. *The Business of America Is Lobbying: How Corporations Became Politicized and Politics Became More Corporate* (New York: Oxford University Press, 2015).

Druzin, Rye. "South Texas School Board Approves $531 Million in Tax Breaks for Exxon Plant." *San Antonio Express-News*. March 22, 2017. updated January 9, 2018, https://www.expressnews.com/business/eagle-ford-energy/article/South-Texas-school-board-approves-1-2-billion-in-11021080.php

Duffin, Erin. "Total Lobbying Spending in the U.S. 1998-2018." Statista. April 29, 2019. https://www.statista.com/statistics/257337/total-lobbying-spending-in-the-us/

Dunbar, John. "Congress Gives NASCAR A Boost with A Tax Break for Improving Speedways." The Center for Public Integrity. https://apps.publicintegrity.org/tax-breaks-the-favored-few/#racetracks

Durst, Ron, and Robert Williams. "Farm Bill Income Cap for Program Payment Eligibility Affects Few Farms." United States Department of Agricultural Economic Research Service. August 01, 2016. Farm Economy. https://www.ers.usda.gov/amber-waves/2016/august/farm-bill-income-cap-for-program-payment-eligibility-affects-few-farms/

Dwoskin, Elizabeth. "Google Reaped Millions in Tax Breaks as It Secretly Expanded Its Real Estate Footprint Across the U.S." *The Washington Post*. February 15, 2019. Business. https://www.washingtonpost.com/business/economy/google-reaped-millions-of-tax-breaks-as-it-secretly-expanded-its-real-estate-footprint-across-the-us/2019/02/15/7912e10e-3136-11e9-813a-0ab2f17e305b_story.html

Dwyer, Jim. "Pushing New Yorkers Beyond the End of the Line." *The New York Times*. November 28, 2017. https://www.nytimes.

com/2017/11/28/nyregion/new-york-subway-funding-real-estate.
html

Dzieza, Josh. "Foxconn Is Confusing the Hell Out of Washington."
The Verge. April 10, 2019. https://www.theverge.com/2019/4/10/
18296793/foxconn-wisconsin-location-factory-innovation-centers-
technology-hub-no-news

Eastman, Scott, and Nicole Kaeding. "Opportunity Zones: What We
Know and What We Don't." Tax Foundation. January 8, 2019.
https://taxfoundation.org/opportunity-zones-what-we-know-and-
what-we-dont/

Eastman, Scott. "Measuring Opportunity Zone Success." Tax Foundation.
May 29, 2019. https://taxfoundation.org/measuring-opportunity-
zone-success/

Eastman, Scott. "The Home Mortgage Interest Deduction." Tax Foundation.
October 15, 2019. https://taxfoundation.org/home-mortgage-interest-
deduction/

Eder, Steve, and Ben Protess. "Developers Seek $6 Million Tax Break for
Trump-Managed Hotel." *The New York Times.* February 9, 2018.
https://www.nytimes.com/2018/02/09/business/trump-hotel-
mississippi-tax-break.html?hp&action=click&pgtype=Homepage&
clickSource=story-heading&module=first-column-region&region=
top-news&WT.nav=top-news

Eder, Steve. "When Picking Apples on a Farm With 5,000 Rules, Watch
Out for Ladders." *The New York Times.* December 27, 2017. https://
www.nytimes.com/2017/12/27/business/picking-apples-on-a-farm-
with-5000-rules-watch-out-for-the-ladders.html

Editorial Board. "America's Nutty Farm Subsidies Cause Damage at
Home and Abroad." *The Washington Post.* April 26, 2016. https://
www.washingtonpost.com/opinions/americas-nutty-farm-subsidies-
cause-damage-at-home-and-abroad/2016/04/26/22f51fa6-07fb-
11e6-bdcb-0133da18418d_story.html?utm_term=.46697ddb0f26

Editorial Board. "Give the D.C. United Stadium Plan's Tax Breaks a
Final Review." *The Washington Post.* November 28, 2014. https://
www.washingtonpost.com/opinions/give-the-dc-united-stadium-
plans-tax-breaks-a-final-review/2014/11/28/483d97be-75a5-11e4-
a755-e32227229e7b_story.html?utm_term=.9a8b85c7f54f

Editorial Board. "The Trade-War Growth Slowdown." *Wall Street Journal*. July 26, 2019. Opinion. https://www.wsj.com/articles/the-trade-war-growth-slowdown-11564182695?mod=hp_opin_pos_2

"Editorial: Nuclear Subsidy Plan Bows to PSEG Demand." *My Central Jersey, USA Today Network*. April 6, 2018. Opinion. https://www.mycentraljersey.com/story/opinion/editorials/2018/04/06/editorial-nuclear-subsidy-plan-bows-pseg-demand/33609071

Edwards, Chris. "Advantages of Low Capital Gains Tax Rates." Tax & Budget Bulletin. no. 66 (December 2012). https://www.cato.org/sites/cato.org/files/pubs/pdf/tbb-066.pdf

Edwards, Chris. "Agricultural Subsidies." Cato Institute. April 16, 2018. https://www.downsizinggovernment.org/agriculture/subsidies

Edwards, Chris. "Repealing the Federal Estate Tax." Tax and Budget Bulletin. no 36 (June 2006). https://www.cato.org/sites/cato.org/files/pubs/pdf/tbb-0606-36.pdf

Edwards, Chris. "Taxing Wealth and Capital Income." Tax and Budget Bulletin. no. 85 (August 1, 2019). https://www.cato.org/publications/tax-budget-bulletin/taxing-wealth-capital-income

Edwards, Chris. "The Senate Tax Bill Favors the Middle Class, Not the Rich." Cato Institute. December 5, 2017. Commentary. https://www.cato.org/publications/commentary/senate-tax-bill-favors-middle-class-not-rich

Elkind, Peter. "The Billion-Dollar Loophole." Fortune. December 20, 2017. https://fortune.com/2017/12/20/conservation-easement-tax-deduction-loophole/

Ember, Sydney, and Brooks Barnes. "Disney Ends Ban on *Los Angeles Times* Amid Fierce Backlash." *The New York Times*. November 7, 2017. https://www.nytimes.com/2017/11/07/business/disney-la-times.html

Erickson, Amanda. "The Birth of Zoning Codes, A History." *CityLab*. June 19, 2012. https://www.citylab.com/equity/2012/06/birth-zoning-codes-history/2275/

"EWG's Farm Subsidy Database." Environmental Working Group. https://farm.ewg.org/search.php

"Expertise." Ogilvy Government Relations. https://www.ogilvygr.com/expertise/

"Exxon Mobil Corporate Tax Dodger." Institute for Policy Studies. Americans for Tax Fairness. https://americansfortaxfairness.org/files/ Exon_PR_final.pdf

"Facebook Market Cap: 541.20B for Aug. 8, 2019." https://ycharts. com/companies/FB/market_cap

"Facts & Figures." Crop Insurance. https://cropinsuranceinamerica.org/ about-crop-insurance/facts-figures/

Fagan, Mark. *Lobbying: Business, Law and Public Policy: Why and How 12,000 People Spend $3+ Billion Impacting Our Government* (Vandeplas Publishing, 2015).

Fahrenthold, David A. "This is the Portrait of Donald Trump That His Charity Bought for $20,000." *The Washington Post*. November 1, 2016. Politics, https://www.washingtonpost.com/news/post-politics/ wp/2016/11/01/this-is-the-portrait-of-himself-that-donald-trump- bought-with-20000-from-his-charity/?utm_term=.d1bbc9d959de

Fausset, Richard. "A School Board Says No to Big Oil, and Alarms Sound in Business-Friendly Louisiana." *The New York Times*. February 5, 2019. https://www.nytimes.com/2019/02/05/us/louisiana-itep-exxon- mobil.html

"Federalist No. 10 (1787)." Bill of Rights Institute. https://billofrights institute.org/founding-documents/primary-source-documents/ the-federalist-papers/federalist-papers-no-10

Feeney, Scott. "To Stop Monster Homes, Legalize Apartments." *San Francisco Examiner*. October 29, 2017. Opinion. https://www. sfexaminer.com/opinion/to-stop-monster-homes-legalize-apartments/

Fichtner, Jason J., and Adam N. Michel. "Can a Research and Development Tax Credit Be Properly Designed for Economic Efficiency?" Mercatus Center. July 2015. https://www.mercatus.org/ system/files/Fichtner-R-D-Tax-Credit.pdf

Fichtner, Jason J., and Adam N. Michel. "The Research and Development Tax Credit Suffers from Design and Implementation Problems." Mercatus Center. August 5, 2015. https://www.mercatus.org/ publication/research-and-development-tax-credit-suffers-design- and-implementation-problems

Fleischer, Victor. "How A Carried Interest Tax Could Raise $180 Billion." *The New York Times*. June 5, 2015. https://www.nytimes.

com/2015/06/06/business/dealbook/how-a-carried-interest-tax-could-raise-180-billion.html

Florida, Richard. "Support a Non-Aggression Pact for Amazon's HQ2." Change.org (petition). https://www.change.org/p/elected-officials-and-community-leaders-of-amazon-hq2-finalist-cities-support-a-non-aggression-pact-for-amazon-s-hq2

Foley, Jonathan. "It's Time to Rethink America's Corn System." Scientific American. March 5, 2013. https://www.scientificamerican.com/article/time-to-rethink-corn/

"Fortune Telling License Application." City of Annapolis; Office of the City Clerk. https://www.annapolis.gov/DocumentCenter/View/860/Fortune-Telling-License-Application-PDF

Frank, Allan Dodds. "Trump Organization Seeks Hefty Tax Break for Westchester Golf Club." *ABCNews*, June 21, 2017. https://abcnews.go.com/Politics/trump-organization-seeks-hefty-tax-break-westchester-golf/story?id=48179222

Frank, Robert. "Jeff Bezos Is Now the Richest Man in the World with $90 Billion." *CBNC*. October 27, 2017. https://www.cnbc.com/2017/10/27/jeff-bezos-is-now-the-richest-man-in-the-world-with-90-billion.html

Frankel, Matthew. "Here's How the U.S. Tax System is Changing for 2018 and Beyond." TLBJ|CPA. December 30, 2017. http://www.tlbjcpa.com/your-complete-guide-to-the-2018-tax-changes

Frankel, Todd. C. "The Strange Case of Ford's Attempt to Avoid the 'Chicken Tax'." *The Washington Post*. July 6, 2018. Business. https://www.bbc.com/news/business-45875405https://www.washingtonpost.com/business/economy/the-strange-case-of-fords-attempt-to-avoid-thechicken-tax/2018/07/06/643624fa-796a-11e8-8df3-007495a78738_story.html

Frankovic, Kathy. "People Are Unwilling to See Tax Deductions Go Even If They Don't Benefit from Them." YouGov. October 30, 2017. https://today.yougov.com/topics/politics/articles-reports/2017/10/30/tax-deductions-are-hard-part

Friedman, Milton, "Landon Lecture Series on Public Issues." Kansas State University. April 27, 1978. https://www.k-state.edu/landon/speakers/milton-friedman/transcript.html

Furman, Jason, Katheryn Russ, and Jay Shambaugh. "US Tariffs Are an Arbitrary and Regressive Tax." *Vox*. January 12, 2017. https://voxeu.org/article/us-tariffs-are-arbitrary-and-regressive-tax

G., Peter. "Why Not Let Americans Work at Home?" The Heritage Foundation. January 30, 1984. Jobs and Labor. https://www.heritage.org/jobs-and-labor/report/why-not-let-americans-work-home

Gajanan, Mahita. "Trump's Trade War with China Could Cost the Average Family Up to $2,300 a Year, Report Estimates." *Time*. May 14, 2019. https://time.com/5587197/trump-china-trade-war-cost-families/

Galbraith, Rob. "Exelon Lobbyist Bragged About Profitability of Cuomo's Nuclear Bailout." Eyes on the Ties. March 27, 2018. https://news.littlesis.org/2018/03/27/exelon-lobbyist-bragged-about-profitability-of-cuomos-nuclear-bailout/

Gale, William G. "Chipping Away at the Mortgage Deduction." *Wall Street Journal*. April 9, 2019. https://www.wsj.com/articles/chipping-away-at-the-mortgage-deduction-11554851420

Gangitano, Alex. "Biz Group Takes Victory Lap on Ex-Im Bank." The Hill. May 10, 2019. https://thehill.com/business-a-lobbying/business-a-lobbying/443000-biz-groups-take-victory-lap-on-ex-im-bank

Gardner, Matthew. "Amazon in Its Prime: Doubles Profits, Pays $0 in Federal Income Taxes." Institute on Taxation and Economic Policy. February 13, 2019. https://itep.org/amazon-in-its-prime-doubles-profits-pays-0-in-federal-income-taxes/?ftag=MSFd61514f

Gardner, Timothy. "U.S. Company XCoal Energy to Sell Steam Coal to Fuel-Strapped Ukraine." *Reuters*. July 31, 2017. https://www.reuters.com/article/us-usa-coal-ukraine/u-s-company-xcoal-energy-to-sell-steam-coal-to-fuel-strapped-ukraine-idUSKBN1AG22Q

Garofalo, Pat, and Travis Waldron. "If You Build It, They Might Not Come: The Risky Economics of Sports Stadiums." *The Atlantic*. September 7, 2012. Business. https://www.theatlantic.com/business/archive/2012/09/if-you-build-it-they-might-not-come-the-risky-economics-of-sports-stadiums/260900/

Garside, M. "U.S. Gas and Oil Industry Annual Revenue 2010-2017." Statista. September 26, 2019. https://www.statista.com/statistics/294614/revenue-of-the-gas-and-oil-industry-in-the-us/

Garza, Olga, and Annet Nalukwago. "Chapter 313: Attracting Jobs and Investment, State Law Aims at Local Development." Fiscal Notes. April 2016. https://comptroller.texas.gov/economy/fiscal-notes/2016/april/chap313.php

Gelles, David. "They're Rich and They're Mad About Taxes (Too Low!)." *The New York Times*. February 12, 2019. https://www.nytimes.com/2019/02/12/business/rich-people-against-tax-cut.html

Ghilarducci, Teresa. "Why Some of the Rich Want to Pay More Taxes." *Forbes*. February 11, 2019. https://www.forbes.com/sites/teresaghilarducci/2019/02/11/why-some-of-the-rich-want-to-pay-more-taxes/#38f6194b6cf9

"Giving Statistics." Charity Navigator. 2019. https://www.charitynavigator.org/index.cfm?bay=content.view&cpid=42

Glaeser, Edward L., and Bryce A. Ward. "The Causes and Consequences of Land Use Regulation: Evidence from Greater Boston." *The Journal of Urban Economics* 65. no. 3. (May 2009). doi: https://doi.org/10.1016/j.jue.2008.06.003

Glenn, Heidi. "America's 'Complacent Class': How Self-Segregation Is Leading to Stagnation." *NPR*. March 2, 2017. https://www.npr.org/2017/03/02/517915510/americas-complacent-class-how-self-segregation-is-leading-to-stagnation

Gold, Alexander K., Austin J. Drukker, and Ted Gayer. "Why the Federal Government Should Stop Spending Billions on Private Sports Stadiums." *Brookings Institution*. September 8, 2016. https://www.brookings.edu/research/why-the-federal-government-should-stop-spending-billions-on-private-sports-stadiums/

Goldenberg, Suzanne, and Helena Bengtsson. "Biggest US Coal Company Funded Dozens of Groups Questioning Climate Change" *The Guardian*. June 13, 2016. https://www.theguardian.com/environment/2016/jun/13/peabody-energy-coal-mining-climate-change-denial-funding

"Gov. Edwards Ties Industrial Tax Breaks to Job Creation and Local Approval." Office of the Governor (press release). June 24, 2016. http://gov.louisiana.gov/news/gov-edwards-ties-industrial-tax-breaks-to-job-creation-and-local-approval

Gowen, Annie. "'I Don't Know How We're Going to Survive This.' Some Once-Loyal Farmers Begin to Doubt Trump." *The Washington Post*. June 21, 2019. National. https://www.washingtonpost.com/national/i-dont-know-how-were-going-to-survive-this-once-loyal-farmers-begin-to-doubt-trump/2019/06/21/04a32c65-c385-4052-8cd7-5cb4ef2119cc_story.html?utm_term=.5d6455d9939a

Graham, Bob, and Pionnula Ni Aolain. "Saudi Arabia Still Isn't Doing Enough to Fight the Financing of Terrorism." *The Washington Post*. February 19, 2019. Opinions. https://www.washingtonpost.com/opinions/global-opinions/saudi-arabia-still-isnt-doing-enough-to-fight-the-financing-of-terrorism/2019/02/19/bdb300d4-3454-11e9-a400-e481bf264fdc_story.html

Grennes, Thomas. "Does the Jones Act Endanger American Seamen?" Regulation (Fall 2017). https://object.cato.org/sites/cato.org/files/serials/files/regulation/2017/9/regulation-v40n3-7_2.pdf

Grenville, Stephen. "What Did the 2008 Crisis Cost America?" *The Interpreter*. August 23, 2018. https://www.lowyinstitute.org/the-interpreter/what-did-2008-crisis-cost-america

Griffiths, Benjamin W., Gürcan Gülen, James S. Dyer, David Spence, and Carey W. King. "Federal Financial Support for Electricity Generation Technologies." White Paper. UTEI/2016. no. 11 (January 11, 2016).

"Gross Private Domestic Investment." Federal Reserve Economic Data. 2019. https://fred.stlouisfed.org/series/GPDI

Grossman, Karl. "Why 'One of the Largest Tax Increases in Recent History' is Buried in Your Electric Bill." *Riverhead Local*. June 17, 2018. https://riverheadlocal.com/2018/06/17/why-one-of-the-largest-tax-increases-in-recent-history-is-buried-in-your-electric-bill/

Grundy, Adam. "Nonemployer Statistics and County Business Patterns Data Tell the Full Story." United States Census Bureau. September 18, 2018. https://www.census.gov/library/stories/2018/09/three-fourths-nations-businesses-do-not-have-paid-employees.html

Hackbarth, Sean. "How Excessive Regulations Stifle Small Businesses." U.S. Chamber of Commerce. May 29, 2014. https://www.uschamber.com/above-the-fold/how-excessive-regulations-stifle-small-businesses

Hansen, Louis. "Solar City Agrees to Settle Government Fraud Claims." *The Mercury News.* September 22, 2017. https://www.mercurynews. com/2017/09/22/solarcity-agrees-to-settle-government-fraud-claims/

Harkinson, Josh. "Taxpayer Subsidies Helped Tesla Motors, So Why Does Elon Musk Slam Them?" *Mother Jones.* September/ October 2013. http://www.motherjones.com/politics/2013/10/tesla-motors-free-ride-elon-musk-government-subsidies/

"Harmonized Tariff Schedule (2019 Revision 12)." https://hts.usitc.gov/? query=orange%20juice

Harned, Karen R., Esq. "A Forward on Checks and Balances." The Fourth Branch & Underground Regulations. September 2015. https://www. nfib.com/pdfs/fourth-branch-underground-regulations-nfib.pdf

Harris, Shane, Greg Miller, and Josh Dawsey. "CIA Concludes Saudi Crown Prince Ordered Jamal Khashoggi's Assassination." *The Washington Post.* November 16, 2018. National Security. https://www.washingtonpost. com/world/national-security/cia-concludes-saudi-crown-prince-ordered-jamal-khashoggis-assassination/2018/11/16/98c89fe6-e9b2-11e8-a939-9469f1166f9d_story.html

Hegseth, Pete. "Ex-Im Bank's Phony 'National Security' Cred: Column." *USA Today.* May 14, 2015. Opinion. https://www.usatoday.com/ story/opinion/2015/05/14/export-import-bank-economy-security-column/27188991/

Heller, Chris. "The Impossible Fight Against America's Stadiums." *Pacific Standard.* September 2, 2015. Economics. https://psmag. com/economics/the-shady-money-behind-americas-sports-stadiums

Hellerstein, Daniel M. "The US Conservation Reserve Program: The Evolution of an Enrollment Mechanism." Land Use Policy. no. 63 (April 2017): 601-610, https://doi.org/10.1016/j.landusepol.2015.07.017

Hengehold, Kevin. "Subsidy or Investment: Arizona's Energy Future." *Arizona Community Press.* October 2, 2015. http://azcommunitypress. org/2013/10/02/subsidy-or-investment-arizonas-energy-future/

Hershbein, Brad, David Boddy, and Melissa S. Kearney. "Nearly 30 Percent of Workers in the U.S. Need a License to Perform Their Job: It Is Time to Examine Occupational Licensing Practices." *Brookings Institute.* January 27, 2015. https://www.brookings.edu/blog/up-front/2015/01/27/nearly-30-percent-of-workers-in-the-u-s-need-a-license-to-perform-their-job-it-is-time-to-examine-occupational-licensing-practices/

Hersher, Rebecca. "How $85 Million Failed to Build a Swanky Hotel in Kabul." *NPR*. November 17, 2016. https://www.npr.org/sections/thetwo-way/2016/11/17/502428985/how-85-million-failed-to-build-a-swanky-hotel-in-kabul

Hill, Kyle. "There's No Magic in Venture-Backed Home Care." Medium. February 24, 2017. https://medium.com/@kaleazy/theres-no-magic-in-venture-backed-home-care-8f5389528279

Hiltzik, Michael. "The Revolving Door Spins Faster: Ex-Congressmen Become 'Stealth Lobbyists'." *Los Angeles Times*. January 6, 2015. Business. https://www.latimes.com/business/hiltzik/la-fi-mh-the-revolving-door-20150106-column.html

Hirsch, Jerry. "Elon Musk's Growing Empire Is Fueled by $4.9 Billion in Government Subsidies." *Los Angeles Times*. May 30, 2015. Business. http://www.latimes.com/business/la-fi-hy-musk-subsidies-20150531-story.html

Ho, Catherine. "Ex-Im Backers Spent Record Amounts Lobbying Government in 2015." *The Washington Post*. January 28, 2016. PowerPost. https://www.washingtonpost.com/news/powerpost/wp/2016/01/28/ex-im-backers-spent-record-amounts-lobbying-government-in-2015/

Holland, Steve, and Ginger Gibson. "Trump to Impose Steep Tariffs on Steel, Aluminum; Stokes Trade War Fears." *Reuters*. March 1, 2018. https://www.reuters.com/article/us-usa-trade-trump/trump-to-impose-steep-tariffs-on-steel-aluminum-stoking-trade-war-talk-idUSKCN1GD4ZW

Hopper, Reed. "PLF Testifies on WOTUS Rule." Pacific Legal Foundation (blog). November 30, 2017. https://pacificlegal.org/plf-testifies-on-wotus-rule/

"How High Are Sales Taxes in Your State?" Tax Foundation. January 1, 2019. https://files.taxfoundation.org/20190130101615/LOST-Jan-2019-Final-03-e1548861386125.png

Hsieh, Chang-Tai, and Enrico Moretti. "Housing Constraints and Spatial Misallocation." *American Economic Journal: Macroeconomics 2019* 11. no. 2. (April 2019). doi:10.3386/w21154

Hudson, Chris, and Donald Bryson. "Yelling 'Cut!' for Moviemaking Tax Breaks." *Wall Street Journal.* September 18, 2015. https://www.wsj. com/articles/yelling-cut-for-moviemaking-tax-breaks-1442613935

Hughes, Kim. "94-Year-Old Family Produce Biz Andy Boy Gives Millions to Charity." *SamaritanMag.* May 28, 2014. https://www. samaritanmag.com/features/94-year-old-family-produce-biz-andy-boy-gives-millions-charity

Hultin, Suzanne. "The National Occupational Licensing Database; Executive Summary." National Conference of State Legislatures. June 19, 2019. http://www.ncsl.org/research/labor-and-employment/occupational-licensing-statute-database.aspx

Iacurci, Greg. "Filial Law Puts Kids on the Hook for Parents' Health-Care Costs." *Investment News.* November 22, 2017. https://www. investmentnews.com/article/20171122/FREE/171129951/filial-laws-put-kids-on-the-hook-for-parents-health-care-costs

Ikenson, Daniel J., "Trade on Trial, Again." Cato Institute. May/June 2016. CATO Policy Report. https://www.cato.org/policy-report/mayjune-2016/trade-trial-again

ILSR. "Number of Banks in the U.S., 1966-2017." Institute for Local Self-Reliance (graph). May 14, 2019. https://ilsr.org/number-banks-u-s-1966-2014/

"IRS 'Dirty Dozen' List of Tax Scams for 2018 Contains Warning to Avoid Improper Claims for Business Credits." Internal Revenue Service. March 13, 2018. https://www.irs.gov/newsroom/irs-dirty-dozen-list-of-tax-scams-for-2018-contains-warning-to-avoid-improper-claims-for-business-credits

"ITEP Microsimulation Tax Model — Frequently Asked Questions." Institute on Taxation and Economic Policy. https://itep.org/modelfaq/

"Jack A. Fusco Executive Compensation." Salary.com. https://www1.salary. com/Jack-A-Fusco-Salary-Bonus-Stock-Options-for-CHENIERE-ENERGY-INC.html

Jay Evensen. "Why Give Tax Breaks to Super-Rich Companies Like Facebook?" *DesertNews.* June 6, 2018. https://www.deseretnews.com/article/900020686/why-give-tax-breaks-to-super-rich-companies-like-facebook.html

Jensen, Nathan. "Texas Chapter 313 Program: Evaluating Economic Development Strategies." University of Texas at Austin. http://www.natemjensen.com/wp-content/uploads/2017/02/Jensen_TEXAS-CHAPTER-313-PROGRAM-2-Pager.pdf

Johnson, Allen Benjamin III, "America's Corporate Welfare Bank Is Forced to Tighten Its Belt." *Morning Consult.* April 4, 2018. Opinion. https://morningconsult.com/opinions/americas-corporate-welfare-bank-is-forced-to-tighten-its-belt/

Johnston, Jake. "USAID Failing to Ensure Sustainability of Programs in Haiti, Says GAO Report." Center for Economic and Policy Research. June 4, 2015. http://cepr.net/blogs/haiti-relief-and-reconstruction-watch/usaid-failing-to-ensure-sustainability-of-programs-in-haiti-says-gao-report

Jordan, Heather. "How Much Money Did Dow CEO Andrew N. Liveris Make in 2016?" *Mlive.* May 10, 2017. https://www.mlive.com/news/saginaw/2017/05/ceo_pay_report_shows_dows_live.html

Jordan, Mary, and Kevin Sullivan. "'Smothered' and 'Shoved Aside' in Rural America." *The Washington Post.* December 29, 2017. https://www.washingtonpost.com/graphics/2017/national/iowa-farm-waters-trump/

Josephs, Leslie. "Boeing Loses Trade Case Over Bombardier Passenger Jets." *CNBC.* January 26, 2018. https://www.cnbc.com/2018/01/26/boeing-loses-trade-case-over-bombardier-passenger-jets.html

Kaufman, Dan. "Did Scott Walker and Donald Trump Deal Away the Wisconsin Governor's Race to Foxconn?" *The New Yorker.* November 3, 2018. https://www.newyorker.com/news/dispatch/did-scott-walker-and-donald-trump-deal-away-the-governors-race-to-foxconn

Kiel, Paul, and Dan Nguyen. "Bailout Tracker: Tracking Every Dollar and Every Recipient." ProPublica. February 25, 2019. https://projects.propublica.org/bailout/

Kim, E. Tammy. "Do Corporations Like Amazon and Foxconn Need Public Assistance?" *NYR Daily.* March 14, 2019. https://www.nybooks.com/daily/2019/03/14/do-corporations-like-amazon-and-foxconn-need-public-assistance/

Kincaid, Breanne. "2018 Proposition 65 State Impact Report." Center for Accountability in Science. June 2018. https://www.accountablescience.

com/wp-content/uploads/2018/06/2018-Proposition-65-State-Impact-Report.pdf

King, Lawton. "Ex-Im Bank Approves $694 Million to Finance Export of U.S. Mining and Rail Equipment to Australia." Export-Import Bank of the United States (press release). December 19, 2013. https://www.exim.gov/news/ex-im-bank-approves-694-million-finance-export-us-mining-and-rail-equipment-australia

"Kirby Corporation Annual Report." Kirby Corporation. 2018. http://www.annualreports.com/HostedData/AnnualReports/PDF/NYSE_KEX_2018.pdf

Kleiner, Sarah. "A Controversial Tax Incentive for Racehorse Owners Is Back on Track." The Center for Public Integrity. https://apps.publicintegrity.org/tax-breaks-the-favored-few/#racehorse-owners

Koch, Charles G. "Charles Koch: This is the One Issue Where Bernie Sanders is Right." *The Washington Post*. February 18, 2016. Opinion. https://www.washingtonpost.com/opinions/charles-koch-this-is-the-one-issue-where-bernie-sanders-is-right/2016/02/18/cdd2c228-d5c1-11e5-be55-2cc3c1e4b76b_story.html

Krancer, Michael L. "UpstreamPA 2017 Conference." Silent Majority Strategies LLC. March 21, 2017. http://www.upstreampa.com/Presentations/Krancer.pdf

Krugman, Paul. "Tariff Tantrums and Recession Risks." *The New York Times*. August 7, 2019. Opinion. https://www.nytimes.com/2019/08/07/opinion/tariff-tantrums-and-recession-risks.html

Kuo, Mercy A. "Upping the Ante in the US-China Trade War: Insights from Nien Su." *The Diplomat*. May 21, 2019. https://thediplomat.com/2019/05/upping-the-ante-in-the-us-china-trade-war/

Lawler, Joseph. "Koch Group Warns Cities Against 'Corporate Welfare' for Amazon." *Washington Examiner*. February 21, 2018 https://www.washingtonexaminer.com/koch-group-warns-cities-against-corporate-welfare-for-amazon

Lawrence, Peter. "Congress Agrees to Historic Funding for HUD in Fiscal Year 2018 Omnibus Spending Bill." HUD Resource Center. March 22, 2018. https://www.novoco.com/notes-from-novogradac/congress-agrees-historic-funding-hud-fiscal-year-2018-omnibus-spending-bill

Layne, Rachel. "Microsoft Reaches $1 Trillion Market Value for the First Time." *CBS News*. April 25, 2019. https://www.cbsnews.com/news/microsoft-1-trillion-market-value-reached-today/

Lee, Don. "Limited Success of Chinese Tire Tariffs Shows Why Donald Trump's Trade Prescription May Not Work." *Los Angeles Times*. July 24, 2016. Business. https://www.latimes.com/business/la-fi-tariffs-trade-analysis-20160724-snap-story.html

Lee, Fiona. "After Going Viral, Outer Sunset 'Pod Guy' Selling Custom Pods." *Hoodline*. August 4, 2016. https://hoodline.com/2016/04/after-going-viral-outer-sunset-pod-guy-selling-custom-pods

Leschin-Hoar, Clare. "U.S. to Ship Peanuts to Feed Haitian Kids; Aid Groups Say 'This Is Wrong'." *NPR*. May 5, 2016. Food for Thought. https://www.npr.org/sections/thesalt/2016/05/05/476876371/u-s-to-ship-peanuts-to-feed-haitian-kids-aid-groups-say-this-is-wrong

"Levi's Stadium is a Model for Privately Financed Venues." *San Francisco Chronicle*. February 5, 2016. Opinion/Editorials. https://www.sfchronicle.com/opinion/editorials/article/Levi-s-Stadium-is-a-model-for-privately-6808683.php

Levine, Bertram J. *The Art of Lobbying: Building Trust and Selling Policy* (Washington, D.C.: CQ Press, 2009).

Levinthal, Dave. "Congress Packed Budget Bill with Special Breaks for Washington Insiders." The Center for Public Integrity. March 13, 2018. https://apps.publicintegrity.org/tax-breaks-the-favored-few/

Litman, Julie. "Some Developers 'Terrified' Of Entering San Francisco's Development Process, But City Is Working to Improve It." *Bisnow*. April 15, 2018. https://www.bisnow.com/san-francisco/news/construction-development/san-francisco-policy-87227

"List of Presidents of the United States by Net Worth." Wikipedia. https://en.wikipedia.org/wiki/List_of_Presidents_of_the_United_States_by_net_worth

"Lobbying Database." OpenSecrets.org. https://www.opensecrets.org/lobby/

Looney, Adam. "Abuse of Tax Deductions for Charitable Donations of Conservation Lands Are on the Rise." Brookings Institute. June 1, 2017. https://www.brookings.edu/research/abuse-of-tax-deductions-for-charitable-donations-of-conservation-lands-are-on-the-rise/

Looney, Adam. "Estimating the Rising Cost of a Surprising Tax Shelter: The Syndicated Conservation Easement." Brookings Institute. December 20, 2017. Up Front. https://www.brookings.edu/blog/up-front/2017/12/20/estimating-the-rising-cost-of-a-surprising-tax-shelter-the-syndicated-conservation-easement/

Loris, Nicolas, and Bryan Cosby. "How 'Green' Energy Subsidies Transfer Wealth to the Rich." *The Daily Signal.* July 18, 2018. Energy/Commentary, https://www.dailysignal.com/2018/07/18/how-green-energy-subsidies-transfer-wealth-to-the-rich/

"*Lost.*" Wikipedia (TV series). https://en.wikipedia.org/wiki/Lost_(TV_series)

Loudenback, Tanza. "Crazy-High Rent, Record-low Homeownership, and Overcrowding: California Has a Plan to Solve the Housing Crisis, but Not Without a Fight." *Business Insider.* March 12, 2017. http://www.businessinsider.com/granny-flat-law-solution-california-affordable-housing-shortage-2017-3

Luigi Zingales. *A Capitalism for the People* (New York: Basic Books, 2012).

Luzkow, Jack Lawrence. *Monopoly Restored How the Super-Rich Robbed Main Street* (Palgrave Macmillan, 2018).

MacMillan, Douglas, Eliot Brown, and Peter Grant. "Google Plans Large New York City Expansion." *Wall Street Journal.* November 7, 2018. https://www.wsj.com/articles/google-plans-large-new-york-city-expansion-1541636579

Malanga, Steven. "When Will States Get Smart and Stop Subsidizing Movies?" *Los Angeles Times.* August 13, 2017. https://www.latimes.com/opinion/op-ed/la-oe-malanga-hollywood-subsidies-20170813-story.html

Mamoowala, Asheem. "Are San Francisco Buildings as Tall as They Could Be?" Mapbox (blog). October 23, 2017. https://blog.mapbox.com/are-san-francisco-buildings-as-tall-as-they-could-be-77ecc4a3d32a

Mangu-Ward, Katherine. "Dangerous Toys, Strange Bedfellows." Reason. June/2009. Regulation. https://reason.com/2009/05/18/dangerous-toys-strange-bedfell?print

"Manure Applicator Certification." Iowa Department of Natural Resources. https://www.iowadnr.gov/Environmental-Protection/Land-Quality/Animal-Feeding-Operations/Applicator-Certification

"MAP Funding Allocations — FY 2019." United States Department of Agriculture: Foreign Agricultural Service. https://www.fas.usda.gov/programs/market-access-program-map/map-funding-allocations-fy-2019

"Marc R. Bitzer Executive Compensation." Salary.com. https://www1.salary.com/Marc-R-Bitzer-Salary-Bonus-Stock-Options-for-WHIRLPOOL-CORP.html

"Mark Zuckerberg: Real Time Net Worth $70.6B." *Forbes.* accessed July 15, 2019. https://www.forbes.com/profile/mark-zuckerberg/#6973235b3e06

Marks, Gene, and Ben Gran. "7 Myths About the Research and Development Tax Credit for Small Business Owners." *The Hartford.* March 7, 2017. updated August 26, 2019, https://sba.thehartford.com/finance/7-myths-about-the-research-and-development-tax-credit/

Marroquin, Art. "Studies to Start for Freeway Improvements Near Raiders Stadium Site." *Las Vegas Review-Journal.* October 9, 2017. https://www.reviewjournal.com/local/local-las-vegas/studies-to-start-for-freeway-improvements-near-raiders-stadium-site/

"Mattel Inc." https://www.opensecrets.org/lobby/clientsum.php?id=D000000571&year=2008

McAndrews, Michael. "Yard Goats Owner Josh Solomon: 'Real Estate Is in My Blood'." *Hartford Magazine.* July 01, 2017. https://www.courant.com/hartford-magazine/hc-hm-josh-solomon-yard-goats-20170701-story.html

McLaughlin, Ralph. "Who Will Win the Homebuilding Race of 2017?" Trulia Research. August 16, 2017. https://www.trulia.com/blog/trends/homebuilding/

Melchior, Jillian Kay. "Trump's Support for Ethanol Is Bad for Taxpayers and Their Cars." *National Review.* January 21, 2016 https://www.nationalreview.com/2016/01/donald-trump-ethanol-subsidy-support-bad-taxpayers/

Metcalf, Tom, and Suzanne Woolley. "'We Are Part of the Problem': Billionaires and Heirs Demand Wealth Tax." *Bloomberg.* June 24, 2019. https://www.bloomberg.com/news/articles/2019-06-24/billionaires-from-soros-to-pritzker-heirs-call-for-wealth-tax

Mettler, Katie. "Extreme Weather Is Pummeling the Midwest, and Farmers Are in Deep Trouble." *MSN.* May 30, 2019. Money. https://www.msn.com/en-us/money/markets/extreme-weather-is-pummeling-the-midwest-and-farmers-are-in-deep-trouble/ar-AAC9bTJ#page=2

Meyer, Jared. "No Matter Who Wins at the Oscars, Taxpayers Lose on Film Subsidies." Reason. February 26, 2016. https://reason.com/2016/02/26/no-matter-who-wins-at-the-oscars-taxpaye

Michels, Patrick. "Free Lunch." *The Texas Observer.* https://www.texasobserver.org/chapter-313-texas-tax-incentive/

"Microsoft Seeks Delays in Finishing Third West Des Moines Data Center." Business Record. December 26, 2018. https://businessrecord.com/Content/Tech-Innovation/Technology/Article/Microsoft-seeks-delays-in-finishing-third-West-Des-Moines-data-center/172/834/85097

"Microsoft Word - Billionaire Chart BW_RC." https://cdn.ewg.org/sites/default/files/blog/Billionaire_Chart_BW_RC.pdf?_ga=2.83119636.360598995.1497477451-842112084.1489101636

Miller, Daniel. "How One Election Changed Disneyland's Relationship with Its Hometown." *LA Times.* September 26, 2017. https://www.latimes.com/projects/la-fi-disney-anaheim-city-council/

Miller, Daniel. "Is Disney Paying Its Share in Anaheim?" *LA Times.* September 24, 2017. https://www.latimes.com/projects/la-fi-disney-anaheim-deals/

Miller, John J. "Taxpayers Take the Puck." *National Review.* May 24, 2012. https://www.nationalreview.com/magazine/2012/06/11/taxpayers-take-puck/

Mitchell, Matthew D., and Tamera Winter. "The Opportunity Cost of Corporate Welfare." Mercatus Center. May 22, 2018. https://www.mercatus.org/publications/corporate-welfare/opportunity-cost-corporate-welfare

Molla, Rani. "CEO's — Especially Those in Tech - Are Making More Money Than Ever: Worker Pay, However, Is Stagnating." *Vox Media.* May 2, 2019. https://www.vox.com/recode/2019/5/2/18522927/ceo-pay-ratio-tech-employee-salary-2018

Moon, Emily. "The Trump Administration Will Pay Farmers $16 Billion For Its Trade War." *Pacific Standard.* July 26, 2019. https://psmag.

com/news/the-trump-administration-will-pay-farmers-16-billion-for-its-trade-war

Moran, Tyler. "Tariffs Hit Poor Americans Hardest." Peterson Institute for International Economics. July 31, 2014. https://www.piie.com/blogs/trade-investment-policy-watch/tariffs-hit-poor-americans hardest? utm_source=Bruegel%20Updates&utm_campaign=651aba2df0-Blogs%20review%20%2022/1/2017&utm_medium=email&utm_term=0_eb026b984a-651aba2df0-278510293

Moretti, Enrico. "Fires Aren't the Only Threat to the California Dream." *The New York Times*. November 3, 2017. https://www.nytimes.com/2017/11/03/opinion/california-fires-housing.html? searchResultPosition=1

Mullen, Regina. "There's Never Been a Better Time to Claim R&D Tax Credits in the US: Here's Why." Replicon. August 4, 2017. https://www.replicon.com/blog/theres-never-better-time-claim-rd-tax-credits-us-heres/

"N250294: The Tariff Classification of a Men's Knit Jacket from China." U.S. Customs and Border Protection Securing America's Borders. March 11, 2014. https://rulings.cbp.gov/ruling/N250294

Nabil, Ryan, and Vincent H. Smith. "Ryan Nabil and Vincent H. Smith: $20 Billion In Farm Subsidies Doesn't Reach the Poor, Leaves Them Hungry." *La Crosse Tribune*. January 20, 2017. Commentary. https://lacrossetribune.com/news/opinion/editorial/columnists/ryan-nabil-and-vincent-h-smith-billion-in-farm-subsidies/article_f7df0bf4-d6ce-58ae-94c4-5cb596a44989.html

Narayan, Chandrika. "'Apocalyptic' Devastation in Puerto Rico, and Little Help in Sight." *CNN US*. September 26, 2017. https://www.cnn.com/2017/09/25/us/hurricane-maria-puerto-rico/index.html

"National Chicken Council Thanks USDA for Special Purchase of Chicken." National Chicken Council. August 16, 2011. https://www.nationalchickencouncil.org/national-chicken-council-thanks-usda-for-special-purchase-of-chicken/

Nellis, Stephen. "Apple to Build Iowa Data Center, Get $207.8 Million in Incentives." *Reuters*. August 24, 2017. https://www.reuters.com/article/us-apple-iowa/apple-to-build-iowa-data-center-get-207-8-million-in-incentives-idUSKCN1B422L

"New Survey: Americans Believe Washington Has Not Learned the Hard Lessons from Bailouts-A Decade Later." Charles Koch Institute. September 19, 2018. https://www.charleskochinstitute.org/news/tarp-bailouts-anniversary/

"Newcomers to the World's Most Powerful People List." *Forbes*. https://www.forbes.com/pictures/5af099a8a7ea436b547c830d/darren-woods-34/#32ce1d5d1fb7

Newton, John, Ph.D. "Change on the Horizon for the Conservation Reserve Program?" American Farm Bureau Federation. May 15, 2017. https://www.fb.org/market-intel/change-on-the-horizon-for-the-conservation-reserve-program

"NFL Stadium Funding Information." *CBS Minnesota*. December 2, 2011. https://cbsminnesota.files.wordpress.com/2011/12/nfl-funding-summary-12-2-11.pdf

Nicklaus, David, "Bonuses Bring Arch Coal CEO's Pay to $9.8 Million." *St. Louis Post-Dispatch*. March 21, 2018. https://www.stltoday.com/business/columns/david-nicklaus/bonuses-bring-arch-coal-ceo-s-pay-to-million/article_e95bc108-0da9-5962-b60a-e88f9c580c76.html

Noguchi, Yuki. "New Round of Tariffs Takes A Bigger Bite of Consumers' Budget." *NPR*. May 10, 2019. https://www.npr.org/2019/05/10/721921317/new-round-of-tariffs-take-a-bigger-bite-of-consumers-budget

"Oil and Gas Tax Benefits." Western Capital, INC., Energy Development. http://www.oilandgasjointventures.com/tax-benefits.html

Omarzu, Tim. "Google Building $600 Million Data Center Near Chattanooga." *Times Free Press*. June 25, 2015. https://www.timesfreepress.com/news/local/story/2015/jun/25/goodbye-coal-plant-hello-google-google-plans/311380/

"OPIC Investments Increased Chile's Energy Capacity, but Weak Processes and Internal Controls Diminish OPIC's Ability to Gauge Project Effects and Risks (audit report 9-OPC-19-002-P)." Office of Inspector General; U.S. Agency for International Development. February 1, 2019. https://www.oversight.gov/sites/default/files/oig-reports/9-OPC-19-002-P.pdf

Orton, Kathy. "Federal Government Spends More Subsidizing Homeowners Than It Does Helping People Avoid Homelessness."

The Washington Post. October 11, 2017. Where We Live. https://www. washingtonpost.com/news/where-we-live/wp/2017/10/11/the-federal-government-spends-more-than-twice-as-much-subsidizing-homeowners-as-it-does-helping-people-avoid-homelessness/?utm_term=.735942f18218

Ostrower, Jon. "Delta CEO Reiterates Objections to Ex-Im Bank Widebody-Jet Financing: Richard Anderson Also Warns of 'Huge Bubble' in Single-Aisle Jets." *Wall Street Journal.* June 24, 2014. https://www.wsj.com/articles/delta-head-warns-of-single-aisle-jet-bubble-1403651272

"Our Approach." J.F. Lehman & Company. https://www.jflpartners. com/approach

"Our Mission." Sunlight Foundation. https://sunlightfoundation.com/ about/

"Our Vision and Mission: Inform, Empower & Advocate." Center for Responsive Politics. http://www.opensecrets.org/about/

Owens, Jeremy C. "Why Governments Are Giving Billions in Tax Breaks to Apple, Amazon and Other Tech Giants." *MarketWatch.* October 14, 2016. https://www.marketwatch.com/story/why-governments-are-giving-billions-in-tax-breaks-to-apple-amazon-and-other-tech-giants-2016-10-13

Parker, Mario. "Koch Brothers Build Biofuel Giant Aided by Mandates They Abhor." *Bloomberg.* November 2, 2016. https://www.bloomberg. com/news/articles/2016-11-02/koch-brothers-build-biofuel-giant-aided-by-mandates-they-abhor

Patel, Jugal K., and Alicia Parlapiano. "The Senate's Official Scorekeeper Says the Republican Tax Plan Would Add $1 Trillion to the Deficit." *The New York Times.* December 1, 2017. https://www.nytimes.com/ interactive/2017/11/28/us/politics/tax-bill-deficits.html

Pathé, Simone, and Bridget Bowman. "Wealth of Congress: 14 Vulnerable Incumbents Are Worth At Least $1 Million." *Roll Call.* February 27, 2018. Politics. https://www.rollcall.com/news/politics/ wealth-congress-vulnerable-incumbents-worth-least-1-million

Perkins, Madeleine Sheehan. "The Coal Industry Is Collapsing, and Coal Workers Allege That Executives Are Making the Situation

Worse." *Business Insider,* July 1, 2017, https://www.businessinsider. com/from-the-ashes-highlights-plight-of-coal-workers-2017-6

Perry, Mark J. "Inconvenient Energy Fact: It Takes 79 Solar Workers to Produce Same Amount of Electric Power as One Coal Worker." Carpe Diem AEI. May 3, 2017. https://www.aei.org/publication/ inconvenient-energy-fact-it-takes-79-solar-workers-to-produce-same-amount-of-electric-power-as-one-coal-worker/

Peters, Alan H., and Peter S. Fisher. "State Enterprise Zone Programs: Have They Worked?" Upjohn Institute for Employment Research. 2002. https://doi.org/10.17848/9781417524433

Phillips, Shane. "The Disconnect Between Liberal Aspirations and Liberal Housing Policy Is Killing Coastal U.S. Cities." Market Urbanism. January 27, 2017. http://marketurbanism.com/2017/01/27/the-disconnect-between-liberal-aspirations-and-liberal-housing-policy-is-killing-coastal-u-s-cities/

Pogol, Gina. "How the Mortgage Interest Tax Deduction Lowers Your Payment." The Mortgage Reports. July 20, 2017. https:// themortgagereports.com/30247/how-the-mortgage-interest-tax-deduction-lowers-your-payment

"President's Decision on Solar Tariffs is a Loss for America." Solar Energies Industries Association (press release), January 22, 2018. https://seia.org/news/presidents-decision-solar-tariffs-loss-america

Prevost, Lisa. *Snob Zones: Fear, Prejudice, and Real Estate* (Boston: Beacon Press, May 7, 2013).

"Production and Exports." U.S. Grains Council. 2019. Corn. https:// grains.org/buying-selling/corn/

"Profile for 2018 Election Cycle." OpenSecrets.org. Pinnacle West Capital. Contributions. https://www.opensecrets.org/orgs/summary. php?id=D000000658&cycle=2018

"Profile for 2018 Election Cycle." OpenSecrets.org. Pinnacle West Capital. Top Recipients. https://www.opensecrets.org/orgs/summary. php?id=D000000658&cycle=2018

"Profile for the 2016 Election Cycle." OpenSecrets.org. Exelon Corp. https://www.opensecrets.org/orgs/summary.php?id=D000000368& cycle=2016

"Projected Spending Under the 2014 Farm Bill." United State Department of Agriculture Economic Research Service. August 20, 2019. https://www.ers.usda.gov/topics/farm-economy/farm-commodity-policy/projected-spending-under-the-2014-farm-bill/

"Projected Spending Under the 2014 Farm Bill." United States Department of Agriculture Economic Research Services. https://www.ers.usda.gov/topics/farm-economy/farm-commodity-policy/projected-spending-under-the-2014-farm-bill/

Puzzanghera, Jim. "A Decade After the Financial Crisis, Many Americans Are Still Struggling to Recover." *The Seattle Times*. September 10, 2018. updated September 11, 2018. Nation & World. https://www.seattletimes.com/nation-world/a-decade-after-the-financial-crisis-many-americans-are-still-struggling-to-recover/

"Quick Facts: Jackson County, Alabama." United States Census Bureau. https://www.census.gov/quickfacts/jacksoncountyalabama

"R.A. Walker Executive Compensation." Salary.com. https://www1.salary.com/R-A-Walker-Salary-Bonus-Stock-Options-for-ANADARKO-PETROLEUM-CORP.html

"Raise the Tax Rates on Long-Term Capital Gains and Qualified Dividends by 2 Percentage Points." Congressional Budget Office. December 8, 2016. https://www.cbo.gov/budget-options/2016/52249

Rappeport, Alan. "A $12 Billion Program to Help Farmers Stung by Trump's Trade War Has Aided Few." *The New York Times*. November 19, 2018. https://www.nytimes.com/2018/11/19/us/politics/farming-trump-trade-war.html

Rappeport, Alan. "Trump Promised to Kill Carried Interest. Lobbyists Kept It Alive." *The New York Times*. December 22, 2017. https://www.nytimes.com/2017/12/22/business/trump-carried-interest-lobbyists.html

Rauch, Jonathan. *Government's End: Why Washington Stopped Working* (New York: Perseus Books Group, 1999).

"Razing Appalachia." produced by Sasha Waters. *PBS SoCal*. 2003. Independent Film. 54:00. http://www.pbs.org/independentlens/razingappalachia/mtop.html

"Reg Stats." Columbian College of Arts & Sciences. https://regulatorystudies.columbian.gwu.edu/reg-stats

Reklaitis, Victor. "Trump's New FERC Chairman Could Give New Life to Plan to Help Coal and Nuclear Power Plants, Analysts Say." MarketWatch. October 26, 2018. https://www.marketwatch.com/story/trumps-new-ferc-chairman-could-give-new-life-to-plan-to-help-coal-and-nuclear-power-plants-analysts-say-2018-10-25

"Restaurants: New Warning." CA.gov. August 30, 2016. Proposition 65. https://www.p65warnings.ca.gov/places/restaurants

Ric Edelman. *The Truth About Money* (Harper Collins, 2003).

Rich, Gillian. "Boeing, GE, Caterpillar Overseas Sales Hopes Just Got A Big Lift." *Investor's Business Daily*. May 8, 2019. News. https://www.investors.com/news/export-import-bank-quorum-bank-of-boeing-ge-caterpillar/

Rivera, Daniel. "U.S. Sugar Program Hurts Businesses and Kills Jobs." Competitive Enterprise Institute(blog). November 10, 2011. https://cei.org/blog/us-sugar-program-hurts-businesses-and-kills-jobs

"Robert Raben's Approach to Lobbying Highlighted by CQ Magazine." The Raben Group. February 13, 2018. https://rabengroup.com/2018/02/robert-rabens-approach-lobbying-highlighted-cq-magazine/

Roberts, Chris. "New Record Rents in SF: $3,410 For 1 Bedroom." *NBC Bay Area*. February 04, 2015. https://www.nbcbayarea.com/news/local/Record-Rents-in-San-Francisco-290737151.html

Robinson, Jessica. "A Unanimous Supreme Court Ruling, But Still No House for Idaho Couple." *My News Network*. October 2, 2013. https://www.nwnewsnetwork.org/post/unanimous-supreme-court-ruling-still-no-house-idaho-couple-0

Rolnik, Guy. "Meet the Sugar Barons Who Used Both Sides of American Politics to Get Billions in Subsidies." ProMarket (blog). September 19, 2016. https://promarket.org/sugar-industry-buys-academia-politicians/

Romell, Rick. "Foxconn Falls Short of First Job-Creation Hurdle but Reiterates Ultimate Employment Pledge." *Milwaukee Journal Sentinel*. January 18, 2019. https://www.jsonline.com/story/money/business/2019/01/18/foxconn-falls-short-first-jobs-hurdle-reiterates-13-000-job-pledge/2617038002/

Rosa, Isabel, and Renée Johnson. "Federal Crop Insurance: Specialty Crops." Congressional Research Service. January 14, 2019. https://fas.org/sgp/crs/misc/R45459.pdf

Rosenberg, Eli. "An Angry Historian Ripped the Ultrarich Over Tax Avoidance at Davos. Then One Was Given the Mic." *The Washington Post*. January 31, 2019. Business. https://www.washingtonpost.com/ business/2019/01/31/an-angry-historian-ripped-ultra-rich-over-tax-avoidance-davos-then-one-was-given-mic/?utm_term=.ed376f5dd3d9

Rosenwald, Michael S. "Cloud Centers Bring High-Tech Flash but Not Many Jobs to Beaten-Down Towns." *The Washington Post*. November 24, 2011. Business. https://www.washingtonpost.com/business/economy/ cloud-centers-bring-high-tech-flash-but-not-many-jobs-to-beaten-down-towns/2011/11/08/gIQAccTQtN_story.html

Rubin, Richard. "Donald Trump's Donations Put Him in Line for Conservation Tax Breaks." *Wall Street Journal*. March 10, 2016. https:// www.wsj.com/articles/donald-trumps-land-donations-put-him-in-line-for-conservation-tax-breaks-1457656717#livefyre-comment

Rubinstein, Dana. "Facebook and Google Say They Didn't Get State Subsidies. Why Should Amazon?" *Politico New York*. November 8, 2018. https://www.politico.com/states/new-york/albany/story/ 2018/11/08/facebook-and-google-say-they-didnt-get-state-subsidies-why-should-amazon-688859

Rucinski, Tracy. "Arch Coal Files for Bankruptcy, Hit by Mining Downturn." *Reuters*. January 10, 2016. https://www.reuters.com/ article/us-arch-coal-restructuring-idUSKCN0UP0MR20160111

Ruge, Mark, Sarah Beason, and Elle Stuart. "Fiscal Still Matters: How Social Media and Even Mainstream Media Publications Got It Wrong on the Jones Act and Puerto Rico." *The Maritime Executive*. February 25, 2018. https://www.maritime-executive.com/magazine/ facts-still-matter

Rushe, Dominic. "'It's a Huge Subsidy': The $4.8bn Gamble to Lure Foxconn to America." *The Guardian Weekly*. July 2, 2018. https://www.theguardian.com/cities/2018/jul/02/its-a-huge-subsidy-the-48bn-gamble-to-lure-foxconn-to-america

"Sackett v. EPA: How One Couple's Battle against the Feds Might Protect Your Land." ReasonTV (YouTube). March 7, 2012. https:// youtu.be/40iHXAOjJ3U

Sandefur, Timothy. *The Permission Society: How the Ruling Class Turns Our Freedoms into Privileges and What We Can Do About It.* (New York: Encounter Books, 2016).

Satow, Julie. "Pied-à-Neighborhood." *The New York Times.* October 24, 2014. https://www.nytimes.com/2014/10/26/realestate/pieds-terre-owners-dominate-some-new-york-buildings.html

Sawe, Benjamin Elisha. "The Biggest Industries in the United States." World Atlas. https://www.worldatlas.com/articles/which-are-the-biggest-industries-in-the-united-states.html

Sawhill, Isabel V., and Eleanor Krause. "American Workers Need a Pay Raise - the Estate Tax Could Help." Brookings Institute. November 2, 2017. Social Mobility Memos. https://www.brookings.edu/blog/social-mobility-memos/2017/11/02/american-workers-need-a-pay-raise-the-estate-tax-could-help/

Schechinger, Anne Weir, and Craig Cox. "Double Dipping: How Taxpayers Subsidize Farmers Twice for Crop Losses." Environmental Working Group. November 14, 2017. https://www.ewg.org/research/subsidy-layer-cake

Scheinin, Richard. "$216,181: That's the Household Income Needed to Buy a House in San Jose Metro Area, Report Says." *The Mercury News.* November 21, 2017. http://www.mercurynews.com/2017/11/20/216181-thats-the-household-income-needed-to-buy-a-house-in-san-jose-metro-area-report-says/

Schleicher, David. "Stuck! The Law and Economics of Residential Stability" (The Yale Law Journal, Vol. 127, 2017). https://papers.ssrn.com/sol3/papers.cfm?abstract_id=2896309

Schmidt, Samantha. "'Herd Retirement': A Nice Dairy Industry Term for Slaughtering 500,000 Productive Cows." *The Washington Post.* January 19, 2017. Morning Mix. https://www.washingtonpost.com/news/morning-mix/wp/2017/01/19/herd-retirement-a-nice-dairy-industry-term-for-slaughtering-500000-productive-cows/?utm_term=.87b8c23b3cb9

Schneider, Mike. "Mickey Vs. the Tax Man: Disney, Universal Fight Tax Bills." *US News.* March 23, 2017. https://www.usnews.com/news/best-states/florida/articles/2017-03-23/disney-universal-battle-tax-bill-for-florida-theme-parks/

Schnurman, Mitchell. "Tax Breaks 'R' Us: Texas Ponies Up the Big Bucks for Corporate Incentives, Again." *Dallas News*. June 2, 2019. https://www.dallasnews.com/opinion/commentary/2019/06/02/tax-breaks-r-us-texas-ponies-big-bucks-corporate-incentives-again

Schoenberg, Shira. "Gov. Charlie Baker Tries to Address Housing 'Crisis' in Massachusetts." *Masslive.com*. January 30, 2018. http://www.masslive.com/politics/index.ssf/2018/01/gov_charlie_baker_tries_to_add.html

Sechler, Bob. "Senate Panel Weighs Future of State's Tax Abatement Law." *Statesman*. April 18, 2017. updated September 25, 2018. Business. https://www.statesman.com/business/20170418/senate-panel-weighs-future-of-states-tax-abatement-law

Shapiro, Ilya. "EPA Actions Should Be Subject to Judicial Review." Cato Institute. January 9, 2012. https://www.cato.org/blog/epa-actions-should-be-subject-judicial-review

Shields, Dennis A. "U.S. Peanut Program and Issues." Congressional Research Service(report). August 19, 2015. https://www.fb.org/files/2018FarmBill/CRS_Report_on_Peanuts.pdf

Shugart II, William F. "How the Ethanol Mandate Is Killing the American Prairie." *Investor's Business Daily*. April 13, 2017. Commentary. https://www.investors.com/politics/commentary/how-the-ethanol-mandate-is-killing-the-american-prairie/

Siegel, Karen R., PhD, Kai McKeever Bullard, PhD, Giuseppina Imperatore, MD, Henry S. Kahn, MD, Aryeh D. Stein, PhD, Mohammed K. Ali, MBChB, K. M. Narayan, MD. "Association of Higher Consumption of Foods Derived from Subsidized Commodities with Adverse Cardiometabolic Risk Among US Adults." *JAMA Internal Medicine* (August 2016). doi:10.1001/jamainternmed.2016.2410

Siegel, Rachel. "Senators Urge USDA to Stop Trump Farm Bailout Money from Going to Foreign-Owned Companies." *The Washington Post*. March 30, 2019. Economic Policy, https://www.washingtonpost.com/us-policy/2019/05/30/senators-urge-usda-stop-trump-farm-bailout-money-going-foreign-owned-companies/

Simon, Ruth, and Richard Rubin. "As States Pick 'Opportunity Zones' for Tax Breaks, A Debate Over Who Benefits." *Wall Street Journal*. March

20, 2018. https://www.wsj.com/articles/will-new-tax-incentives-for-poor-communities-work-some-are-skeptical-1521547201

Smith, Christine. "Why Economists Don't Like the Mortgage Interest Deduction." Open Vault Blog. May 9, 2018. https://www.stlouisfed.org/open-vault/2018/may/why-economists-dont-like-mortgage-interest-deduction

Smith, Frederick W., William Brock, and Charlene Barshefsky. "We Need to Get Back to a Pro-Trade Consensus. But It'll Take a Fight." *The Washington Post*. August 18, 2019. Opinions. https://www.washingtonpost.com/opinions/we-need-to-get-back-to-a-pro-trade-consensus-but-itll-take-a-fight/2019/08/18/d74c64c8-c062-11e9-b873-63ace636af08_story.html

Smith, Vincent H. "Should Washington End Agriculture Subsidies?" *Wall Street Journal*. July 12, 2015. Business Leadership. https://www.wsj.com/articles/should-washington-end-agriculture-subsidies-1436757020

Somin, Ilya, and The Volokh Conspiracy. "Political Ignorance and The Captured Economy." *The Washington Post*. November 16, 2017. https://www.washingtonpost.com/news/volokh-conspiracy/wp/2017/11/16/political-ignorance-and-the-captured-economy/?utm_term=.839269372b47

Sopko, John F. "SIGAR-17-13-SP Review Letter: Abandonment of OPIC Projects in Kabul." Office of the Special Inspector General for Afghanistan Reconstruction. November 14, 2016. https://www.sigar.mil/pdf/special%20projects/SIGAR-17-13-SP.pdf

Sorkin, Andrew Ross, Diana B. Henriques, Edmund L. Andrews, and Joe Nocera. "As Credit Crisis Spiraled, Alarm Led to Action." *The New York Times*. October 1, 2008. https://www.nytimes.com/2008/10/02/business/02crisis.html

Sorkin, Andrew Ross. "Tax the Rich? Here's How to Do It (Sensibly)." *The New York Times*. February 25, 2019. DealBook. https://www.nytimes.com/2019/02/25/business/dealbook/taxes-wealthy.html?searchResultPosition=1

SR. "US Tires: Tariff Expirations Will Not Hurt Bridgestone." Selective Rationality. October 2, 2012. http://selectiverationality.com/us-tires-tariff-expirations-will-not-hurt-bridgestone/

Staff. "USDA Awards Contracts for Chicken Purchase Program." Sosland
Publishing Company. September 27, 2013. Meat+Poultry. https://
www.meatpoultry.com/articles/8806-usda-awards-contracts-for-
chicken-purchase-program

Stanley-Becker, Isaac. "Disney's CEO Made 1,424 Times as Much as His
Employees. An Heir to the Disney Fortune Thinks That's 'Insane.'."
The Washington Post. April 22, 2019. Morning Mix. https://www.
washingtonpost.com/nation/2019/04/22/disneys-ceo-made-times-
much-his-employees-an-heir-disney-fortune-thinks-thats-insane/?utm_
term=.cbfff2140e36

Stein, Jeff. "Two U.S. Senators Applying for Bailout Money for
Farmers Under White House Program." *The Washington Post.*
September 28, 2018. Business. https://www.washingtonpost.com/
business/2018/09/28/sen-charles-grassley-apply-bailout-money-
farmers-under-white-house-program/

Stephens, Joe, and Carol D. Leonnig. "Solyndra: Politics Infused
Obama Energy Programs." *The Washington Post.* December 25,
2011. https://www.washingtonpost.com/solyndra-politics-infused-
obama-energy-programs/2011/12/14/gIQA4HllHP_story.html?
utm_term=.0a3ddf42ae05

Stewart, James B. "A Tax Loophole for the Rich That Just Won't Die."
The New York Times. November 9, 2017. https://www.nytimes.
com/2017/11/09/business/carried-interest-tax-loophole.html

"Subsidy Tracker Individual Entry." Good Jobs First. Subsidy Tracker:
Anadarko Petroleum. https://subsidytracker.goodjobsfirst.org/subsidy-
tracker/tx-anadarko-petroleum

"Subsidy Tracker Individual Entry." Good Jobs First. Subsidy Tracker:
Exxon Mobil. https://subsidytracker.goodjobsfirst.org/subsidy-tracker/
la-exxonmobil

"Subsidy Tracker Individual Entry." Good Jobs First. Subsidy Tracker:
Clean Coal Power Operations (KY) LLC. https://subsidytracker.
goodjobsfirst.org/subsidy-tracker/ky-clean-coal-power-operations-
ky-llc

"Subsidy Tracker Individual Entry." Good Jobs First. Subsidy Tracker:
Summit Power Group. https://subsidytracker.goodjobsfirst.org/
subsidy-tracker/tx-summit-power-group

"Subsidy Tracker Individual Entry." Good Jobs First. Subsidy Tracker: Apple, https://subsidytracker.goodjobsfirst.org/subsidy-tracker/nc-apple

"Subsidy Tracker Individual Entry." Good Jobs First. Subsidy Tracker: Microsoft." https://subsidytracker.goodjobsfirst.org/subsidy-tracker/ia-microsoft

"Subsidy Tracker Parent Company Summary: Foxconn Technology Group (Hon Hai Precision Industry Company)." Good Jobs First. https://subsidytracker.goodjobsfirst.org/prog.php?parent=foxconn-technology-group-hon-hai-precisi

"Subsidy Tracker Parent Company Summary: Peabody Energy." Good Jobs First. https://subsidytracker.goodjobsfirst.org/prog.php?parent=peabody-energy

"Subsidy Tracker Parent Company Summary." Good Jobs First. Subsidy Tracker: Kinder Morgan. https://subsidytracker.goodjobsfirst.org/prog.php?parent=kinder-morgan

"Subsidy Tracker Parent Company Summary." Good Jobs First. Subsidy Tracker: Cheniere Energy. https://subsidytracker.goodjobsfirst.org/prog.php?parent=cheniere-energy

"Subsidy Tracker Parent Company Summary." Good Jobs First. Subsidy Tracker: Anadarko Petroleum. https://subsidytracker.goodjobsfirst.org/parent/anadarko-petroleum

"Subsidy Tracker Parent Company Summary." Good Jobs First. Subsidy Tracker: Exxon Mobil. https://subsidytracker.goodjobsfirst.org/prog.php?parent=exxon-mobil

"Subsidy Tracker Parent Company Summary." Good Jobs First. Subsidy Tracker: Chevron. https://subsidytracker.goodjobsfirst.org/prog.php?parent=chevron

"Subsidy Tracker Parent Company Summary." Good Jobs First. Subsidy Tracker: Alpha Natural Resources. https://subsidytracker.goodjobsfirst.org/prog.php?parent=alpha-natural-resources

"Subsidy Tracker Parent Company Summary." Good Jobs First. Subsidy Tracker: Facebook. https://subsidytracker.goodjobsfirst.org/prog.php?parent=facebook

Sumner, Daniel A., Joseph W. Glauber, and Parke E. Wilde. "Poverty, Hunger, and US Agricultural Policy: Do Farm Programs Affect the Nutrition of Poor Americans?" American Enterprise Institute.

January 9, 2017. http://www.aei.org/publication/poverty-hunger-and-us-agricultural-policy-do-farm-programs-affect-the-nutrition-of-poor-americans/

Surowiecki, James. "Special Interest." *The New Yorker*. March 7, 2010. https://www.newyorker.com/magazine/2010/03/15/special-interest-2

Swanson, Ana. "Why A Weird Legal Dispute About Whether the Snuggie Is A Blanket Actually Matters A Lot." *The Washington Post*. March 6, 2017. Economic Policy. Analysis. https://www.washingtonpost.com/news/wonk/wp/2017/03/06/why-a-weird-legal-dispute-about-whether-the-snuggie-is-a-blanket-actually-matters-a-lot/

Tannenwald, Robert. "State Film Subsidies: Not Much Bang for Too Many Bucks." Center on Budget and Policy Priorities. December 9, 2010. https://www.cbpp.org/sites/default/files/atoms/files/11-17-10sfp.pdf

"Taxpayers Stuck with Unsold Ferries in Default." *Maui Tomorrow*. August 11, 2011. http://maui-tomorrow.org/superferry-an-economic-disaster-for-state-and-federal-taxpayers/

Teles, Steven M. "Kludgeocracy in America." National Affairs. Fall 2013. https://www.nationalaffairs.com/publications/detail/kludgeocracy-in-america

Tesoro, Len. "Debunking Myths About Federal Oil & Gas Subsidies." *Forbes*. February 22, 2016. https://www.forbes.com/sites/drillinginfo/2016/02/22/debunking-myths-about-federal-oil-gas-subsidies/#2ed28cdd6e1c

"Texas Farm Subsidy Information." EWG's Farm Subsidy Database. https://farm.ewg.org/region.php?fips=48000&progcode=total

The Data Team. "Donald Trump Hopes to Save America's Failing Coal-Fired Power Plants." *The Economist*. June 6, 2018. https://www.economist.com/graphic-detail/2018/06/06/donald-trump-hopes-to-save-americas-failing-coal-fired-power-plants

"The Database Tracks $368 Billion in Farm Subsidies from Commodity, Crop Insurance, Disaster Programs and Conservation Payments Paid Between 1995 and 2017." EWG's Farm Subsidy Database. https://farm.ewg.org/?_ga=1.147549623.1607116893.1473806254

The Editors. "How the Jones Act Blocks Natural Disaster Relief: View." *Bloomberg*. January 2, 2013. Opinion. https://www.bloomberg.

com/opinion/articles/2013-01-01/how-a-disaster-called-the-jones-act-blocks-disaster-relief-view

The President's Constitutional Duty to Faithfully Execute the Laws: Hearing Before the Committee on the Judiciary House of Representatives, First Session. 113th Cong. 113-55 (December 3, 2013) (Oral Testimony and Prepared Statement of Jonathan Turley, Shapiro Professor of Public Interest Law, George Washington University). https://www. govinfo.gov/content/pkg/CHRG-113hhrg85762/html/CHRG-113hhrg85762.htm

"The Tax Break-Down: Intangible Drilling Costs." The Committee for a Responsible Federal Budget (blog). October 17, 2013. http://www. crfb.org/blogs/tax-break-down-intangible-drilling-costs

"The U.S. Coal Industry: Historical Trends and Recent Developments." EveryCRSReport.com. August 18, 2017. https://www.everycrsreport. com/reports/R44922.html

"The Wrong Remedy: Faced with a Housing Crisis, California Could Further Restrict Supply." *The Economist.* May 12, 2018. https://www. economist.com/united-states/2018/05/10/faced-with-a-housing-crisis-california-could-further-restrict-supply

Thompson, Derek. "The Shame of the Mortgage-Interest Deduction." *The Atlantic.* May 14, 2017. Business. https://www.theatlantic.com/ business/archive/2017/05/shame-mortgage-interest-deduction/ 526635/

"TPC." Tax Policy Center. https://www.taxpolicycenter.org/sites/default/ files/20190516_tpc_1_pager.pdf

"Trailblazers: The New Zealand Story." Free to Choose Network. directed by James Trusty and Maureen Castle Trusty. 2016. https:// www.freetochoosenetwork.org/programs/new_zealand/credits.php

Trump, Donald J. "Presidential Executive Order on Reducing Regulation and Controlling Regulatory Costs." The White House. January 30, 2017. https://www.whitehouse.gov/presidential-actions/presidential-executive-order-reducing-regulation-controlling-regulatory-costs/

Trump, Donald, Chris Christie, Ted Cruz, Julianna Goldman, Michael Scherer, Anne Gearan, Manu Raju, Ruth Marcus, and Ken Burns, interview by John Dickerson. Face the Nation. August 23, 2015.

https://www.cbsnews.com/news/face-the-nation-transcripts-august-23-2015-trump-christie-cruz/

Turner, Sylvester. "Official City of Houston Zoning Letter" City of Houston. January 1, 2019. http://www.houstontx.gov/planning/Forms/devregs/2019-coh-no-zoning-letter.pdf

University of Chicago. "Longer Commutes Disadvantage African-American Workers." *ScienceDaily*. February 15, 2014. https://www.sciencedaily.com/releases/2014/02/140215122416.htm

"U.S. Commercial Service U.S.-Caribbean Business Conference." District Export Council of South Florida and the Department of Commerce's U.S. Commercial Service (paper brochure). June 2019.

"Understanding the True Cost of CPSIA Testing Requirements." Handmade Toy Alliance. October 1, 2009. http://handmadetoyalliance.blogspot.com/2009/09/understanding-true-costs-of-cpsia.html

"USDA Subsidy Information for Doug Dallas Sombke." Environmental Working Group. https://farm.ewg.org/persondetail.php?custnumber=A07736446

Valentina, Adriana. "Model Group to Build a 'Unique' Restaurant in Fort Wayne." *Indiana Construction News*. April 22, 2019. https://www.indianaconstructionnews.com/2019/04/22/model-group-to-build-a-unique-restaurant-in-fort-wayne/

Vance, Ashlee. *Elon Musk Tesla, SpaceX, and the Quest for a Fantastic Future* (Harper Collins, 2015). Kindle. https://play.google.com/store/books/details/Ashlee_Vance_Elon_Musk?id=Yd99BAAAQBAJ

"Vegetable Farming Industry in the US - Market Research Report." IBIS World. May 2019. https://www.ibisworld.com/industry-trends/market-research-reports/agriculture-forestry-fishing-hunting/crop-production/vegetable-farming.html

Velotta, Richard N. "Exact Cost of Raiders' Las Vegas Stadium Still Unknown." *Las Vegas Review-Journal*. June 12, 2017. https://www.reviewjournal.com/business/stadium/exact-cost-of-raiders-las-vegas-stadium-still-unknown/

Vinik, Danny. "Under Trump, Regulation Slows to a Crawl." *Politico*. June 7, 2017. The Agenda. https://www.politico.com/agenda/story/2017/06/07/trump-regulation-slowdown-000446

"Violation Tracker Parent Company Summary: Arch Coal." Good Jobs First. https://violationtracker.goodjobsfirst.org/parent/arch-coal

"Wage and Hour Division (WHD)." U.S. Department of Labor. https://www.dol.gov/whd/programs/dbra/faqs/calculat.htm

Wang, Dong D., MD, MSc, Yanping Li, PhD, Stephanie E. Chiuve, ScD., Meir J. Stampfer, MD, DrPH, JoAnn E. Manson, MD, DrPH, Eric B. Rimm, ScD, Walter C. Willett, MD, DrPH, Frank B. Hu, MD, PhD. "Association of Specific Dietary Fats with Total and Cause-Specific Mortality," *JAMA Internal Medicine* (August 2016). doi:10.1001/jamainternmed.2016.2417

Wang, Yanan. "Man Moves to San Francisco, Pays $400 a Month to Sleep in Wooden Box in Friends' Living Room." *The Washington Post.* March 29, 2016. https://www.washingtonpost.com/news/morning-mix/wp/2016/03/29/man-moves-to-san-francisco-pays-400-a-month-to-sleep-in-wooden-box-inside-friends-living-room/?utm_term=.2ed9ef57b152

"Warren Buffett." *Forbes.* https://www.forbes.com/profile/warren-buffett/#477e723c4639

Watson, Kathryn. "'You All Just Got A Lot Richer,' Trump Tells Friends, Referencing Tax Overhaul." *CBS News.* December 24, 2017. https://www.cbsnews.com/news/trump-mar-a-lago-christmas-trip/

Weisenthal, Joe. "The New York Times Goes to Bat for Big Toymakers." *Business Insider.* February 19, 2009. https://www.businessinsider.com/the-new-york-times-goes-to-bat-for-big-toymakers-2009-2

Weissmann, Jordan. "America's Dumbest Tax Loophole: The Florida Rent-a-Cow Scam." *The Atlantic.* April 17, 2012. https://www.theatlantic.com/business/archive/2012/04/americas-dumbest-tax-loophole-the-florida-rent-a-cow-scam/255874/

Wesoff, Eric. "Executives Bonuses Kept Coming in 2011." *GreenTech Media.* November 2, 2011. https://www.greentechmedia.com/articles/print/Solyndra-Executive-Bonuses-Kept-Coming-in-2011

Wesoff, Eric. "Solyndra CEO and CFO Pleading the Fifth: Part 2." *GreenTech Media.* September 21, 2011. https://www.greentechmedia.com/articles/read/solyndra-ceo-and-cfo-pleading-the-fifth#gs.qe5ez9

"What Is U.S. Electricity Generation by Energy Source?" U.S. Energy Information Administration. https://www.eia.gov/tools/faqs/faq.php?id=427&t=3

Will, George. "Washington Post: Whirlpool, Lobbyists Putting Tariffs on Spin Cycle." *Waco Tribune-Herald*. December 16, 2017. https://www.wacotrib.com/townnews/commerce/george-will-washington-post-whirlpool-lobbyists-putting-tariffs-on-spin/article_6182df28-9ebb-5db5-93e6-56c4ad51205f.html

Wilson, Scott. "As Gentrification Escalates in Calif., People Wonder: Where Can the Homeless Go?" *The Washington Post*. May 6, 2018. https://www.washingtonpost.com/national/as-gentrification-escalates-in-calif-people-wonder-where-can-the-homeless-go/2018/05/06/d2b1018a-4a43-11e8-9072-f6d4bc32f223_story.html?utm_term=.286fbd7e06f8

Winkler, Elizabeth. "'Snob Zoning' Is Racial Housing Segregation by Another Name." *The Washington Post*. September 25, 2017. https://www.washingtonpost.com/news/wonk/wp/2017/09/25/snob-zoning-is-racial-housing-segregation-by-another-name/?utm_term=.95229dc09383

Wolla, Scott A. "The Economics of Subsidizing Sports Stadiums." Economic Research; Federal Reserve Bank of St. Louis. May 2017. https://research.stlouisfed.org/publications/page1-econ/2017-05-01/the-economics-of-subsidizing-sports-stadiums

Worstall, Tim. "Union Wages Increase Construction Costs By 20% - Abolish Davis Bacon." *Forbes*. August 31, 2016. https://www.forbes.com/sites/timworstall/2016/08/31/union-wages-increase-construction-costs-by-20-abolish-davis-bacon/#4ddb6541406e

"Wyden Presses FERC: Trump Administration's Coal Bailout Will Raise American's Utility Rates." Ron Wyden United States Senator for Oregon (press release). June 12, 2018. https://www.wyden.senate.gov/news/press-releases/wyden-presses-ferc-trump-administrations-coal-bailout-will-raise-americans-utility-rates

Yglesias, Matthew. "Silicon Valley's Profound Housing Crisis, in One Sentence." *Vox*. June 07, 2016. https://www.vox.com/2016/6/7/11877378/silicon-valley-housing-crisis

York, Erica. "Nearly 90 Percent of Taxpayers Are Projected to take the TCJA's Expanded Standard Deduction." Tax Foundation. September 26, 2018. https://taxfoundation.org/90-percent-taxpayers-projected-tcja-expanded-standard-deduction/

Young, Ryan. "REINing in Regulatory Overreach." Competitive Enterprise Institute. November 15, 2016. https://cei.org/content/reining-regulatory-overreach

Young, Ryan. "This Week in Ridiculous Regulations: 2016 Wrap-Up." Competitive Enterprise Institute (blog). January 3, 2017. https://cei.org/blog/week-ridiculous-regulations-2016-wrap

Young, Ryan. "Virtuous Capitalism, or, Why So Little Rent-Seeking?" Competitive Enterprise Institute. October 20, 2015. https://cei.org/blog/virtuous-capitalism-or-why-so-little-rent-seeking

Yuen, Stacy. "Keeping Up with The Jones Act." *Hawaii Business Magazine*. August 4, 2012. Government. https://www.hawaiibusiness.com/keeping-up-with-the-jones-act/

Zarroli, Jim. "As Trump Built His Real Estate Empire, Tax Breaks Played a Pivotal Role." *NPR*. May 18, 2017. https://www.npr.org/2017/05/18/528998663/as-trump-built-his-real-estate-empire-tax-breaks-played-a-pivotal-role

Zibreg, Christian. "Apple Gave Tim Cook a $12 Million Bonus as His Total 2018 Compensation Hits $136 Million." *iDownloadBlog*. January 9, 2019. https://www.idownloadblog.com/2019/01/09/tim-cook-compensation-fiscal-2018/

Zipp, Yvonne. "A New Law Hurts Small Toy Stores and Toymakers." *The Christian Science Monitor*. January 9, 2009. https://www.csmonitor.com/The-Culture/The-Home-Forum/2009/0109/p25s23-hfgn.html

Zipp, Yvonne. "A New Law Hurts Small Toy Stores and Toymakers." *The Christian Science Monitor*. January 9, 2009. https://www.csmonitor.com/The-Culture/The-Home-Forum/2009/0109/p25s23-hfgn.html

Index